1, 2, 4, 5, 8, 10, 11

MANAGEMENT AND SUPERVISION OF LAW ENFORCEMENT PERSONNEL

by
Donald J. Schroeder, Ph. D.
Frank Lombardo
and
Jerry Strollo

GOULD PUBLICATIONS

COPYRIGHT © 1995
by J. & B. Gould
Printed in the U.S.A.

Published by
J.B.L. PUBLICATIONS, INC.
61 Prospect Ave.
Binghamton, NY 13901
(607) 724-3000

Distributed by
GOULD PUBLICATIONS
199 State Street
Binghamton, NY 13901
(607) 724-3000

DEDICATION

To our fathers:

> James J. Schroeder,
> *N.Y.C. Police Sergeant, Retired,*

> Sebastiano Lombardo,
> *Master Sergeant and World War Veteran,*

> Angelo J. Strollo,
> *N.Y.C. Fireman 1st Grade, Retired*

...For their guidance, advice, and traditional work ethic.

As all good managers and supervisors do, they led by example.

AUTHORS

Dr. Donald Schroeder holds a Ph.D. in Criminal Justice. He is also a retired Police Captain, having held both field and staff assignments in the N.Y.C. Police Department. One such staff assignment involved his acting as police liaison from the N.Y.C. Police Department to the Educational Testing Service of Princeton, New Jersey. He has taught criminal justice subjects at John Jay College and has co-authored several texts on police promotion. Dr. Schroeder has acted as a consultant to governmental personnel agencies throughout the country, assisting them in the preparation, administration and evaluation of criminal justice promotional examinations. At the present, Dr. Schroeder provides assistance to individuals and study groups competing in management assessment exercises.

Frank Lombardo is a retired Deputy Inspector of the New York City Police Department who has also worked with the San Francisco Police Department with assignments that included patrol, vice/narcotics criminal investigations and staff assignments such as personnel. His classroom experience consists of teaching at John Jay College of Criminal Justice and St. John's University. The co-author of several texts on police entry and promotional exams, he has been a consultant to civil service agencies in the writing, administration, and scoring of exams. Currently engaged in the tutoring of candidates for police promotion, he holds a Masters in Urban Affairs.

Gerald J. Strollo is a retired New York City Police Captain whose 26 year police career included assignments in patrol, investigations and staff positions. He holds a Bachelor of Science degree in Criminal Justice Administration, and possesses various N.Y. State criminal justice instructor certifications. He currently works as a police subject matter consultant and additionally instructs individuals in police and private security matters.

FOREWORD

Altogether, we, the three authors, have over sixty years of service as law enforcement supervisors. During these years of service we have developed an overwhelming affinity for the men and women of the law enforcement community all over the country who, on a daily basis, risk their lives so that others may enjoy the many freedoms of our great country. It was this affinity that motivated us to write this book.

It is our hope that law enforcement personnel of all ranks can benefit in two ways from what is written on the following pages. We believe that current law enforcement managers and supervisors who want to improve their on-the-job performance can do so by following the time proven principles of management and supervision provided in this book. In addition, we firmly believe that law enforcement personnel of all ranks who aspire to be promoted will be well served by using this work in their preparation for such advancement.

If we help you via this book to achieve your goals, whatever they may be, we will be deeply gratified. Good luck to you and yours, and may God bless you for the work you do.

For ease of grammatical construction, the use of pronouns such as he is intended to refer to he or she without any implication of gender. However, when the intent is to appropriately identify gender then the use of pronouns such as he and she and so on will be used.

MANAGEMENT AND SUPERVISION OF LAW ENFORCEMENT PERSONNEL

TABLE OF CONTENTS

© 1995 by J. & B. Gould
Printed in the U.S.A.   Ms

TABLE OF CONTENTS
(Continued)

© 1995 by J. & B. Gould
Printed in the U.S.A.   Ms

ix

TABLE OF CONTENTS
(Continued)

TABLE OF CONTENTS
(Continued)

TABLE OF CONTENTS
(Continued)

Chapter   *Page*

TABLE OF CONTENTS
(Continued)

MANAGEMENT AND SUPERVISION OF LAW ENFORCEMENT PERSONNEL

CHAPTER 1
THE SPECIAL ROLE OF THE SUPERVISOR IN LAW ENFORCEMENT

Management is the process of directing and controlling the resources of an organization, such as its personnel, materials and equipment, so as to achieve the goals of the organization. Supervision is the management of workers. While all supervisors are managers, all managers are not supervisors. Management doesn't necessarily involve a direct relationship with workers. Immediate contact with workers is the essential ingredient in the supervisory process. As managers ascend the hierarchy of an agency, they usually become less involved in supervisory tasks.

As is true in any organization, law enforcement agencies need competent managers as well as productive workers. However, because of the absence of widespread lateral entry, law enforcement agencies usually select their managers from among incumbent workers in the lower ranks. Today's workers become tomorrow's leaders. Given this fact, top administrators must make a special effort to ensure high quality management and supervision.

From a legal standpoint, the entry level selection process in any law enforcement agency must be geared to select candidates who have the ability to perform as effective entry level officers. However, the skills needed to be an effective manager go beyond the skills needed to be an effective worker.

Fortunately, managerial and supervisory skills can be learned. "Management is a topic about which much has been written. In the last 100 years an organized body of knowledge concerning the subject has developed. [It is] believe[d] that by studying the management process you can increase your effectiveness as a manager."[1] Effective managers and supervisors can be developed from among the rank and file. But, such development requires two things: motivated personnel and adequate training.

Agencies need highly motivated personnel who are willing to make the effort to develop the special skills required of managers. Ideally this motivation should come mostly from within an individual. However, it is advisable for an agency to fuel this motivation by making each managerial position a desirable one to attain. Agencies should also provide incentives for those willing to make the special effort to add to their expertise.

Adequate training is the second requirement for developing effective managers from incumbent workers. An agency must provide adequate initial training for all newly promoted personnel and continuing training for incumbent managers. Law enforcement agencies who provide only cursory training for their management personnel must be willing to live with mediocrity.

IMPORTANCE OF THE FIRST LEVEL SUPERVISOR

The importance of high quality first level supervision cannot be overstated. It is the first level supervisor who is in the best position to ensure that the goals of the agency are being accomplished. Although this is true of any organization, the complex goals of law enforcement coupled with the need for teamwork make the first level supervisor's position an extremely demanding one. Of all its supervisory personnel, the success of the agency is dependent on its first level supervisors.

The Unique Role of the First Level Supervisor

The role of the first level supervisor can be understood best by first dividing law enforcement personnel into three groups: the workers (officers and agents), first level supervisors (usually sergeants), and higher level managers (usually lieutenants and above). The first level supervisor occupies the ambivalent position in the middle. He is required to represent management to the workers, but he is also required to speak to management for

2

the workers. Fulfilling this ambivalent role is a demanding task requiring great courage. This is particularly evident when a supervisor sides with the workers in a dispute with management. If the facts indicate that workers have a legitimate grievance, the supervisor must support them. But, blindly supporting workers simply to gain their loyalty is detrimental in the long run. All else being equal, in any situation that pits the needs of the agency against the needs of the worker, the needs of the agency must prevail.

TRANSITION FROM WORKER TO SUPERVISOR

In any occupation, the transition from worker to supervisor is a difficult one. For the first time an individual is responsible for the actions of others and must utilize skills unique to supervising. The difficulty of this transition makes a probationary period imperative for all newly promoted personnel.

Common Errors of the Transition Period

Transitions are further complicated by mistakes made by new supervisors that create negative impressions among the workers. For this reason it is recommended that newly appointed supervisors in large departments be transferred after successfully completing their probationary period. More importantly, new supervisors must avoid the common pitfalls of the transition period. Please note that, while these errors are usually committed by newly promoted supervisors, all supervisors at every level need to avoid them.

Over-supervising

Over-supervision is the most common error made by new supervisors. Ironically, it is often brought on by a positive trait—conscientiousness. In their zeal to get the job done, they forget that their new position requires them to delegate authority to their subordinates. Instead, they become overly involved in controlling the routine activities of their subordinates and, even worse, they do the actual work themselves, often under the mistaken belief that they will win the favor of their subordinates.

However, most workers resent such an approach and often view it as indicative of a lack of confidence in their abilities. To complicate the matter even more, over-supervision also curtails worker initiative, creates morale problems and decreases respect for the supervisor.

Striving for Popularity

Often, individuals fail to successfully make the change from follower to leader because they mistakenly believe that they must strive for popularity with their subordinates. New supervisors must distinguish between popularity and respect. Popularity is not a requisite for the job of supervisor, but respect is. All supervisors, especially new ones, must understand the need to separate themselves from their subordinates. This does not mean that old friendships must end, nor that there is no room in the supervisor-subordinate relationship for friendship. It means that such friendship should never be allowed to interfere with a supervisor's objectivity.

Actions that win popularity with some subordinates incur unpopularity with others. Favoritism is a double-edged sword. While it may make a supervisor popular with the recipient of the special treatment, it more often alienates those workers who are not the beneficiaries of that treatment. Ironically, even those who receive the special treatment may lose respect for the supervisor.

Excessive Revamping

In general, people resist change. For this reason, with one exception, a new supervisor should make it clear that he has no intention of making any immediate changes. He should state that his initial intent is to maintain the status quo. Then, after a period of observation and evaluation, any change deemed necessary should be made gradually after obtaining appropriate input from those who will be affected. Obtaining such input is important since "employees who participate in planning and implementing a change are better able to understand the reasons for the change."[2] The exception to the rule occurs when a supervisor

4

is assigned to a unit following instances of gross incompetence in that unit which dictate the need for immediate change.

Building False Hopes

In almost every law enforcement agency, there are unpopular or outdated conditions that remain unchanged because of budgetary or legal considerations. When such a condition is brought to the attention of a supervisor, it is a mistake for that supervisor to promise to change it. Although such a promise translates into instant popularity, that popularity turns to resentment when the supervisor is unable to fulfill that promise. On the other hand, it is a supervisor's obligation to identify and, insofar as possible, to correct problems in the work environment. But, there is a difference between attempting change and guaranteeing change. It is the latter that should be avoided.

Avoiding Accountability

Accountability is having to answer to someone for the way one meets one's responsibilities. All supervisors are accountable to management for their own actions and, in appropriate circumstances, for the actions of their subordinates.

Inappropriately attempting to avoid accountability by shifting blame to others destroys respect. Unfortunately, this is a common mistake of newly promoted supervisors. An experienced supervisor realizes that he cannot escape accountability for a delegated duty. "In other words, you can delegate responsibility but you cannot delegate accountability."[3]

Another error occurs when a supervisor attributes an unpopular policy, rule, or procedure to top management. Supervisors should not hide behind management when exacting compliance with unpopular edicts. To imply that a certain policy, rule or procedure is inappropriate but must be enforced because of the mandates of superiors is wrong. Saying, "Although I don't agree, that's the way our bosses want it, so that's how it has to be done," is an example of an inappropriate attempt to shift blame. Supervisors represent management to their subordinates. Therefore, if a supervisor believes a particular management position is in error or unfair, then he is responsible for making this position known to management. But, until the position is changed, the supervisor must defend and support it as if it were his own.

Overexerting Authority

Authority is the power to command others. By virtue of their position, supervisors have the authority to issue orders and give instructions to subordinates. The way supervisors exert this authority impacts supervisor-subordinate relationships. The quickest way to alienate subordinates is to act like a dictator. "Dictators sow seeds of distrust. Employees can sense this and will resent it. Employees who believe you [a supervisor] have no confidence in their ability or their integrity, will usually become argumentative, aggressive and uncooperative."[4] A new supervisor should not seek to prove to his subordinates how much he knows during his first few days on the job. Instead, he should spend this time learning about his subordinates and seeking their advice. It is a mistake for any supervisor in non-emergency situations to rely too heavily on direct orders. As will be discussed later, undue reliance on direct orders, in other than emergency situations, causes resentment. New supervisors should resort to a show of authority only when necessary.

SKILLS NEEDED BY A SUPERVISOR

Effective workers do not always make quality supervisors. This does not mean that the skills needed by workers are not needed by supervisors. It means that good supervisors need additional skills. Most experts agree that the basic skills required of all managers can be grouped into three broad categories: technical skills, interpersonal skills, and analytical skills. The type of skill most often used depends on a manager's position and current circumstances. In general, first level supervisors are more dependent on technical skills than upper level managers are. "It's assumed, especially in large organizations, that Chief Executives can utilize the technical abilities of their subordinates."[5]

Technical Skills

Technical skills involve specialized knowledge and the ability to apply that knowledge. These skills are not usually possessed by the general population and are needed to do a specific job. For example, the technical skills required of a field officer include knowledge of and the ability to apply statutory law, case law, and various regulations. Newly appointed entry level officers learn the technical skills required of them during their formal entry level training.

A good supervisor does not need to possess all of the technical skills of his workers, nor does he have to be more technically proficient than any worker in his unit. This is especially true in those units which perform highly specialized functions, such as a crime scene unit. However, technical proficiency is an extremely valuable asset. Remember, a primary responsibility of all supervisors is to train their subordinates. Obviously only a supervisor with the required technical skills can meet this responsibility. In addition, influencing subordinates is easier given strong technical skills. Many workers resent being supervised by someone who lacks the technical skills needed to do the job. Conversely, a supervisor with exceptional technical skills can earn the respect of his subordinates by displaying those skills.

Also, when a supervisor responds to an incident, strong technical skills can be useful. Supervisors respond to the scene of an incident which requires police intervention when (1) the nature of the incident is such that agency regulations require the supervisor to respond, or (2) upon hearing the assignment on the radio the supervisor decides to respond, or (3) the assigned officer requests the supervisor's assistance. It is in this third situation that the technically skilled supervisor gains respect in the eyes of his subordinates.

In situations which do not require immediate action, supervisors who are unsure of how to deal with a problem should postpone any decision until the correct course of action is determined. However, in emergency situations, the worst decision is no decision. "You can get into more management difficulty by repeatedly refusing to make decisions than by occasionally making an incorrect one."[6] Here the supervisor who is uncertain must order the most reasonable course of action. When this occurs, a supervisor is obligated to find out what should have been done. Remember, even wise men make mistakes, but only fools make the same mistake twice.

All supervisors have a responsibility to maintain a high level of technical skills. This is especially true of first level supervisors. However, except in extraordinary circumstances, a supervisor should not do the work of his subordinates.

Understanding the Local Government Structure

Besides understanding the goals, policies and regulations of their own agency, supervisors must understand the workings of local government and certain private agencies. Law enforcement must work fluidly with emergency medical services, correctional services, the state attorney's office, welfare agencies, and victims' advocacy groups.

Interpersonal Skills

Interpersonal skills are those skills needed to work in harmony with subordinates, peers, and superiors. Good supervisors must be able to get along with people. They must be human relations specialists. Poor personal relations with workers or other managers rated highest on a list of why supervisors fail.[7]

While interpersonal skills are needed by all supervisors, it is first line supervisors who have the greatest need for them. Given that the essential ingredient in the supervisory process is the immediate contact with workers, an individual with poor interpersonal skills has difficulty directing others without offending them. Such a person could have excellent technical and analytical skills and still not be effective as a supervisor, since most subordinates have no tolerance for a supervisor who offends them personally. For this reason interpersonal skills are the most valuable skills for a supervisor to develop.

Certain basic tendencies define a person with highly developed interpersonal skills:

-They communicate effectively.
-They earn respect.

-They manage participatively.
-They are considerate.
-They maintain objectivity.

Supervisors Must Communicate Effectively

Since law enforcement demands team work, the ability to communicate effectively is the most valuable interpersonal skill needed by supervisors. Though usually issuing routine orders, supervisors must also issue orders in emergency situations where prompt and coordinated action is needed to preserve life. In addition, supervisors often counsel subordinates regarding work-related and personal problems. For these reasons, strong communications skills are essential to a supervisor.

Supervisors Must Earn Respect

Informed supervisors rely on their rank only as a last resort or in an emergency. Although they derive their official authority from management, they must earn the respect and confidence of their subordinates before this official authority translates into actual authority. The first step in achieving this respect is to set a good example. They cannot set themselves above the rules. Their personal conduct must demonstrate the same qualities they demand of others.

Supervisors Must Manage Participatively

Supervisors with good interpersonal skills allow those affected to participate in the management process. This creates a healthy atmosphere which encourages subordinates to contribute. Gaining input from others may delay decision making, but it facilitates implementation. Of course, there are times when participative management is not appropriate, such as emergency situations when time is of the essence.

Supervisors Must Be Considerate

Supervisors with good interpersonal skills are concerned about the feelings and welfare of others. As a general rule, they praise subordinates in public and criticize them in private. They practice empathy by placing themselves in the position of a subordinate in order to understand that perspective. Tolerant and understanding, they recognize that all subordinates are different and cannot be handled in a uniform manner. Finally, they maintain an "open door" policy; they are ready to listen to the suggestions and grievances of their subordinates. "When we listen without judgment, we open lines of communication; we show people we care."[8]

Supervisors Must Maintain Objectivity

Objectivity is vital to developing a harmonious work group. A cooperative effort cannot be sustained if the supervisor plays favorites. This is more important today because of the heterogeneous work force.

Analytical Skills

The third set of skills required of good supervisors is analytical. Supervisors must analyze problems, finding their sources and formulating their solutions. Problem solving is at the heart of law enforcement work. The decentralization of public services demands strong analytical skills. Because of their seven day a week, twenty-four hour a day availability, field officers are contacted by private citizens even if the citizen's problem does not involve law enforcement. In turn, officers who cannot solve these problems often ask for the assistance of their supervisor, who must analyze the situation and direct an effective course of action. Supervisors must also anticipate potential problems and act to prevent them. They must understand the potential impact of their decisions beyond their own unit. For these reasons, supervisors must be familiar with the systematic method of problem solving.

Too often supervisors treat symptoms of problems, not the causes. They may also act too quickly and without sufficient facts. "The temptation is great for most supervisors to take the first course of action that appears to be valid when attempting to solve problems or make decisions. This quick-fix approach more often than not leads to difficulties later."[9] The systematic approach to problem solving is the only approach that should be used and will be discussed in detail later. The point is that this systematic approach requires analytical skills.

SKILLS NEEDED BY A FEMALE SUPERVISOR

The job of being a supervisor is the same for both males and females. The basic skills needed for success are the same. Male supervisors and female supervisors alike have to get the job done through people. Some experts maintain that, in general, women empathize more and listen better than men. These qualities would make women better suited to be supervisors. However, others argue that women are generally passive rather than assertive. They view women as lacking flexibility and avoiding risks. These qualities would make women in general less suited to be supervisors. The question is whether newly promoted female supervisors should receive special training. Should agency policy make a distinction between men and women because they may have different strengths and weaknesses?

To make a gender distinction in supervisory training programs based on generalities is not recommended. A woman who wants to be an effective supervisor should take the same approach that a male with similar aspirations should. Both must develop and maintain technical, interpersonal, and analytical skills. Every newly promoted supervisor, male or female, should do a personal inventory of his or her skills and strive to correct any weaknesses.

BASIC SUPERVISORY RESPONSIBILITIES

The success or failure of a law enforcement agency depends more on the quality of its first level supervision than on the quality of supervision at any other managerial level. First level supervisors are responsible for ensuring that subordinates deliver high quality service. Although it is impossible to list all the duties and responsibilities of every law enforcement supervisor, all supervisors have certain fundamental roles.

The Special Role of the Supervisor

Supervisors Must Be Effective Leaders

Supervisors are responsible for their units accomplishing their work. This simple statement belies the complexity of the situation. Only the uninformed believe that working through others is a simple process revolving around a "do what I say or else" mentality. Such an approach does not work anymore. "Supervisors have to cope with a new work ethic, which doesn't respond well to iron-handed whip-cracking—once a common management style. Force won't work against this new ethic. You can't make today's employees work; you have to make them want to work."[10] Working through others is a complex task as can be seen in a typical definition of leadership: "Leadership is the process of influencing organizational members to use their energies willingly and appropriately to facilitate the achievement of the police department's goals."[11]

The leadership role is the most important of the supervisor's roles because it permeates all of the others. The complexity of the role is emphasized by the term "willingly" in the above definition. To get a subordinate to do a job appropriately is a challenge, but to get it done willingly is an even greater challenge—even under ordinary circumstances when the supervisor and the subordinate are both present at the work site. However, at the operational level in the typical law enforcement agency, ninety percent of the time, the supervisor is not present. Therefore, getting unsupervised subordinates to willingly do a good job is the greatest of all leadership accomplishments. To achieve this accomplishment, a person must become a human relations expert, an expert at handling people.

Supervisors Must Be Linking Pins

Teamwork in law enforcement is not limited to members of the same unit but extends to other units in the organization. Further, it requires that agency policy be properly interpreted to the unit in order to maintain harmonious relations with upper management. It is the supervisor's job to act as a linking pin in order to achieve this cooperation. Therefore, every line supervisor is actually a member of three groups.

To understand the supervisor's role as a linking pin, consider the example of a first level patrol supervisor we will call Sergeant Rems (see Figure 1-1). The first group with which Sergeant Rems is involved is comprised of Lieutenant Watch Commander 2 and the lieutenant's subordinate supervisors, such as Sergeant 2. The second group is made up of Sergeant Rems's peers, Sergeants One, Two and Four. The third group includes Sergeant Rems and the field officers over which Sergeant Rems has immediate supervisory responsibility. Consequently, Sergeant Rems must interact with the watch commander and all of the supervisors who report to the watch commander, with his peers who are the supervisors of other units, and with the field officers in his own unit. He must link together the activities of each of these three groups. Thus, each line supervisor must function as a competent link between other agency managers and his own personnel. This requires engaging in both horizontal and vertical communication as will be discussed later.

FIGURE 1-1
THE SUPERVISOR AS A LINKING PIN

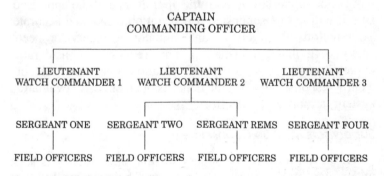

Supervisors Must Be Focal Points

The activities of any law enforcement unit center around an informed supervisor. As the one person who should know the most about the strengths and weaknesses of the unit, the immediate supervisor of a unit who shuns disturbing information is avoiding responsibility and inviting problems. Therefore, the immediate supervisor of a group of workers must remain abreast of all conditions that could impact that group.

To do this the supervisor must utilize both formal and informal communications networks.

As the focal point of operational activity, a supervisor is responsible for eliminating duplicated effort, solving problems, and simplifying procedures. Fulfilling this role requires direct communication and both formal and informal conferences.

Supervisors Must Be Disciplinarians

The term disciplinarian often conjures images of a person who punishes. However, the informed law enforcement supervisor relies primarily on training and attitude correction to prevent and correct deficiencies and uses chastisement or punishment as a last resort. An entire chapter is devoted to this topic since the immediate line supervisor shoulders the greatest responsibility for maintaining discipline.

Supervisors Must Be Evaluators

The evaluator role is perhaps the most exacting of all the roles of immediate supervisors. The evaluation process is worthless if it is not supported by both the appraisers and the appraised. But, it will not be supported if it is not objective and accurate. To function effectively as an evaluator, a supervisor needs accurate firsthand information. This requires a considerable expenditure of time and effort. Evaluation is not a periodic, but a daily responsibility. Yet the benefits of an effective evaluation system far outweigh the effort.

Supervisors Must Be Counselors

Of all the roles of the supervisor that of counselor is least understood by supervisors themselves. Their responsibility to counsel subordinates experiencing personal problems is obscured by two common misconceptions: (1) that an employee's personal problems are not the supervisor's business, and, (2) that supervisory counseling involves professional therapy.

An employee's personal problems should become the supervisor's business when (1) the problem impacts on the employee's work, or (2) the employee asks for the supervisor's

14

help, or (3) the employee's problem results in a personnel complaint. Under any of these circumstances, the supervisor is obligated to counsel the subordinate.

The counseling role of a supervisor does not include any form of professional therapy, unless the supervisor is specifically qualified to administer such therapy. Instead, a supervisor should help when he can and refer to qualified counselors when he cannot.[12] Fulfilling the supervisor's counseling role is addressed in detail later. The point here is that supervisors should familiarize themselves with the symptoms of personal problems so that timely intervention and appropriate referral can prevent an escalation of the problem.

Supervisors Must Be Early Detectors

The supervisor is in a unique position to serve as an early detector of subordinates' behavioral patterns which may lead to work related problems. When a person is motivated to engage in a particular behavior and that behavior becomes blocked or impossible, frustration develops. Some of the more common behavioral patterns which often develop as a response to frustrations are as follows:

a. Aggression. Often when an employee is frustrated, he responds with aggression. Such aggression may be overt, such as direct verbal or even physical confrontation, or covert, such as doing exactly what he is told, no more and no less, often carrying out a supervisor's order to an absurd extreme.

b. Regressive behavior. This involves returning to behavioral responses developed during childhood. For example, if a person responded to frustration in his early years of development by having a temper tantrum, he might regress into similar behavior to deal with frustrations as an adult.

c. Rationalization. Here an employee may respond to frustration by attempting to find an acceptable explanation for the frustration rather than face the real cause. For example, because of Officer Ginty's mediocre performance, he is continually passed over when choice assignments are given. However, Ginty rationalizes that the reason for this is that the department is waiting for a real choice assignment to open up before selecting him.

d. Sublimation. This occurs when a person cannot adequately deal with a work-related frustration, such as achieving promotion. The person then transfers his energies outside the agency. Officer Ginty just cannot pass the supervisor's exam after several attempts. He then decides to moonlight by opening a small landscaping company with several employees whom he will personally supervise. Ginty has become a supervisor by sublimating his energies in another direction. The danger is that it might result in a loss of interest at work.

e. Fixation. This occurs when a person repeatedly has the same response to a frustration, despite the fact that such response has been ineffective in the past. They get so stuck or fixated on the problem that they never deal with or modify their response to it. This is exemplified by the employee who continues to make the same mistake even though he has been corrected in the past.

f. Guilt Complex. This is exhibited by actions which seek to make up for or atone for past inappropriate behavior, real or imagined. Employees experiencing guilt complex may exhibit behavior which constantly seeks to please others regardless of the self sacrifices it costs them personally.

g. Inferiority Complex. Most individuals wish to succeed. At times, when this success is blocked, frustration sets in and feelings of inadequacy develop. Curiously, the response to such feelings among some people is to set even higher goals or to constantly prove oneself. People who feel inferior usually try to compensate. Unfortunately, they usually compensate at the expense of others. A person with an inferiority complex always tries to out do everyone else, will try to make themselves look good at the expense of others, and may even resort to bully-like behavior.

h. Anxiety. Everyone experiences concern and worry at one time or another, but some employees may experience anxiety and not be able to articulate why. They say, "I feel worried about something, but I don't know exactly what it is." In extreme cases the employee may feel like he is about to "go to pieces." It is this pervasive, dark-cloud anxiety which seems to overtake an employee that should alert a supervisor.

16

i. Job Stress. The field of law enforcement provides work stressors not found in most other occupations. Law enforcement personnel find themselves on a roller-coaster ride rising from prolonged periods of continuous boredom and tedium to times of danger and excitement. In addition law enforcement personnel often are called upon to deal with cultures, lifestyles, and problems which they have never experienced. To all of this, some seem to properly handle the stress, but other employees react in the extreme by either becoming overly emotionally involved in the problems of those they serve or becoming overly callous to their needs or even displaying cruelty to those they come in contact with.

Conversations with supervisors often provide subordinates with the opportunity to relive unpleasant or even traumatic events they have experienced. When this occurs the event can be more realistically viewed and dealt with by the subordinate. This process is known as catharsis. Supervisors should allow this process to take place not only to allow a more realistic appraisal of a past event by a subordinate, but also to detect behavioral patterns of subordinates which may lead to work-related problems.

However, a word of caution is needed for the supervisor. The supervisor must be careful when attempting to label the behavior of a subordinate. Labeling tends to oversimplify the behaviors of subordinates. In addition, the label does not offer clear clues as to the cause(s) of such behavior. The supervisor should be aware of such behaviors and frustration responses and help the subordinate seek proper assistance when these behaviors impact negatively on the subordinate's work.

TEST YOUR UNDERSTANDING

1. Discuss the supervisor's ambivalent role.

2. Identify and discuss the most common errors made by first level supervisors during their transition from worker to supervisor.

3. Identify and discuss the three basic skill areas needed to become effective supervisors.

4. Identify and discuss the fundamental roles of the law enforcement supervisor.

FOOTNOTES

1. Herbert G. Hicks and C. Ray Gullett, *Management,* 4th ed. (New York: McGraw-Hill Book Company, 1981), p. 7.

2. Ricky W. Griffin, *Management.* (Boston, MA: Houghton Mifflin Company, 1984), p. 358.

3. Lester R. Bittel, *What Every Supervisor Should Know.* New York: McGraw-Hill Book Company, 1974), p. 127.

4. Margot Robinson, *Egos and Eggshells - Managing for Success in Today's Workplace.* (North Carolina: Stanton and Harper Books, 1993), p. 27.

5. Harold Koontz, Cyril O'Donnell and Heinz Weihrich, *Management,* 8th ed. (New York: McGraw-Hill Book Company, 1984), p. 403.

6. Loren B. Belker, *The First-Time Manager,* 3rd ed. (New York: AMACOM, 1993), p. 19.

7. Lester R. Bittel, p. 32.

8. Matthew J. Culligan, Suzanne Deakins and Arthur H. Young, *Back to Basics Management: The Lost Craft of Leadership.* (New York: Facts on File, 1993), p. 14.

9. W. Richard Plunkett, *Supervision: Diversity and Teams in the Workplace.* (Boston, MA: Allyn and Bacon, 1994), p. 7.

10. Margot Robinson, p. 11.

11. Charles R. Swanson and Leonard Territo, *Police Administration.* (New York: MacMillan Publishing company, 1983), p. 98.

12. Marian E. Hayes, *Managing Performance - A Comprehensive Guide to Effective Supervision.* (California: Crisp Publications, Inc., 1990) p. 34.

SUGGESTED READINGS

Allen, Louis A.
The Profession of Management.
New York: McGraw-Hill Book Company, 1964.

Benton, Lewis.
Supervision and Management.
New York: McGraw-Hill Book Company, 1972.

Bethel, Sheila Murray.
Twelve Qualities That Make You A Leader.
New York: G.P. Putnam's Sons, 1990.

Koontz, Harold and Cyril J. O'Donnell.
Principles of Management, 5th ed.
New York: McGraw-Hill Book Company, 1972.

Kotter, John P.
The Leadership Factor.
New York: The Free Press, 1988.

CHAPTER 2
THE MANAGERIAL FUNCTIONS OF
THE LAW ENFORCEMENT SUPERVISOR

MANAGEMENT DEFINED

Management is a process or activity whereby the human and material resources of a formal organization are coordinated to achieve specific goals. Management also refers to those people whose job it is to accomplish those goals through others.

The Formal Organization

A formal organization exists when a group of people interact together to achieve stated purposes.

"The four essential elements of any formal organization are as follows:

1. A clear understanding about stated purposes and goals.
2. A division of labor among specialists.
3. A rational organization or design.
4. A hierarchy of authority and accountability."[1]

The Hierarchy of Authority and Accountability

Formal organizations are composed of workers and managers. The managers form a hierarchy which is comprised of three levels: top, middle and operating. This hierarchy is often depicted as a pyramid.

Managers who direct the activities of workers are on the operating level, which forms the base of the pyramid since most of an agency's managers are there. It is there that first level supervisors are found. Recall that all supervisors are managers, and that as one ascends the hierarchy one usually performs more managerial and less supervisory functions. Managers who direct the activities of other managers are never found on the operating level.

The middle and top levels of the pyramid are occupied by managers who direct the activities of other managers. The primary functions of top and middle managers are planning, directing, and controlling. But, these functions are also performed by managers on the operating level. It is a difference of degree and not of kind.

FORMAL MANAGERIAL AUTHORITY

Formal managerial authority is the power or right to command, enforce obedience, or make decisions. Every manager needs formal managerial authority to issue orders, since it is the job of a manager to work through others. "Organizations are structured on superior-subordinate relationships. As a result, authority is a universal element in all formal organizations."[2] Formal managerial authority is bestowed upon a manager by virtue of his assignment. It follows that as an individual manager changes assignments in an agency, the scope of his formal authority also changes. This is especially true as one moves vertically on the managerial pyramid as opposed to moving horizontally.

Line, Staff and Functional Authority

Law enforcement managers should understand the distinction among line, staff, and functional authority. While they are all forms of formal authority, they are quite different.

Line Authority

Line authority allows managers to exercise direct control over subordinates. Given line authority over someone, a manager can issue orders to that person and expect compliance. And, if that compliance isn't realized, the line manager can discipline that person. Their authority flows in a direct "line" down to their subordinates. "The word line refers to a position (or positions) of command authority with the responsibility for coordinating the functions under it."[3] It must flow downward. One doesn't have line authority over one's peers, only over one's subordinates. The most common example of line authority is a patrol supervisor's authority over the officers under his immediate command.

Staff Authority

Staff authority is possessed by all managers who act in an advisory capacity to other managers. "Every large organization has a number of people with superior knowledge and skills whose primary duty consists of aiding others to do a better job. The specialists who do the aiding are ordinarily referred to as staff people, whereas those whom they aid are referred to as line people."[4] The gathering and dissemination of intelligence, the providing of communication services, and the conducting of legal research are examples of staff specialties. When such a specialist exercises staff authority, that individual is usually acting in a purely advisory capacity, and the line manager is not obligated to follow the advice. Pure staff authority is not binding; the advice can be ignored. Of course, in such a situation, the line manager must take full responsibility for this action. But this is true whether or not the line manager follows the advice of the staff manager. A line manager cannot be relieved of responsibility for following the advice of a staff specialist.

The situation is complicated by the fact that managers who exercise staff authority also possess line authority. These managers exercise staff authority when they advise other managers but exercise line authority when they direct their own subordinates.

Functional Authority

As stated above, a manager with staff authority, in most cases, acts in an advisory capacity since line managers are not obligated to follow the advice. The exception exists when a staff manager also possesses functional authority. Functional authority exists when a staff specialist is authorized by agency policy to issue binding orders. Consider, for example, a staff manager who is in charge of payroll. That manager could be given functional authority to issue orders and instructions which must be followed by everyone in the agency. For example, he could issue orders specifying the procedures for authorizing overtime. Such procedures must be followed. Interestingly, functional authority can flow in any direction. All managers at all levels can be bound by functional authority.

23

Examples of Line, Staff, and Functional Authority

a. When a patrol sergeant orders an officer under his command to follow a certain course of action, as long as the order is a lawful one, the officer is bound to obey the order and may be disciplined by the sergeant for failing to comply. This is an example of line authority.

b. When a manager who is a community relations specialist offers advice on policing a street demonstration to a watch commander, unless the specialist has functional authority over such procedures, the commander can either follow the advice or ignore it. This is an example of pure staff authority.

c. When a manager who is a community relations specialist directs the activities of one of his own subordinates at a street demonstration, the subordinate must comply. This is an example of a manager with staff authority exercising line authority.

d. When a manager who is a community relations specialist is empowered by department policy to issue a directive on the investigation of certain incidents, such as bias incidents, then all department managers are bound to follow that directive. This is an example of a manager with staff authority exercising functional authority.

Job Descriptions

Managers must know the scope of their formal authority. A manager who is unsure of his authority is hampered in two ways. He may unintentionally exceed his authority and thereby interfere with the authority of other managers. Or, he may unnecessarily involve another manager in a decision under the mistaken belief that he does not have sufficient authority. For these reasons, top level managers should make job descriptions available for every managerial position. These descriptions should outline the duties of the job. "As jobs are analyzed, duties and responsibilities are brought into focus and areas of overlapping or neglected duties come to light."[5] Then the holder of the job must be given authority commensurate with those responsibilities. Job descriptions, therefore, should be as specific as possible. In the absence of detailed job descriptions it is not

24

reasonable to hold a manager accountable for either exceeding his authority or failing to exercise it.

Perceived Authority

Managers need more than formal managerial authority to perform effectively. Authority also comes from the opinion, respect and esteem of others. "Martin Luther King had very little legitimate power, but by the force of his personality, his ideas, and his ability to preach, he strongly influenced the behavior of many people."[6] This type of authority is called perceived authority since it emanates from the perception of subordinates. This explains how two managers could have the same formal managerial authority and differ greatly in their effectiveness. The greater the extent of a manager's perceived authority, the better that manager can influence his subordinates and the greater his ability to exercise power over them. Managers bolster their perceived authority mostly via their ability to direct others fairly without becoming overbearing. Perceived authority is also bolstered by technical skills, experience, and the respect of peers and higher level managers.

Authority, Responsibility, and Accountability

Authority, responsibility and accountability cannot be separated nor are they the sole province of managers. Every member of an agency who has duties to perform needs the authority to perform them, has the responsibility to execute them and has the accountability for their performance.

Consider the following:
A patrol sergeant's job description requires the submission of a monthly report on the arrest activity of all subordinates. Agency procedures specify that this report must be delivered to the watch commander by the fifth day of each month. One month a sergeant neglects to hand in this report by the due date. After that date, the sergeant is approached by the watch commander and asked to explain the failure.

In this example, the sergeant's authority to gather the required information from his subordinates comes from his job description. His responsibility was to prepare the required report and submit it to the watch commander by the fifth of each month. When the sergeant neglected to meet this responsibility, the watch commander held him accountable. Authority, responsibility, and accountability are inseparable. When one is present, the other two must also be present.

There is an important distinction concerning accountability. Workers can be held accountable only for their own actions. But supervisors can be held accountable for the actions of others. This occurs when a supervisor delegates authority to a subordinate.

THE DELEGATION PROCESS

One principal function of all managers is to delegate authority, to entrust their authority to other people. Delegation is strictly a management function. Workers cannot delegate; only managers can delegate. But, since delegation is always downwards, managers cannot delegate to their peers, and they cannot delegate to their superiors. They can delegate only to subordinate managers and workers. These subordinate managers and workers can be given an entire task or different parts of the same task. Or the supervisor can delegate the routine parts and reserve the important parts for himself. When a task lends itself to delegation but is of unusual importance, it should be delegated with the stipulation that the final product needs the supervisor's approval.

A delegated task should not be rescinded simply because the worker complains of its difficulty or needs additional training. The only acceptable reason for revoking delegated authority is that the delegated assignment is so far beyond a worker's capabilities that even additional training would not assure the task's completion.

A first level supervisor must delegate authority in order to function effectively. A supervisor who is reluctant to delegate creates problems for himself, his subordinates, and his bosses. However, while it is imperative for a supervisor to delegate, if the delegation process is not completely understood or properly

26

utilized and controlled, additional problems can develop. The delegation process requires good judgment, since there are no definitive rules for the delegation of authority.

Although there are no definitive rules, the reasons for delegating authority should be understood, as well as the failures of delegating. It must be understood that delegation creates dual responsibility and accountability, as explained later. It should also be understood that certain tasks should not be delegated and that there are certain steps to be followed when a supervisor entrusts his authority to a subordinate.

Delegation as an Essential Process

Delegation is an essential process for several reasons.

First, it prevents slowdowns in services. These slowdowns occur when supervisors mistakenly feel that they must be in direct control of all activity. This feeling is most common in new supervisors.

Consider the following:

Statistics indicate that locations in a sergeant's jurisdiction need traffic surveys to determine if hazards exist. The surveys are standard and require no special skills. It is the analyzing of the surveys that requires special skills. Nevertheless, the sergeant schedules the surveys at a pace which allows him to be present when each one is conducted. In the meantime, a fatal accident occurs at one of the locations due to be surveyed. Investigation reveals that the cause of the accident would have been uncovered by the survey.

This example emphasizes how delays in services can have serious ramifications. The sergeant should have delegated the making of the surveys to his officers and spent his time analyzing the surveys and planning needed improvements.

A second reason why delegation is an essential process is that it allows supervisors to spend more time on planning, directing, and controlling. "These 'priorities' are normally long-term as opposed to urgent and may fall victim to procrastination while [supervisors] concentrate on immediate—and less important—concerns."[7] Routine tasks are the most appropriate ones to delegate since their delegation enables the supervisor to spend time on more important managerial functions. "Lack of effectiveness on the part of managers can usually be attributed to insufficient time being devoted to the priority activities."[8]

A third reason why delegation is essential is that it increases subordinates' skills. Though routine tasks are the most appropriate ones to delegate, a supervisor should also delegate some more complex ones. "Delegation is sharing your job with the people who work for you. This includes the highly visible, important tasks as well as the routine."[9] Subordinates who perform tasks usually performed by supervisors are given an opportunity to increase their technical skills. In addition, this entrusting of additional authority develops subordinates' confidence in their own abilities which often motivates them to seek positions of greater responsibilities.

Yet another reason why delegation is essential is that it benefits the agency. First, it is economical, since routine tasks are performed at the lowest possible level. Delegation also aids the agency in its personnel development, allowing supervisors to train subordinates. Besides increasing the technical skills of workers, delegation also enhances worker initiative and creates a pool of employees who are able to fill in for supervisors. Such practices also increase job satisfaction by offsetting the monotony of a patrol officer's routine tasks. "Taking orders is tedious. Making decisions is fun. Rote assignments are boring. New challenges stimulate. Being a cog in a machine makes workers stale. Being contributors makes them enthusiastic."[10]

Failures to Delegate

Despite the advantages of delegating, some supervisors are reluctant to relinquish their authority to subordinates for several reasons.

Supervisors often fail to recognize the benefits of delegation. This is the most common reason why supervisors fail to delegate. This problem is best dealt with via the agency's supervisory training program. Newly promoted supervisors must be exposed to the benefits of delegating and the agency's policy of rewarding supervisors who delegate effectively.

Supervisors may also believe that delegation threatens their job security. These supervisors feel that once talented subordinates know their job, those subordinates will become their competition. In actuality, this is paranoia given the job security guaranteed tenured civil servants. This concern might be valid only in private industry and those law enforcement agencies which do not offer civil service tenure. Nonetheless, an agency policy which rewards the developing of subordinates to perform supervisory tasks is the best way to deter these concerns.

Other supervisors may fear that subordinates cannot do the job as well as they can. This concerns overly conscientious supervisors or supervisors who overestimate their own competence. They fear a substandard performance will reflect poorly on them or believe that they are the only ones who can do their job. Both of these obstacles can be overcome by understanding the delegation steps. Basically, routine tasks should be delegated to all subordinates to improve their competence. Then, once competent workers are developed, they can gradually be given authority to perform more complex tasks.

Dual Responsibility and Accountability

As noted, authority, responsibility and accountability are inseparable. When supervisors delegate their authority, they do not rid themselves of their responsibility or their accountability. In effect, the delegation process creates a dual responsibility and accountability. The worker given the authority is responsible and accountable for the task, but, so is the supervisor who delegated the authority. Otherwise, supervisors could avoid being held responsible for difficult jobs simply by delegating them to subordinates. In fact, the primary burden of responsibility and accountability rests with the supervisor and not with the subordinate.

Tasks Not To Be Delegated

Although it is not possible to list all the tasks which lend themselves to delegation, it is possible to list those tasks of the supervisor which should NOT be delegated. Those tasks not excluded can be delegated.

1. Tasks the supervisor either does not understand or does not know how to perform. Obviously, if a supervisor cannot give clear instructions or advice to the subordinate, then the delegation should not be made.

2. Tasks beyond the capability of a subordinate. While complex tasks are suitable to the delegation process, such tasks should not be delegated to subordinates who lack the skills or abilities to complete them.

3. Tasks which involve the rewarding or punishing subordinates. Subordinates strive to please a supervisor because that supervisor alone has the authority to reward or punish them. A supervisor who delegates this authority loses this control.

4. Tasks involving serious personnel problems. A supervisor has to be seen as concerned about subordinates. Delegating the handling of personnel problems implies that a supervisor lacks this concern.

5. Tasks formulating important policy. Few supervisors can delegate this authority, since policy is developed by top management. Given policies' widespread effects, top managers should not delegate the responsibility of formulating policy.

6. Offensive or distasteful tasks. Though such tasks sometimes lend themselves to delegation, if they are the only ones being delegated, subordinates will become resentful.

Basic Steps in the Delegation Process

The delegation process should be viewed as having six basic steps:

Step One - Choosing the Task

Choosing the task includes making sure a task is suitable for delegation and deciding what the subordinate is to do. Remember, if the task is not clear to the supervisor, it will not be communicated clearly to the worker. When the task is a simple one, little time need be spent on this step. But, if the task is a complex one, this step requires significant reflection.

Step Two - Selecting the Subordinate

Selection of the subordinate is the most important step in the entire delegation process. The temptation for many supervisors, knowing they will be given credit for successful delegations, is to delegate to only the most competent of their subordinates. This undermines the training benefit of delegation. A supervisor's delegations should be spread out among as many subordinates as possible, though assignments should be made only to those capable of carrying them out. In most cases, this capability must be built gradually. Thus a supervisor must know the strengths and weaknesses of subordinates in order to efficiently delegate.

Step Three - Giving the Assignment

The subordinate receiving the assignment must be told exactly what is to be accomplished. Assumptions have no place in the delegation process. Other guidelines also govern the process of giving the assignments as follows:

1. Written instructions are recommended in two instances. The first is when the task is very complex. The second is when the delegating supervisor will not be available for consultation and the task is other than a routine assignment. However, even when written instructions are given, they should be discussed in person.

2. The subordinate should be told why he was chosen.

3. The importance and necessity of the task should be reviewed.

4. Any resources available to assist in the task should be identified, e.g., staff units within the agency or private agencies.

Step Four - Setting Management Controls

Steps four and five are accomplished during the assignment of the task, and many managerial experts include them as part of that step. But because of their importance, it is recommended that they be viewed as separate steps.

To varying extents, every delegated assignment must be controlled, and it is the supervisor's responsibility to implement these controls. A simple delegation can be controlled by (a) setting a reasonable due date, and by (b) obtaining feedback at its completion. A longer, more complex delegation is best controlled by a series of due dates that require the submission of progress reports. These dates can be tied to goals of the task, or they can be made on a weekly or monthly basis, depending on the nature and length of the assignment. In setting the due dates, unless the time frames are predetermined by a definite need, subordinates should play a role in deciding these time frames. Once agreed upon, these dates must be recorded by the supervisor, ideally on a calendar. Then, it is incumbent upon the supervisor to follow up. One final word about due dates, they must be specific. General statements, such as "Get it done as soon as possible" are not effective control devices. "Get it done by May 4th", is specific and effective.

Step Five - Checking Understanding

The subordinate must be required to restate the assignment. Queries such as "Do you understand?" or "Do you have any questions?" are not sufficient. The supervisor must make certain the subordinate understands the assignment. In the absence of such understanding, the subordinate cannot be held accountable. Only when the subordinate is able to explain the assignment and the agreed upon time frames should a supervisor be satisfied.

Consider the following:

A simple delegation has been made, and the supervisor is setting management controls.

Supervisor: Let's talk about a due date. It seems to me that you should be able to take care of this matter within the next three days. What do you think?

Officer: Three days sounds reasonable to me.

Supervisor: Fine. Today is June 1st. Your due date is June 4th. By that time I will expect feedback from you in the form of a brief written report.

Officer: Yes sir.

32

Supervisor: Great. Now, tell me in your own words exactly what you believe I am asking you to do and how long you have to do it.

In this example, the supervisor adequately covered steps four and five. The supervisor correctly:

1. Established a specific due date.
2. Obtained input from the worker as to the appropriateness of that due date.
3. Described how feedback would be provided.
4. Checked for understanding.

This is an example of how a simple delegation is controlled. If the delegated task is one which will take a long time, then interim due dates should be established. In such a situation, evaluation should not be withheld until the very end. Evaluating, therefore, includes checking progress as well as checking results.

Step Six - Following Up

Remember, when a supervisor delegates his authority to a subordinate, the supervisor maintains final responsibility and accountability. Thus supervisors must follow up on all delegations to ensure that action has been taken, goals have been satisfied, and deadlines have been met. When a lengthy task has been delegated, this follow-up should not be put off until the completion of the task. Rather, periodic evaluation should be made to ensure that progress is being made.

If follow-up reveals either above average or below average performance, the supervisor should inform the worker. With an above average performance, the worker should be rewarded with praise and an official note in the personnel folder. If the performance was below average, the supervisor should review with the worker what went wrong and how similar errors can be avoided in the future.

SPAN OF CONTROL

Span of control is a managerial principle which emphasizes that there is a limit to the number of subordinates a supervisor can effectively manage. Most management experts agree that top level managers should have a more narrow span of control than other managers, and that as one moves down the managerial hierarchy, the span of control can broaden. These same experts often maintain that a top level manager's span of control should never exceed five to one. This means that a top level manager should not directly supervise more than five subordinates.

The optimal span of control most often recommended at the level of operations varies but rarely exceeds twelve to one. The emerging theory, however, is that so many factors impact span of control that it is futile to attempt to determine an optimal span of control for law enforcement supervisors in general, especially those at the level of operations. "[R]ecent operational management theorists have taken the position that there are too many underlying variables in a management situation for us to specify any particular number of subordinates that a manager can effectively supervise. Thus, the principle of the span of management states that 'there is a limit to the number of subordinates a manager can effectively supervise, but the exact number will depend on the impact of underlying factors.'"[11] Besides, the reality of the situation is that the ratio of officers to supervisors is determined more by budgetary considerations than by management theory. However, a narrow span of control of about six to one is always preferable to a broader span of control of about twelve to one. Unfortunately, some law enforcement agencies in this country will continue to exceed the bounds of effective supervisory spans of control, The best way to combat this problem is to understand the factors which impact on the span of control, as well as the negative effects of these factors, though overcoming some of these effects is not realistically possible.

Factors Impacting Span of Control

The number of workers that can be effectively supervised by one supervisor is impacted by the following:

1. Capabilities of the supervisor. The more capable the supervisor, the more subordinates he can effectively supervise.

2. Capabilities of the subordinates. Highly capable subordinates require less supervision.

3. Work performed by subordinates. The simpler the task, the less the need for close supervision. Conversely, complex work requires more supervision.

4. Extent of the supervisor's non-supervisory tasks. If the supervisor has a number of non-supervisory responsibilities, he will be able to supervise fewer subordinates. Also, supervisors who are required to complete an inordinate amount of paperwork have less time for supervisory tasks.

5. Willingness of the supervisor to delegate. Supervisors reluctant to delegate authority can not effectively maintain a broad span of control.

6. Physical distance between the supervisor and the workers. If the subordinates and supervisor are in the same location, as in an office, more subordinates can be supervised than if they are spread over a large geographical area, as in patrol operations.

7. Quality of the agency's formal training program. Better trained employees require less supervision.

8. Rate of turnover. A high rate of personnel turnover forces supervisors to conduct considerable on-the-job training. The time needed for such training limits their effective span of control.

Though certain of the above factors cannot be changed, span of control can be expanded. A critical review of non-supervisory tasks can reveal activities that can be shifted from field supervisors without impacting services to the community. Also, delegating authority can quickly and easily broaden span of control without bureaucratic entanglements.

Organizational change can also increase or decrease existing spans of control if it involves adding or eliminating a supervisory level in the management hierarchy. Adding a level automatically creates a more narrow span of control since it increases the number of supervisors. Removing a level results in a broader span of control by decreasing the number of supervisors.

CHAIN OF COMMAND

Chain of command is the term used to describe the lines or chains of authority in an organization as they flow from the highest manager down through the intermediate managers to the managers at the level of operations.

All of a manager's communication must be channeled through either that manager's immediate subordinate or through that manager's immediate superior. Except when exigencies exist, all official communications must follow this communication path. This is known as following the chain of command. This rule is necessitated by the need for all managers to remain informed. Violating the chain of command creates misunderstanding and confusion in the organization.

Workers are also expected to adhere to the chain of command, channeling communications through their immediate supervisor, unless exigencies exist.

Any supervisor or worker who violates the chain of command must prove the need to prevent one of the links in the chain from obtaining the information being communicated. One example of a justifiable violation involves an allegation of serious misconduct implicating someone in the chain.

Time constraints do not justify violating the chain of command. If time is of the essence, a manager can communicate directly with someone, provided a duplicate of the communication is sent through channels. In that way the chain of command is preserved.

UNITY OF COMMAND

Unity of command is often confused with chain of command. While there are similarities, they are in fact quite different. Chain of command controls communications; unity of command controls subordinates.

Unity of command requires that every employee be under the direct control of only one supervisor, his immediate supervisor. Unity of command prevents the confusion caused by conflicting orders from different sources. "The more complete an individual's reporting relationships to a single supervisor, the smaller the problem of conflicting instructions and the greater the feeling of personal responsibility for results."[12] If accountability is to exist and priorities are to be set, then employees must receive uniform direction from only one supervisor. Furthermore, violations of this principle often cause friction among supervisors and undermine the authority of immediate supervisors.

The principle of unity of command does not apply under two circumstances: (1) in an emergency situation in which the immediate supervisor is unavailable and prompt supervisory intervention is required, and (2) in a potentially damaging situation in which the department's reputation is endangered and the immediate supervisor is unavailable.

For example, assume that a supervisor, a lieutenant from a staff unit, is in the vicinity of a hostage situation. Responding to the location, the lieutenant is the only ranking officer on the scene. A few patrol officers not under his command are present, and others are due to arrive within minutes. Immediate supervisory attention is required to coordinate the activities of the officers in order to protect the lives of the hostages and bystanders. Under these circumstances the lieutenant is authorized to take command pending the arrival of the appropriate patrol supervisor.

Or, assume a supervisor observes a uniformed officer of the department's juvenile division involved in a heated argument with a civilian. No supervisor from the juvenile division is present. The officer is engaged in conduct bordering on unprofessional before several witnesses. Despite the fact that the officer in the dispute is not assigned to the supervisor's unit, the supervisor is not bound by the unity of command. This is so since, unless the supervisor intervenes promptly, the officer's conduct could damage the reputation of the department.

However, the most common violation of unity of command does not involve intervention from outside commands. Instead, it involves supervisors and subordinates assigned to the same command. It occurs when ranking officers such as lieutenants and captains deal directly with operating personnel instead of dealing with them through their immediate supervisors. Unfortunately, workers are harmed most by this breach of procedure. Given the fact that it is risky to call a superior's attention to poor management practices, unity of command should be routinely covered in training programs.

MANAGEMENT BY OBJECTIVES

Management by objectives is a management principle which recognizes the fact that subordinates are more committed to achieving goals when they have played a role in the setting of those goals. Although there is no one recommended approach to management by objectives, there are certain steps that should be included.

Step One - Setting Goals

Objectives are the goals of a unit that must be reached within a specified time period. If achieved, they must result in improved operations. Goal setting must occur during periodic meetings between managers and their subordinate managers. It is equally important that all goals are mutually accepted and arrived at through negotiation. The goals must be both realistic and challenging. Also, goals must be clearly and concisely stated and must not involve an unreasonable expenditure of resources.

Step Two - Identifying Needs

Goals must be analyzed and resources identified. If the means of achieving a goal are beyond either the capabilities of those responsible or beyond the available resources, the goal should either be amended or discarded.

Step Three - Setting Timetables

Goals become objectives when time frames are set. But besides the completion date, time frames for progress reports should also be established via negotiation.

Step Four - Evaluating Results

Management by objectives should be a continuing process. The end of each cycle involves an evaluation of results. This evaluation then serves as a springboard for the entire cycle to begin again. While the initial few cycles will seem difficult, proficiency usually increases as the cycles continue. When used properly, management by objectives develops managerial ability and improves organizational performance.

TEST YOUR UNDERSTANDING

1. What is the difference between line and staff authority?

2. What can a manager learn from his job description?

3. Discuss why delegation is an essential process.

4. Discuss four causes of delegation failure.

5. What tasks should not be delegated?

6. Discuss the basic steps in the delegation process.

7. Discuss some factors which impact on span of control.

8. When can the chain of command be violated?

9. Discuss the four step approach to management by objectives.

FOOTNOTES

1. W. Richard Plunkett, *Supervision: Diversity and Teams in the Workplace.* (Boston, MA: Allyn and Bacon, 1994), p. 67.

2. William G. Scott, D.B.A., Terrence R. Mitchell, Ph.D., and Phillip H. Birnbaum, Ph.D., *Organization Theory: a structural and behavioral analysis.* (Homewood, IL: Irwin, 1981), p. 27.

3. Ibid., p. 31.

4. John M. Pfiffner and Marshall Fels, *The Supervision of Personnel Human Relations In the Management of Men.* (Englewood Cliffs, NJ: Prentice-Hall, Inc., 1964), p. 73.

5. Harold Koontz and Heinz Weihrich, *Management,* 9th ed. (New York: McGraw-Hill Book Co., 1988), p. 278.

6. Ibid., p. 208.

7. Harold L. Taylor, *Delegate - The Key to Successful Management.* (New York: Beaufort Books, 1984), p. 35.

8. Ibid., p. 35.

9. Taylor, p. 82.

10. James M. Jenks and John M. Kelly, *Don't Do. Delegate!.* (New York: Franklin Watts, 1985), p. 38.

11. Koontz and Weihrich, p. 167.

12. Koontz and Weihrich, p. 290.

SUGGESTED READINGS

Allen, Louis A.
The Management Profession.
New York: McGraw-Hill Book Co., 1964.

Dale, Ernest.
Organization.
New York: American Management Association, 1967.

Davis, Ralph C.
Fundamentals of Top Management.
New York: Harper and Row, 1951.

Durkheim, Emile.
The Division of Labor in Society.
New York: The Free Press, 1947.

Koontz, Harold and Cyril J. O'Donnell.
Principles of Management, 5th ed.
New York: McGraw-Hill Book Co., 1972.

Maynard, H.B. [ed.].
Handbook of Business Administration.
New York: McGraw-Hill Book Co., 1967.

Mc Conkey, Dale.
No Nonsense Delegation.
New York: AMACOM, 1974.

CHAPTER 3
THE MANAGERIAL FUNCTION
OF PLANNING

The word "plans" usually implies something graphic, i.e., a blueprint, diagram, or chart. However, graphics only serve as an illustration of an idea. The illustration is not the plan itself, only a small part of it. Actually most plans do not lend themselves to illustration. For example, how could a supervisor illustrate a plan to increase morale?

Planning develops courses of action to bring about objectives by a specific time. It can be reactive or proactive. A supervisor may plan a reaction to a new law. Or a manager noting a low absenteeism rate in one unit may wish to proactively develop a plan promoting a similar rate in other units. Planning may also be about preventing things from happening, such as reducing accidents. Regardless of whether a manager wants to cause something desirable or eliminate something undesirable, planning involves setting objectives and initiating actions to reach those objectives. A continuous process, planning requires revision, modification, and re-evaluation, which may even terminate the plan. Planning is a skill dependent on judgment. This judgment is based on experience, knowledge of the agency, knowledge of the job, awareness of the public, and advice from within the unit.

PLANNING DEFINED

In simplest terms, planning tells managers what is to be accomplished and how it is to be accomplished. "It involves selecting from among alternative future courses of action for the enterprise as a whole and for every department or section within it."[1] Planning is best defined by its five basic steps:

1. Researching the need.
2. Setting the goal.
3. Formulating the plan.
4. Initiating the action.
5. Monitoring the results.

RESEARCHING THE NEED

Before any planning should take place, the need for a plan must be established. Information from inside and outside the agency must be collected and analyzed. Data from within the agency can come in the form of:

Internal reports. These include ongoing reports, such as daily summaries like arrest reports.

Inspections. These include reports done by both supervisors and staff inspection units.

Literature. Recent publications dealing with the problem also help clarify objectives.

Participant information. If gathered correctly, this is the best source of information. This data can be collected through personal interviews, informal conversations, and properly constructed questionnaires.

Regardless of its source, information must be analyzed and corroborated. Fact must be separated from fiction. Research must also be accurately interpreted.

Consider the following:

Prosecutors are complaining that they are losing cases because they cannot reach witnesses. The information on witnesses they are receiving from the officers who initially investigate incidents is not sufficient. A supervisor corroborates that a large number of cases are being lost. The need for a plan is established. A plan is initiated to train officers in the proper completion of the agency's preliminary investigation reports. The problem, however, does not go away. More data reveals that the form used as a preliminary investigation report has not been constructed to collect enough information on witnesses. Therefore, the plan for training officers would never solve the problem. Clarified, the need is for a better form, not better training.

SETTING THE GOAL

Any goal must conform with the overall mission of the agency. Each agency must have a mission statement, a clear statement of what the agency is supposed to do, and where the agency wants to go. It is the reason for the very existence of the organization.

Mission Statements

A typical mission statement of a public sector law enforcement agency reads: "The mission of the New York City Police Department is to enhance the quality of life in our city by working in partnership with the community and in accordance with constitutional rights to enforce the laws, preserve the peace, reduce fear, and provide for a safe environment."[2]

Consider two sub-units of such a typical department, the gun squad and the patrol allocation unit. The gun squad has a plan to infiltrate illegal gun transactions by any means available and intercept illegal firearms. However, this goal conflicts with the mission statement of the agency. Despite the fact that intercepting illegal firearms is in keeping with the mission statement's call to enforce laws, the goal is not in keeping with the statement's call to work in accordance with constitutional rights. By utilizing any means available, their actions violate constitutional rights. On the other hand, the patrol allocation unit has a plan to increase the visibility of patrol officers assigned to neighborhood beats. This goal is in conformance with the department's overall mission of reducing fear and providing for a safe environment. Officers patrolling in a highly visible manner would do just that.

No matter how well-constructed a plan, it must conform with the mission statement of the agency. Some managers will display the mission statement conspicuously as a reminder of what the agency is supposed to do. Too often goals are set which do nothing to achieve the agency's mission. The goals, then, serve the sub-unit, not the agency. This is especially true in staff units that forget they exist to support line units. Their goals may perpetuate their own existence and ignore the overall mission statement.

FORMULATING THE PLAN

In formulating the plan, the supervisor, having established a need for a plan and subsequently set the goal, must determine the range of choices and select one. In establishing a range of choices, initially the supervisor should not be overly restrictive. He should consider all feasible choices and reject only those that have no potential for success. Rejecting choices must be based on logical reasoning and documented facts.

The questions that should be answered in determining if a plan is appropriate include: Are there sufficient resources on hand? Can the necessary support be obtained? Will the plan achieve real results or provide only a temporary solution? When examining resources the supervisor should consider both funding and staff. If there are a sufficient number of people, do they have the necessary skills? If the staff lacks the skills, would it be cost effective to train them? In examining the need for support, such issues as union objection to contractual agreements and local community reaction must be considered. In terms of results, "band-aid" approaches which only temporarily deal with a problem should be avoided. For example, if a plan creates a task force to deal with the prostitution problem, what will happen once the task force is disbanded? Will the same problem again surface? The answer to one question sometimes leads to another question. Thus it is not possible to identify in advance all the questions that should be asked when determining the right choice of action. The selection process is often one of de-selection rather than one of selection. The best choice is the one with the fewest drawbacks.

The chosen plan must also adhere to agency policy, which requires an understanding of policy.

Policy Defined

Policies tell what to do, not how to do it. They have been identified "as guides to thinking in decision making,"[3] and "general statements that guide decisions."[4]

For example, an agency's policy is to prevent vehicular accidents by issuing traffic summonses. This tells what to do, not how to do it. The policy does not indicate when and where to give summonses. Nor does it define the number of drivers or the kind of violations to be cited. A policy does not deal with specifics. It is merely a general statement intended to assist in the mission of the agency.

Understanding Policy

In private industry policy is usually created either by the president or by the board of directors. They create policy to facilitate the business of the company. In law enforcement, policy is usually created by the head of the agency for the same reason.

Policy may be created to accommodate recently passed legislation. For example, a law prohibiting discrimination against gays may result in a policy prohibiting questions about sexual preferences on employment applications. Policy could also be created as a reaction to conditions in the agency. For example, if officers in one-person patrol cars are involved in more vehicular accidents due to driver fatigue, a policy might mandate two-person patrol units so that the driving burdens can be shared.

Regardless of what motivates the policy, its dissemination should be accompanied by an explanation of its need. Simply stapling a policy statement to each member's paycheck does not guarantee that everyone will read and understand it. Training and feedback are necessary to introduce, clarify and reinforce policy. Also, wherever possible, those affected by the policy should assist in its formulation in order to ensure acceptance.

INITIATING THE ACTION

At this point the plan has been formulated. Now representatives of those who will implement the plan should be brought together and advised of: (1) each unit's or person's responsibility, (2) the method of implementation, (3) time schedules, and (4) expected results.

Inherent in the supervisor's duties is the coordination of those involved. Coordination involves creating a balance or harmony between the participants. Time must be allowed for the participants to become accustomed to their new duties. The supervisor should be constantly available for consultation. However, a supervisor should not be overbearing, or the participants will not function independently.

When the plan is put into action, the agency's rules and procedures must be followed.

Rule Defined

No smoking at a crime scene. Keys of unused patrol cars shall be kept at the station house desk unless required by the motor transport division. These are examples of rules. They are inflexible; no exceptions are permitted beyond what is stated by the rule. Rules specifically direct how personnel should act on the job. While rules are necessary, they bring with them certain dangers. Rules may limit the exercise of discretion and good sense. Stern imposition of unreasonable rules may lead individuals to do only what they have to, with little regard for the overall success of the agency. Still rules are necessary, and little effective planning can take place without them.

Procedure Defined

Procedures are the chosen methods for carrying out tasks. Procedures tell how to do something. When compared to policies and rules, procedures fall somewhere in the middle in terms of flexibility. Because procedures are more specific than policies, they are less flexible. And because procedures are less restrictive than rules, they are more flexible. The following illustrates these degrees of flexibility and restrictiveness:

POLICIES	MOST FLEXIBILITY and LEAST RESTRICTIVE
PROCEDURES	LESS FLEXIBILITY and MORE RESTRICTIVE
RULES	LEAST FLEXIBILITY and MOST RESTRICTIVE

MONITORING THE RESULTS

Little goes exactly as planned, and if supervisors do not monitor or evaluate the plan they have set in motion, they have not done a complete job of planning. The supervisor needs to ensure that the resources of the agency are being properly used to accomplish the goal of the plan. That is the supervisory act of controlling, making sure that people and equipment are being used efficiently.

Controls should inform a supervisor if:
1. Goals of the plan are being met (Are we going in the direction we intended?)
2. Predetermined standards are being met (Is the quality at the level it is supposed to be?)
3. Staff is performing the appropriate tasks (Is the right person doing the right job?)
4. Time schedules are being met (Are we on schedule?)
5. Goals of the plan have been obtained (Are we satisfied with the final results?)

Many new supervisors fail to evaluate their plans. They erroneously believe that their work is done once the plan is put into effect. "One must recognize that the activity is dynamic and evolving and should be willing to modify course, allocation of resources, and even goals—if there is reason to do so."[5]

Reaching the goal is the supervisor's responsibility. Just because the authority has been properly delegated, final accountability still rests with the supervisor. Therefore, subordinates alone should not be relied on to bring forward any problems. However, the supervisor that shows concern for problems will be made aware of them by his staff.

TYPES OF PLANS

Not all agencies refer to the same plan by the same name. The best way to separate plans is by the purposes they serve. Managerial plans prepare for the agency's mission; operational plans perform the agency's mission. Under these two main headings are numerous types of plans.

Managerial Plans

a. Organizational Plan—chart of the responsibilities of each unit.
b. Recruitment Plan—outline for identifying, screening and selecting the best candidates for employment.
c. Personnel Evaluation Plan—procedures for continuously evaluating members of the agency.
d. Promotion Plan—publicized procedures for selecting candidates for career advancement.

e. Fiscal Plan—a budget restricting unit operations to allocated funds.

f. Miscellaneous Personnel Plans—procedures for staffing, equipping, and training personnel.

Other managerial plans exist, but their purpose is always to prepare the agency to accomplish its mission.

Operational Plans

a. Patrol Plan—procedures for patrol tasks, such as handling someone threatening to jump from a structure, handcuffing a prisoner, completing arrest forms, and aiding in medical emergencies.

b. Emergency Plan—procedures for general emergencies such as fires, explosions, and large scale disorders.

c. Tactical Plan—procedures for emergencies at specific locations, such as a fire at a gas storage facility, or the flooding of a certain river, or a robbery at a gun dealer.

d. Interdepartmental Plan—procedures coordinating departments outside the agency in situations such as setting up road blocks for escaping felons and searching for missing persons.

e. Community Relations Plan—procedures for dealing with the community, as in organizing blockwatchers programs and limiting false alarms.

No matter what the name of the plan, the steps and requirements remain the same.[6]

SELF-PLANNING

Self-planning is a supervisor planning his own efforts and time. To self-plan is to decide what you will do, when you will do it, how you will do it, all the while evaluating what you have done. Self-planning is the most distasteful act of planning; it calls for looking in the mirror. Though honest self-evaluation is difficult, the rewards are worth it.

Consider the following:

Captain Upwind complains that everything happens to his unit, and because of these recurring emergencies, he cannot get to any routine matters. He seems to run from one crisis to the next. He also complains that his staff does not seem to plan their actions. They seem to treat each situation with the same approach—that is, "let's see how we'll handle this one." He would like to plan his time better, but that's just the trouble, he doesn't have the time. He is envious of Captain Rems who is in charge of a unit where nothing unusual seems to happen. In those rare crises, Rems seems to have enough time to deal with it, and his staff seems "squared away."

Is Captain Upwind's assessment accurate? Does nothing unusual ever happen in Captain Rems's unit? More than likely Rems is engaging in self-planning, and Upwind is not. Why not? Upwind himself states that he cannot get to routine matters. This is at the core of his problem. No supervisor has a surplus of time for planning. He must make time, and the only way to do that is to delegate routine tasks to subordinates. As far as his staff's failure to plan, they are following his example. If the leadership in a unit fails to plan its own actions, the members will probably also fail to plan their actions.

UPDATING PLANS

Planning is a continuous process. Besides evaluating plans, supervisors need to update plans. What if the plan has achieved the anticipated results, but the results are no longer required? Or, what if the plan's results are not sufficient, or produce more problems? Thus plans must be constantly updated. They must be examined to see if the required actions are still needed, and if still needed, if they are effective.

Consider the following:

A plan is created to handle the traffic of weekly rock concerts held at a local sports arena. However, because of an economic downturn, the arena has been torn down and replaced by high rise apartments. Obviously there is no longer a need for the weekly traffic plan.

Or, consider tenants of a housing project being burglarized during the morning hours. To combat this, a patrol plan calls for three police officers to each make at least two vertical sweeps of the area between the hours of 9 A.M. and 11:30 A.M. The morning burglaries decrease dramatically but do not disappear completely. The results are fine, but the actions now seem excessive. The plan is updated, and only two police officers are assigned to make one vertical sweep each. If, however, the burglaries had increased despite the plan, then the sweeps should have been increased. A plan's original actions may not be enough.

In summary, plans are not devised, initiated and then forgotten. They must be constantly re-examined and updated.

TEST YOUR UNDERSTANDING

1. How is planning a continuous process?

2. What are the five basic steps of planning?

3. What impact does the mission statement of an agency have on planning?

4. Define policies, procedures, and rules.

5. Considering policies, procedures, and rules, which of them is the most flexible? Most restrictive?

6. Describe one way to classify plans.

7. Why is self-planning important?

8. Explain the need for updating plans.

FOOTNOTES

1. Harold Koontz, Cyril O'Donnell, and Heinz Weihrich, *Management.* (New York: McGraw-Hill Book Co., 1984), p. 103.

2. *New York City Police Department Patrol Guide.* 1991, p. 1.

3. Harold Koontz, Cyril O'Donnell, and Heinz Weihrich, *Management.* (New York: McGraw-Hill Book Co., 1984), p. 145.

4. Herbert G. Hicks and C. Ray Gullet, *The Management Of Organizations.* (New York: McGraw- Hill Book Co., 1976), p. 271.

5. Ann McKay Thompson and Marcia Donnan, *Management Strategies For Women.* (New York: Simon and Schuster, 1980), p. 119.

6. For an interesting and unique classification of plans based on single-use plans and recurring-use standing plans use, see Herbert G. Hicks, *The Management Of Organizations.* (New York: McGraw-Hill Book Company, 1976), pp. 271-275.

SUGGESTED READINGS

Famularo, Joseph J.
Organization Planning Manual.
New York: AMACOM, 1979.

Ellis, Darryl J. and Peter P. Pekar.
Planning For Non-Planners - Planning Basics For Managers.
New York: AMACOM, 1980.

Glueck, William F.
Strategic Management and Business Policy.
New York: McGraw-Hill, 1984.

Hussey, David E.
Corporate Planning - The Human Factor.
New York: Pergamon Press, 1978.

Linneman, Robert E.
Shirt-Sleeve Approach To Long-Range Planning For the Smaller, Growing Corporation.
Englewood Cliffs, NJ: Prentice-Hall, 1980.

O'Connor, Rochelle.
Evaluating The Company Planning System and the Corporate Planner.
New York: Conference Board, 1982.

Radford, K.J.
Strategic Planning - An Analytical Approach.
Reston, VA: Reston Publishing Company, 1980.

Ryans Jr., John K. and William L Shanklin.
"Strategic Planning, Concepts and Implementation - Test, Readings, and Cases."

Steiner, George Albert.
Strategic Planning - What Every Manager Must Know.
New York: Free Press, 1979

Tregoe, Benjamin B. and John W. Zimmerman.
Top Management Strategy - What It Is and How To Make It Work.
New York: Simon and Schuster, 1980.

CHAPTER 4
THE SUPERVISOR AS A LEADER

Although the traits and principles of leadership, can be easily identified, there exist different leadership styles, which produce different results. Since there is probably no greater measurement of a leader, especially in the eyes of those who are led, than the ability to make decisions, we will discuss the role of the supervisor as a decision maker.

LEADERSHIP DEFINED

Any meaningful definition of leadership must discuss the following:

Delegating Tasks

Leaders must have the ability to get the job done, not solely by their efforts, but through the efforts of subordinates. For new supervisors this is sometimes a difficult concept. For the first time in their careers they are responsible for getting the job done but not required to actually do the physical work necessary to get it done. "Their main responsibility is to facilitate the work of others, not to do the work themselves. They manage the people who literally put their hands on the work." [1]

Consider the following:

In the locker room of a law enforcement facility, the following conversation takes place: Officer Jones complains, "Sergeant Egos is a nice enough guy, but he never lets you do what you're supposed to do. He explains what has to be done and then winds up doing it himself. Take for example the other day. I was handling a serious accident where the driver of one of the vehicles involved was taken to the hospital unconscious. Sergeant Egos responds to the scene and reminds me I had to make a notification to the injured's next of kin because the guy was taken to the hospital. I knew I had to do that and didn't resent him reminding me 'cause I know his job is to make sure the job gets done right. But when I get to the injured man's home to notify the next of kin, guess who's there? Sergeant Egos! Not only is he there but as soon as the door opens and the injured guy's wife appears,

Egos decides to make the notification himself instead of letting me do it like I'm supposed to do."

Officer Smith responds,"What do you care? If he's silly enough to do your work, let him do it. You aren't going to get paid less. I've had the same kind of experience with him. The way I handle it is that I do exactly as he tells me. No less but certainly no more."

As he locks his locker and walks away, Officer Jones comments again, "I guess so, but if he wanted to still physically do the work he should have stayed a cop and not made boss as a sergeant. That kind of stuff doesn't really motivate you to do your best. I lose respect for him when he does that. That's no kind of a leader."

This perception can be expected when a supervisor performs the work of his subordinates. Notice the lack of motivation and respect.

Motivating Workers, Engendering Respect

If leadership involves getting work done through others, then the question should arise, "How does a leader get subordinates to do the work?" A supervisor could by virtue of his position simply demand that the work be done. After all, each employee is paid to work. But that is not a true leader. The real leader motivates subordinates to do the job. By demonstrating that he believes in the job he is asking his subordinates to perform, he wins their respect and loyalty. They know if they honestly try to perform their jobs, the supervisor will guide and support them. They will have his loyalty and he will in turn have theirs. Thus such a supervisor will obtain the willing cooperation of his subordinates.

If a supervisor is to act as a leader he must stand in front of his subordinates and both direct and draw them towards the objective. The supervisor does not act as leader when he stands behind his subordinates and drives them towards an objective. "There is only one real way to lead, and that is to get in front. You've got to lead by pulling and not pushing."[2]   Supervisory leadership is then the ability to get the job done through the efforts of subordinates by winning their respect, confidence and loyalty and motivating them to do the job willingly.

LEADERSHIP: NATURE OR NURTURE?

Is leadership ability something you are born with, or is it something you can develop? It's a little of both. It is not a mutually exclusive situation. While there are certain innate qualities that a leader must have, unless he develops them, he will never become a leader.

Natural Qualities

To be a leader, a person must possess certain qualities. Very often observers of supervisors will comment, "Boy, he's a natural born leader." What is really being said is that such person under very specific circumstances demonstrates the kind of qualities which people, especially those at the operating level in an agency, recognize as characteristic of what they see as a leader.

First, the supervisory leader must possess a certain level of innate intelligence. Though not that of a genius, this level must facilitate the ability to readily grasp facts and reason logically. Also, the actual personalities of supervisory leaders will vary, but certain characteristics consistently appear. For example, the personality of one leader may be more aggressive than that of another, but both must exercise good judgment and make effective decisions if they are to be seen as true leaders. While leaders must have certain innate qualities, it is at least equally important that these qualities be utilized and developed. "Leadership is not something that you learn once and for all. It is an ever-evolving pattern of skills, talents, and ideas that grow and change as you do."[3]

Nurtured Qualities

"Although the requirements for management have some elements that are innate, a major, if not the main, requirement comes from either education or work experience."[4] No leader is born with an inherent knowledge of the job. Knowledge of the job must be learned, developed, and nurtured.

Leadership is also developed through situational experience. Many subordinates recognize that leadership ability is based in part on the leader's past experience in similar situations. A personally learned lesson provides a firm frame of reference for handling similar situations. There is a danger, however, in that it leads to trial and error training for the supervisor. While the experience gained from these trial and error situations aids the supervisor's development as a leader, in the minds of subordinates, it can cause confusion and erode morale.

While it is true that certain individuals possess a larger share of commonly recognized leadership traits, it is equally true that unless these traits are developed and nurtured, no real leadership ability evolves. There are supervisors who may possess all the traits necessary to become leaders; however, they are never recognized by their subordinates as leaders. They never take the time to nurture these innate traits. Somewhat conversely, there are supervisors who do not possess all the traits associated with leaders and yet are seen as leaders. Why? They constantly are developing the leadership traits they do possess. The supervisor who constantly seeks to develop his leadership traits ultimately is the better leader.

LEADERSHIP BY WORD OR EXAMPLE

Are the words of a supervisor enough to qualify him as a leader, or is it the actions of a supervisor which qualify him as a leader? There is no doubt that a supervisor must choose his words carefully, but words alone, as important as they may be, cannot make him a leader.

Leadership Through Words

What a leader says and how he says it are evaluated by subordinates. Based on this evaluation, subordinates act or refrain from acting. Thus a leader must be constantly aware of what he says and how he says it. For example, a leader should understand that subordinates require appropriate recognition. "Employees need to know that they are important, that their work is appreciated, and that their manager has their interests sincerely at heart."[5] Therefore, when it is deserved, the leader should publicly recognize the efforts of subordinates. This can be done during conferences and training sessions. This kind

60

of public praise also has an added benefit for the leader, who will be seen as both informed and willing to give credit.

While what he says is important, how he says it is equally, if not more, important. The leader who gives praise but does it in an overly formal and rote manner would be better off not mentioning the subordinate's accomplishment at all. The same can be said when the praise is excessive. In such instances, it loses its effectiveness and has little or no meaning.

Further, a supervisor will not be seen as a leader when his words do not support the legitimate policies of the agency.

Consider the following:

Lieutenant Bailes is briefing subordinates about an order from the commanding officer which restates the agency's unpopular policy on the personal use of agency telephones. He begins his discussion by saying, "You've all heard this one before but listen up anyway because the commanding officer for some reason feels that it needs repeating." He then proceeds to read the order in a very monotone and unenthusiastic manner.

Bailes is not a leader. A true leader is expected to fully and enthusiastically support the legitimate policies of the agency. Given the way his comments were delivered, he is more likely to be seen as wanting to be part of the overall group, as opposed to being out in front leading the group. But if you are a leader, you are not part of the group. This is not to say that a leader cannot be friendly. He can and should, but he must avoid being familiar and should not subvert unpopular policies through his statements or their delivery.

Leadership Through Actions

Consider the following:

Officer Miller has just graduated from training school. He is talking to Officer Ginty, whom he knew socially prior to starting work for the agency. He says to Officer Ginty, "You know that Sergeant Egos is really great. He told me that his door is always open, and anytime I have anything to say to speak up. He also said that he will be speaking to me from time to time to let me know what is happening in the agency and to get my input into future decisions he might be making. Boy, he's right out of a textbook on leadership; he's a real leader."

"Don't hold your breath," Officer Ginty responds. "He talks a good game but never practices what he preaches. It sure sounds good, but he never backs it up. Don't even think about going to him with anything. He feels like he is being shown up. I really get the feeling he's envious and doesn't like the idea of any of the people that work for him getting ahead. That's not my idea of a leader."

While the things a leader says can demonstrate leadership, they are worthless unless the leader supports them with actions. "Nothing leaders say or do escapes the scrutiny and examination of their followers. This is one of the most important secrets of leadership: Followers mirror the example set for them. You lead first by example."[6] Consider the most obvious example: appearance. If the agency requires uniforms, all the demands for proper attire are of no use if the supervisor maintains a sloppy appearance. Leadership by words does have its place but only when supported by actions.

THE PRINCIPLES OF LEADERSHIP

A leader exercising authority over subordinates would do well to follow established and proven guidelines, though it must be remembered that these principles are intended only as a general guide.

1. Know your job
2. Know your abilities
3. Know your subordinates
4. Delegate fairly
5. Maintain teamwork
6. Use personnel and equipment efficiently
7. Keep subordinates informed
8. Make subordinates feel responsible
9. Do not delegate final accountability
10. Make decisions
11. Be Consistent

Know Your Job

Knowledge of both your job and that of your subordinates is important. This does not mean that a leader must be able to perform the subordinates' jobs as well as they do. Think of a baseball team, for example. Although not able to throw, hit or run as well as the players, the manager still must know and understand the jobs of the players so he can coordinate and evaluate their performance. In sum, he must have enough technical knowledge of the job to guide his subordinates in their duties. If he does not have this level of technical knowledge, he will be seen as unnecessary and burdensome.

Know Your Abilities

A wise leader once said, "The only thing I know for sure is that I don't know it all. But, I'm sure willing to learn it!" The real leader knows his strengths and weaknesses. He has no need to flaunt his strong points, nor does he seek to hide his weaknesses. His efforts are directed towards constant improvement.

Know Your Subordinates

As a supervisor must know his own strengths and weaknesses, so must he know the strengths and weaknesses of his subordinates. This will assist him in two things. First he will be better able to properly assign subordinates based on their strengths, and secondly he will be able to develop subordinates by offering training in the areas of their weaknesses.

Delegate Fairly

A worker cannot do a job unless he knows what is expected of him. When a worker is given a job it is up to the supervisor to make sure that the worker understands what he is supposed to accomplish. As you will hear again and again, if there is any doubt about whether an employee understands instructions, ask him to repeat the instructions in his own words.

Once the delegated duty is understood by the worker, the supervisor must check on its progress. The true leader does not wait for the worker to bring problems to him since it may then be too late to reverse costly errors. Instead, the true leader asks how the work is progressing while it is being done and offers assistance, either in terms of personnel or equipment. "Delegation works most effectively when everyone involved has a voice." [7] Such inquiries should be made delicately and tactfully, lest the supervisor be seen as overbearing. Finally, when delegating fairly, a leader makes sure that expected results have been accomplished. Not to do so is actually unfair to the worker, who may wrongly believe that his work was excellent.

Maintain Teamwork

"Standing alone as one person within an organization, you will have little impact on the world in which you exist. However, when several people work together, great things can be achieved."   *- Marion Hayes*[8]

No individual effort can match the efforts of a well-managed and well-supervised team. To maintain teamwork, workers must be trained to act as a team. This requires each member to know his own job, how his job fits in with the jobs of others and what the ultimate goal is. In order to reach such a state, the workers must be trained by the leader.

Use Personnel and Equipment Efficiently

A leader uses his subordinates and equipment to maximize the benefits. If, as mentioned earlier, a leader seeks teamwork among his subordinates, then each member of the team must be assigned duties consistent with their abilities. Of course, to do this requires a knowledge of the strengths and weaknesses of the workers. Finally, as with people, equipment must be efficiently used. It is the leader's job to see that equipment is adequate and safe.

Keep Subordinates Informed

People, unlike mushrooms, do not develop best in the dark. When appropriate, subordinates should be kept abreast of what is going on in the agency. Not to do so alienates them, makes them suspicious, and encourages rigidity. The mentality

64

develops among the workforce that says, "Since I guess I'm not good enough to be let in on things and trusted, I'll do only what I'm told." Workers should be informed about what is happening whenever it is appropriate so that they can feel more like members of the team.

Make Subordinates Feel Responsible

When a subordinate is given a job to do, he should be made to feel responsible for its successful completion. He should not be made to feel that the mere performance of isolated acts fulfills his obligation. He should feel confident dealing with those problems that are within his abilities or alerting the proper person when problems are beyond his abilities. For example, if the subordinate is aware that deadlines are not going to be met, he must raise this issue with those concerned.

In order for a subordinate to act in such a responsible way, the true leader must be willing to delegate the appropriate amount of authority. In general, supervisors should encourage workers to find better ways of working and solving problems. "The challenge of assuming responsibility appears to be rewarding in itself to many, although not all, employees."[9] By making the subordinate feel responsible, a leader is developing the subordinate. The subordinate will become more confident and enjoy a higher level of job satisfaction.

Do Not Delegate Final Authority

A supervisor delegates enough authority to the subordinate for the subordinate to do the job. However, though the leader has delegated authority, he has not abdicated authority. "The important distinction between delegation and abdication needs to be emphasized. In delegation, the delegator retains residual authority, or the power to recall the authority delegated, while in abdication, the powers of office are assigned to another or others irrevocably." [10]

Make Decisions

Nothing distinguishes a supervisor as a leader in the minds of his subordinates more than a willingness to make decisions in a timely manner based on sound information and facts. A supervisor who fails to make decisions will be seen as unwilling to take required risks. Such a leader will be seen as wanting to cover himself by maintaining a noncommittal posture. By the same token a leader should not be seen as constantly shooting from the hip before taking the time and the effort to gather the facts needed to make a sound decision.

Be Consistent

A supervisor may obtain his authority from his position in the agency, but he can be known as a leader only when "authority is assigned by the governed."[11] Thus if the governed, or the group, assign authority, the leader must maintain the proper image by setting a personal example. An important aspect of his personal example must be consistency in the making of decisions. Nothing will strip a leader of his status quicker than his gaining the unfortunate reputation among his subordinates of not being consistent.

Consider the following:

Officer Ginty is complaining to a co-worker, Officer Days. "You know Captain Egos really isn't a bad guy. I really believe he's interested in the members of the command and tries to look out for them whenever he can. But I can't figure him out. Take for example his stand on the wearing of the uniform cap. At the beginning of the month he really came down on me about wearing the uniform cap when outside the radio car. I had just gotten out of my radio car to check to see what was rattling around in the trunk when he pulls up and chews me out about not having my uniform cap on. I tried to explain to him what I was doing and that I was only out of the car for about 30 seconds but he wouldn't hear it. Then a few days later, I respond to handle an aided case and Officer Casey responds as a back up. Captain Egos happens to be on patrol so he also responds to the scene. I went out of my way to remember to put my cap on before I got out of the radio car. Casey on the other hand doesn't. Guess what happens. Egos looks right at Casey and praises him by telling him what a good thing it is to back each other up. Egos never says anything about Casey not having his uniform cap on. Can you imagine anything like that? I hate when a boss runs hot and cold on something. It makes you not want to follow his lead in anything!"

This feeling is not uncommon among subordinates who view a supervisor as inconsistent. A leader must constantly and scrupulously guard against such inconsistency in his actions and demands. "Leaders walk their talk. In true leaders there is no gap between the theories they espouse and the life they practice."[12]

LEADERSHIP TRAITS

A supervisor should strive to be a leader in mind, body, and spirit. Thus, for ease of examination, the traits a leader possesses can be separated into those of the mind, body, and spirit. However, these traits do not operate isolated in a vacuum, but interact together.

Traits of the Mind

Aware—alert to what is going on in the environment
Intelligent—capable of flexible and creative thought
Articulate—able to simplify and explain situations without offending the listener
Open-minded—willing to take criticism and consider others' ideas

Traits of the Body

Energetic—enthusiastic and able to generate a high level of energy without appearing nervous
Vigorous—physically strong and persistent
Calm—composed and tolerant of stress

Traits of the Spirit

Forceful—assertive and influential
Decisive—able to make and support decisions
Confident—self-assured even in unique situations
Realistic—maintains perspective and, while achievement oriented, can deal with setbacks

Friendly—cooperative, courteous, and cordial but not familiar

Honest—possesses and displays integrity

Supervisors possess these traits to differing degrees. What works best in one situation may prove worthless in another. "Differences in the situation faced by a leader have significant effects upon what traits are or are not effective."[13]

Historically, leadership was automatically equated with position in an organization. Also it was believed that leaders were born, not made. Instead it has been learned that leadership can be developed. "Contemporary thinking about leadership urges us not to be preoccupied with what leaders are, but to concentrate on what leaders do."[14]

LEADERSHIP STYLES

The phrase "style of leadership" refers to a supervisor's manner of leadership, or his attitude towards leadership. Although five styles of leadership have been identified, a supervisor may utilize one or a combination of several styles. While certain supervisors seem to operate best following one particular style, it is the situation that dictates which style works best.

"Several excellent examples of the situational nature of leadership stand out in the biography of former President Lyndon B. Johnson. During his stint in the U.S. Senate, Johnson had an uncanny knack for understanding every other senator's strengths, weaknesses, political aspirations, and self-image. He then tailored his interactions with each one to capitalize on his grasp of that person's make-up. As a result, he was soon designated Senate Democratic majority leader and ultimately inherited the White House."[15] Whatever leadership style is followed, a particular climate will be created. Consider the following kinds of leaders:

1. The "By the Book Leader"
2. The Autocratic Leader
3. The Democratic Leader
4. The Sidelines Leader
5. The Laissez-faire Leader[16]

© 1995 by J. & B. Gould
Printed in the U.S.A.   Ms

The "By the Book Leader"

Consider the following:

Investigator Ginty is describing the unit supervisor, Agent Egos, to an investigator recently assigned to the unit. He says, "As long as you follow the manual you'll have no problem with Egos. But don't go to him with anything that isn't covered in the book. He won't give you an answer. He'll tell you that he'll have to check. That works fine when it's something clerical but when you need action in a field situation, he really slows things down. You won't mind it when you first start but after you get the hang of things, you'll wonder why we need him. Actually all we need is the book. It's better than having him around."

The supervisor who uses this style is ruled by regulation, procedures and policies. He finds comfort in exactly following the manual of procedures. In his view, his authority is based on rules which allow him to act with certainty and safety. However, if it isn't specifically in the book, then he immediately consults his superior. He does not interact with subordinates; he merely leads them through rules and procedures.

Effective when:
    a. the subordinate is new or inexperienced and needs guidance and instruction;
    b. the authority to deviate from rules and procedures is specifically withheld from supervisors;
    c. a new procedure is being implemented;
    d. highly routine and repetitive operations are being performed.

Drawbacks:
    a. creates rigid and inflexible work habits;
    b. makes employees resistant to any change in procedures;
    c. fails to motivate employees;
    d. depicts supervisor as a negative force whose only purpose is to enforce rules;
    e. encourages employees to do only what is required and no more.

The Autocratic Leader

Consider the following:

"One afternoon Sergeant Egos says to me, 'Let's take a walk and go to lunch.' I tell him O.K. and get my coat. We start walking down Market Street and I ask him, 'Where are we headed?' He looks straight ahead, never looks at me and says that when we get to the corner he'll let me know. He picks the restaurant and then insists on ordering the specials 'cause he knows they'll be fresh. That would have been O.K. if I had never eaten lunch before, or if I was a little kid who didn't want to eat his lunch, but really! I thought he was even going to tell me how to chew what I ordered. When you're around him you feel like you're not even there. It was funny though. When the food finally came there was a fly in his soup. I guess I should have told him, but I didn't. I just watched him eat his soup and tell me how good everything was."

The Autocratic Leader does not delegate well. He holds all decision making for himself. By not keeping his subordinates informed, the autocratic leader keeps them dependent on him. Initiative on the part of his subordinates is discouraged, and he is not interested in their desires and goals.

Effective when:
  a. the employee is untrained or resistant to duties;
  b. an emergency exists or when there is no time to explain the reasoning behind instructions;
  c. a firm decision is needed to clarify policies;
  d. near term production concerns override all other concerns;
  e. the leader knows well the specific individual duties of subordinates.

Drawbacks:
  a. works in the short term but cannot be continued over long periods;
  b. creates fear of the leader;
  c. does not develop subordinates;

d. may encourage subordinates to resent the leader and thwart work efforts to show their disapproval;

e. creates an overdependence on the leader, curbing individual self-confidence and teamwork.

The Democratic Leader

Consider the following:

Officer Ginty is describing Sergeant Rems to another officer. Ginty explains, "Rems is the kind of boss who is the boss without having to tell you he is the boss. Like, for example, me and Marino had a car boosting problem in our sector. From the way the cars were being broken into and based on what was being taken we figured it had to be the same bad character or characters. We go to Rems and tell him what we got. First thing out of his mouth is to ask us what we think and more important what do we think we can do about it? Now maybe somebody might have thought, 'Why ask us? Isn't it the job's problem?' Somehow he gets you involved. Somehow he gets you to feel that the job's problems are also your problems. Anyway we tell him that if the job could set up a decoy vehicle, put a surveillance team on it, we think in a week we would have our perps. He never blinks. He tells us to outline on paper the problem and our solution and what we think it will take in terms of resources. You know, personnel, equipment and when and where? We do just that. Two days later he tells us he was able to get us assigned as the surveillance team for a week. I was so pumped up, I would have done it on my own time. Bottom line: on the fourth day two of our 'finer citizens' are caught in the act. Needless to say they both have sheets a mile long and can't wait to make a deal and tell us who the fence is. The detectives do a good job and are able to collar the fence. Once again there is peace in the valley. Seriously though, do you know what Rems does then? He puts a letter of commendation on me and Marino on the bulletin board and has it read out loud at roll calls. We took a lot of ribbing from the other cops but I got to tell you, it made us feel like we really belonged. He never mentioned anything he did, just me and Marino."

The democratic leader is able to get his subordinates to commit to the goals of the agency. He does this by providing

© 1995 by J. & B. Gould
Printed in the U.S.A.   Ms

them with appropriate recognition for their efforts, giving them a sense of belonging and security, and offering them opportunities for job satisfaction. He continually allows them entry into the decision-making process by asking for their suggestions in matters that affect them. He is the kind of leader who builds power by sharing decision-making authority, not hoarding it. He is group-oriented, not self-centered. This style of leadership requires self-confidence, since it does not offer much personal recognition.

Effective when:
    a. time constraints allow members of the group to participate;
    b. a tolerance for errors can be sustained, especially in the early stages of an operation;
    c. the supervisor is available to guide the group to uncover any initial difficulties;
    d. members of the group have an acceptable level of competence;
    e. the issue affects all members of the group (e.g. what type of body armor should be worn).

Drawbacks:
    a. once subordinates experience it, it is difficult to rescind;
    b. results in less than perfect solutions;
    c. may make subordinates suspicious if they have never been included in the decision-making process under previous supervisors;
    d. inappropriate in emergency situations;
    e. inappropriate for serious disciplinary problems.

The Sidelines Leader

Consider the following:
    Lieutenant Rems is asked by the chief of his department how he likes his new assignment which has put him in charge of the department's laboratory. Rems responds, "Well Chief, it's different. I never had any real experience in lab work, but the people assigned here sure seem to know what they're doing. I've always believed in letting my subordinates in on what was going on so

72

that they could have a hand in making decisions, but here they really seem able to take care of business. In the short time I've been here it appears that if there is a choice about a job that needs to be done, they make the choice and do the job. And they do it without any big fanfare and without requiring any supervision. For example, when the crime scene unit goes out on a job, they go out there on their own. They know what to do and touch all the bases. What I have done is set up productivity targets for the work around here. I thought that was important so that I, along with the individual members of the unit, could know how the unit is doing."

A sidelines leader can give subordinates a great deal of decision-making authority because the subordinates are highly expert in what they do. This work is most often extremely specialized or technical, as in that of undercover officers or polygraph operators. The sidelines leader is often geographically removed from the work place but controls the output of subordinates by records and reports. This style of leadership is similar to, but not the same as, the democratic leader. The major difference is that the democratic leader has more interaction with subordinates. Given the high level of expertise of his subordinates, a sidelines leader does not have to guide them as much as the democratic leader.

Effective when:
    a. subordinates are extremely competent;
    b. subordinates are highly motivated;
    c. the supervisor is not experienced in the subordinates' duties.

Drawbacks:
    a. may lull supervisors into a false sense of security while production suffers;
    b. may create feelings of insecurity and detachment from the agency in subordinates;
    c. may make workers feel they have become the supervisors;
    d. allows for the potential for improper conduct or corrupt acts on the part of workers.

The Laissez-faire Leader

Consider the following:

Captain Egos has been recently promoted to his rank and has been in his new assignment for about six weeks. In explaining his new position to a former co-worker he says, "This place is the best. The shop runs itself. I give the cops a free rein and they watch themselves. They love it here, and I must say I got to be quite popular with them. They have made me a firm believer in minimum control."

The laissez-faire leader exercises a minimum of control over subordinates. This style of leadership is as bad as, if not worse than, over-supervising. This type of leader believes in leaving subordinates alone and acts under the mistaken belief that a unit can operate without any guidance. The result is that he does not give any assistance to his workers. Soon the workers begin to feel insecure and indifferent since they believe that no one cares what they do. "Without a leader, the group may have little direction and a lack of control. The result can be inefficiency or, even worse, chaos."[17] To fill this void, an informal leader may spring up to replace the supervisor as a leader. However, he is "totally reliant on his own devices."[18] Because subordinates in such a setting tend to go in separate directions, they do not operate as a team. Thus laissez-faire leadership offers the slimmest chance for success.

Effective when:
   a. informal leaders are available to fill the leadership void.

Drawbacks:
   a. erodes morale and discipline of subordinates;
   b. decreases productivity;
   c. makes subordinates uneasy and uncertain because they are unsure of what is expected of them;
   d. replaces the actual supervisor with an informal leader to whom legitimate resources are unavailable;
   e. least likely to accomplish the goals of the agency.

MEASURING LEADERSHIP ABILITY

Although some argue that leadership ability cannot be accurately or objectively measured, indicators exist which can be used to gauge leadership ability. The following four broad questions lead to other more specific questions, the answers to which reflect a leader's ability.

What is the individual and group attitude toward the job?

a. Do the individual and the group perform up to their full capacity, or do they do just enough to get by?

b. Is there teamwork and harmony among individuals in the unit, or is friction evident in the most routine of tasks?

c. Do the members feel like individuals, or do they feel like faceless workers?

d. Do the members of the group discuss their work in a constructive and positive manner, or are they destructive and negative in their comments?

e. Do the members of the unit treat the public with respect and empathy in a professional manner, or is the public seen as a troublesome bother?

What is the public's opinion of the unit?

a. Are there many civilian complaints, or is the number minimal?

b. Is service seen as professional, or is it seen as adversarial?

c. On the whole are the opinions expressed at local community meetings positive or negative?

d. Is the media's general impression of the unit positive or negative?

e. Do members of the public feel that the unit is approachable, or do they see the unit as self-serving?

How good are the members of the unit and the leader at their jobs?

a. Is the leader constantly trying to improve his performance, or is he content with it?

b. Are the members of the unit constantly trying to improve, or do they feel that further improvement serves no purpose?

c. Does the leader give opportunities for growth and development to members of the unit, or does he guard his status and keep individuals from advancing?

d. Does the unit's level of performance meet the standards required by the agency, or does it fall short?

e. Does the unit work together in a cooperative and willing manner, or are there factions thwarting the overall effort?

f. Does the leader communicate with the members of the unit, or does he keep things from them?

g. Does the unit properly and efficiently use the available resources, or is there waste?

h. Does the leader tell members of the unit how their performance measures against agency standards, or do members rely on gossip to gauge their performance levels?

What is the discipline climate of the unit?

a. Does the leader focus only on the unit's productivity, or is he also concerned with the needs of the individual members?

b. Do the members of the unit feel that the leader is accessible to them if problems develop, or do they feel that his door is closed?

c. Does the unit function well when the leader is absent, or does activity cease?

d. Can the unit function well with minimal supervision, or must the leader be consulted on every action?

e. Can the leader take on additional duties when necessary, or is he over-burdened with routine tasks which are not being delegated?

f. Does the leader trust the members of the unit, or does he feel he has to watch them constantly?

g. Do members of the unit know why they are asked to perform certain tasks, or do they see their work as isolated, independent actions?

These questions can assist a supervisor in measuring his leadership ability.

THE LEADER AS A MOTIVATOR

All too often the novice supervisor confuses motivating workers with manipulating workers.

Motivation Defined

If behavior is compared to a motor, then motivation is its fuel. People behave in a certain manner because there exists some motivation for them to do so. If it can be assumed that an employee's behavior is shaped by his perceptions and expectations, the pivotal role of motivation becomes clear. The goal of motivation is to bring about certain behavior in a worker, and this behavior is beneficial not only to the organization, but also to the worker. Motivation thus creates a two-way street where the goal is seen as desirable by both the agency and the worker.

Consider the following:

Sergeant Rems is aware that a promotional exam for the title of sergeant will be held in about six months. He believes that one of his subordinates, Officer Ginty, could make an excellent supervisor. Rems approaches Ginty and attempts to motivate him to begin to prepare for the pending sergeant's examination. By explaining to Officer Ginty that increased salary and fringe benefits are part of getting promoted, Rems attempts to influence Ginty who is unsure if he wishes to commit the time and effort required to prepare for the exam. However, Rems also appeals to Ginty by pointing out the increased status that comes with becoming a supervisor. Ginty agrees to make the commitment to studying.

Here it is clear that there are personal benefits to Ginty— that is, status, pay and fringe benefits. However, there are also benefits to the agency. The agency will have someone improving his abilities, skills and knowledge on his own time, at no expense to the agency, while gaining a potentially competent candidate for supervisor. This illustrates how to bring about positive behavior which is beneficial to both the organization and the employee.

This is the difference between motivation and manipulation. In manipulation the behavior sought may or may not benefit the worker. It is being sought by the supervisor as something positive for the agency. But in the case of motivation, the agency and the worker both gain from the behavior.

How to Motivate Subordinates

Everyone responds differently to motivators. What motivates one person has little or no effect on another. Also, what motivates a person in one situation may not motivate the same person in another situation. Also, the effects of both positive and negative motivators need to be considered. The following positive motivators are recommended:

Positive Motivators

a. Assign them jobs which challenge their capabilities.

Avoid busy work. Workers who do not see their work as worthy of their talents will see work as a chore which interferes with their lives. However, challenging jobs which they can handle can make them feel important to the agency's efforts.

b. Let them know how they are doing.

Offer them not only praise but also constructive criticism. In considering rewards, it should be noted that monetary rewards are not enduring motivators. Although they seem to work for a short time, their motivational impact tends to fade.

c. Expand their jobs.

After they have proven themselves at challenging tasks for a sufficient period of time, give them a little more to do. Most people want to do more and will accept more, as long as they don't feel arbitrarily overburdened.

d. Recognize that they are doing more.

If they take on the additional duties and perform them well, offer additional recognition. What might be considered additional recognition depends on the individual worker's goals and the

78

capabilities of the agency to reward its work force. The rewards may range from having one's own office, cubicle, or desk, to a designated parking spot.

Negative Motivators

Negative motivation uses or threatens punishment. "Examples are reprimands, threats of being fired, and threats of demotion if performance is unacceptable. Each type has its place in organizations depending on the situation." Mature, self-disciplined persons do not require much external discipline from others. "But it seems certain that our world is still populated by many persons who must depend upon others for their discipline."[19]

THE LEADER AS A DECISION MAKER

As noted earlier, nothing distinguishes a leader more than an ability to make decisions, since much of what a leader does involves gathering facts, drawing conclusions, acting on these facts, and then standing behind his actions. If it becomes clear that the wrong decision has been made, the process repeats itself. In any event, subordinates want the leader to make decisions. Even an occasional bad decision is better than no decision. Leaders who vacillate when it is time to make a decision will lose their status as a leader.

Components of Decision Making

Although situations may call for variations, there are common components in any successful decision-making process.

Gather Facts

Before you perform the acts you must get the facts. It must be clear what is being decided.

Consider the following:
The performance of one of your subordinates, Officer Ginty, has dropped off significantly in the last six months. You also

have received several phone calls from Ginty's creditors asking about the agency's procedure for garnishing an employee's salary. Because you referred Ginty to counseling in the past, you know that he is a member of Gamblers Anonymous and that the counseling unit recommended that he attend meetings regularly. You conclude that Ginty's current problems are a result of his gambling again and further conclude that he is probably not attending meetings. You decide to meet with Ginty, confront him, and warn him that his recent conduct coupled with the decline in his performance could be considered "conduct unbecoming an officer" which could result in disciplinary action. You meet and do exactly as you have decided. However, Ginty soberly informs you that he is not gambling, and that he can document his attendance at meetings. He insists that while he is experiencing financial difficulties, it has nothing to do with gambling. He explains that his brother and sister-in-law were killed in a car crash and as a result their three children are living with Ginty and his wife and two children. Supporting his brother's children has placed a tremendous strain on his finances. He openly admits that he has been distracted and apologizes if his work has suffered. He adds that he and his wife have taken steps to deal with the additional expenses and should soon have things under control.

Get all the facts, first about the problem, then about its severity. Remember, however, this is not always possible in emergency situations where time is of the essence.

Draw Conclusions

Gathered facts must be evaluated as to their validity and analyzed as to their importance. Consider whether the source is valid. Ask how important these facts are in drawing conclusions.

Take Action

Based on the conclusions, alternative actions must be identified. After weighing the effects of each of these alternative actions, a specific course of action must be selected and followed. Those who will carry out the action must be informed, and their actions evaluated to determine if the intended results are obtained.

Be Responsible

After a leader makes a decision, he should stand behind it. However, the results of his decision should be evaluated. If it misses the mark, he should engage in an alternate course of action. The biggest mistake a leader can make is not in initially making the wrong decision, but in obstinately sticking to it.

Making Decisions as a Group

Traditional supervisory practices have in the past frowned on "decisions by committee." However, under certain circumstances, it is now clear that good decisions can be developed by the work group when they are guided by a competent leader. For ease of understanding, decision-making groups can be divided into two types: non-critical and critical.

The Non-critical Group

In this approach to group decision making, the leader explains the problem to the group and asks them to meet and discuss their solutions. He puts no limits on the kinds of solutions that may be offered. The purpose is to obtain the most creative and innovative solutions possible. Sometimes referred to as "brainstorming," it is considered non-critical because each solution is examined by the group without criticism. The group is permitted however to mix and match solutions in their effort to arrive at a viable plan. This method works especially well when new approaches are sought.

The Critical Group

Here the leader also brings the group together to find solutions to a defined problem. Before the meeting, the leader must clearly identify for the attendees what the problem is and any limitations. He must inform them as to such limitations as the actual decision-making authority of the group; will the group only make recommendations on a course of action, or does it have the authority to actually implement a decision?

Aside from maintaining order and encouraging participation, the leader must direct the group in arriving at a decision. This involves allowing constructive criticism of ideas until a consensus is reached. Thus the meeting creates a "critical group." After the meeting the leader must follow up to ensure that any tasks assigned are being performed on time and up to standards. In short, he sees to it that the actions decided on by the group are carried out.

TEST YOUR UNDERSTANDING

1. Any meaningful definition of leadership must contain certain components. Identify and explain these components.

2. Are leaders a product of nature or nurture? Explain your answer.

3. Why are words not enough to establish leadership?

4. Identify and explain the eleven principles of leadership.

5. What is the difference between delegating and abdicating authority?

6. What are commonly accepted leadership traits of the mind, body and spirit?

7. Name five leadership styles and explain when they are used best.

8. Explain four measures of leadership.

9. What is the difference between a leader motivating a subordinate and a leader manipulating a subordinate?

10. Describe how a supervisor can motivate a subordinate.

11. What are the components of decision making?

12. Regarding the group decision-making process, what is the difference between a non-critical and critical group?

FOOTNOTES

1. Ronald S. Burke and Lester R. Bittel, *Introduction to Management Practice.* (New York: McGraw-Hill Book Company, 1981), pp. 484, 487

2. William A. Cohen, Ph.D., *The Art of the Leader.* (NJ: Prentice-Hall, 1990), p. 25

3. Sheila Murray Bethel, *Making a Difference-Twelve Qualities That Make You a Leader.* (New York: G.P. Putnam's Sons, 1990), p. 25

4. John P. Kotter, *The Leadership Factor.* (New York: The Free Press, 1988), p. 34

5. Herbert G. Hicks and C. Ray Gullett, *The Management of Organizations,* 3rd ed. (New York: McGraw-Hill, 1976), p. 449

6. Sheila Murray Bethel, *Making a Difference—Twelve Qualities That Make You a Leader.* (New York: G.P. Putnam's Sons, 1990), p. 13

7. Margot Robinson, M.A., *Egos and Eggshells— Managing for Success In Today's Workplace.* (North Carolina: Stanton and Harper Books, 1993), p. 98

8. Robert B. Maddux, *Team Building, An Exercise In Leadership.* (Los Altos, CA: Crisp Publications, 1986), p. 5

9. Ronald S. Burke and Lester R. Bittel, *Introduction to Management Practice.* (New York: McGraw-Hill Book Company, 1981), p. 491

10. James M. Banovetz, Editor, *Managing The Modern City.* (Washington D.C.: International City Management Association, 1971), p. 164.

11. ibid. p. 164.

12. Warren Bennis, *On Becoming a Leader.* (Reading, MA: Addisson-Wesley Publishing Company, Inc., 1989), p. 160

13. Herbert G. Hicks and C. Ray Gullett, *The Management of Organizations,* 3rd ed. (New York: McGraw-Hill, 1976), p. 479

14. Ricky W. Griffin, *Management.* (Boston, MA: Houghton Mifflin Company, 1984), p. 424

15. Doris Kearns, *Lyndon Johnson and the American Dream.* (New York: Harper and Row, 1976).

16. Charles D. Hale, *Police Patrol, Operations and Management.* (New York: John Wiley and Sons, Inc., 1981), pp. 267-268.

17. Herbert G. Hicks and C. Ray Gullett, *The Management of Organizations,* 3rd ed. (New York: McGraw-Hill, 1976), p. 483

18. James M. Banovetz, Editor, *Managing The Modern City.* (Washington, D.C.: International City Management Association, 1971), p. 121.

19. Cf. Douglas McGregor, *The Human Side of Enterprise.* (New York: McGraw-Hill, 1960), p. 41

SUGGESTED READINGS

Cribbin, James J.
Effective Managerial Leadership.
New York: American Management Association, 1972

Fiedler, Fred E. and M.M. Chemers.
Leadership and Effective Management.
Glenview, IL: Foresman Scott, 1974

George, Jr., Claude S.
Supervision In Action: Managing Others.
Reston, VA: Reston Publishing Company, 1979

Hayes, Marion.
Stepping Up To a Supervisor.
Houston, TX: Executive Roundtable Publications, 1987

Steers, Richard M. and Lyman W. Porter.
Motivation and Work Behavior.
New York: McGraw-Hill, 1975

Vroom, Victor H. and Philip W. Yetton,
Leadership and Decision-Making.
Pittsburgh, PA: University of Pittsburgh Press, 1973

CHAPTER 5
THE SUPERVISOR AS A COMMUNICATOR

The supervisor is charged with the responsibility of getting the job done through others. To do this, he must be able to communicate exactly what is to be done, how it is to be done, and when it is to be done. Today's supervisor, in certain circumstances, must even communicate why a job has to be done. Besides this communication from the supervisor, there is also communication to the supervisor from subordinates, superiors and colleagues. In order to communicate effectively, a supervisor must understand what communication means and how it can be improved.

COMMUNICATION DEFINED

Communication must have a sender, someone who is sending information, and a receiver, someone for whom the information is intended. The information transmitted must be both received and understood by the receiver. In order to establish that understanding has taken place, some indication on the part of the receiver is needed. Much of the difficulty surrounding communication occurs at this point. The sender may have sent the information and the receiver received it, but did the receiver understand the message? For true communication to take place:

    a. a sender must transmit information;

    b. a receiver must accept and understand the information; and

    c. the receiver must indicate that the information was understood.

COMMUNICATION: A TWO-WAY STREET

The comment that communication is a two-way street implies that information is to flow back and forth during the communication process with both the sender and receiver transmitting and listening.

Whose Job Is It?

When a sender communicates information to a receiver, it is incumbent upon the sender to make sure that the receiver really understands what has been communicated. But when a receiver accepts information from the sender, he too has an obligation to make sure that he has understood the information. In addition, the receiver must give some feedback indicating that he has understood the information. The sender should look for this feedback.

For example, you enter a shop and ask the clerk how much a six ounce bottle of brand X is. Without answering you, the clerk disappears into the stockroom to return with the bottle, which he then places on the counter. What happens now? Do you examine the bottle for a price sticker? Do you repeat your original question? What has happened? Were you interested in actually making the purchase or were you shopping for the price to make a future purchase?

Real communication did not take place. Neither the sender nor the receiver took steps to ensure that the transmitted information was understood. This is a shared responsibility. "Only when the sender is able to experience direct feedback from the receiver can he really know what the receiver is hearing and what he is failing to hear. How else can the sender become aware of the hidden meaning—the symbolic significance the receiver is ascribing to his words?" [1]

THE LINKS OF THE COMMUNICATION PROCESS

Certain components link together to make up the communication process or loop. This communication loop is constant and continuous. It may temporarily slow down, but as long as the organization continues and its members interact, the loop exists. The six links in this loop are:

1. A stimulation.
2. An information bin.
3. A sender.
4. A vehicle.
5. A direction.
6. A receiver.

A Stimulation

A stimulation starts the communication process. For example, a supervisor may receive an order from a superior mandating that all officers attend a three-day training course in the law of arrest. This would cause the supervisor to use the communication loop to advise his personnel. Another example of a stimulation is when a supervisor receives information from another supervisor about a common problem. Stimulation could also come from a subordinate who is requesting a transfer for hardship reasons. Stimulation can come from a superior, an equal, a subordinate, or the public. No matter where it comes from, the essence of stimulation is the same. It will ultimately cause information to be transmitted. Even when stimulation comes from within oneself, it is still a communication stimulation. A supervisor deciding on his own to communicate with his subordinates is no less stimulated to communicate then when the communication stimulation emanates from the head of the agency. Stimulation causes a sender to evaluate what has been communicated so that he can access his information bin for the details of the communication he sends along the loop.

An Information Bin

Consider the following:

Sergeant Rems has received a confidential note from a subordinate indicating that another subordinate has a drinking problem that is causing a morale problem. Rems has received a stimulation from the communication loop. This causes him to communicate as a sender in the loop. Before he does communicate, however, he should decide what he will communicate and to whom. In this case Rems should go to his "information bin" and get background information from the subordinate who is the author of the confidential note. After interviewing the subordinate who wrote the note, Rems learns of an incident which allegedly was mishandled by the subject of the complaint. Rems now checks command records to verify this information. Thus an information bin can be an interview, a records search or anything that helps a sender decide what should be communicated and to whom.

By definition, an information bin is any resource which a sender can use to develop the details of the communication.

A Sender

The sender is the person or link in the communication loop who will transmit information to an intended receiver. The sender, along with the receiver, is the cause of more communication problems than any of the other links in the process. The reason for this is obvious; people occupy these links.

A Vehicle

The medium selected by a sender can be verbal, written, physical, or any combination of them. The vehicle usually depends on the receiver and the kind of attitude the sender wishes to project.

The Verbal Medium

This vehicle is the medium of the spoken word. It is appropriate when the receiver is a subordinate or in an informal phone call. It should be used when time is of the essence, such as in emergencies. It is not recommended when a permanent record is required. Conversely, it is recommended when the matter is confidential, sensitive or requires face-to-face communication or tact.

The Written Medium

This vehicle of communication is recommended when a permanent record is needed. It is also useful when the message is complicated and lengthy, or when formally responding to one's superiors. It is particularly recommended when a pictorial representation of what is being communicated is needed.

Physical Signal

This medium is neither spoken nor written. It provides a communication vehicle through the use of commonly accepted non-verbal signals. A frown, a nod, a relaxed stance are all physical signals. While they can be used to project rejection

90

or hostility, they are most often used to convey understanding, approval, or sensitivity.

Using More Than One Vehicle

The sender may use more than one vehicle in the same communication, such as a verbal assent coupled with the physical signal of an affirmative nod. It could also be a phone call followed up by a written memo. The sender and the circumstances surrounding the communication control which medium is to be used.

A Direction

Is the message being sent up to a superior, down to a subordinate, or laterally to the public or a colleague? The direction of the communication will be largely determined by the original stimulation and will subsequently influence the type of vehicle chosen. For example, if communicating a formal request upward to a superior, the written medium should be used.

A Receiver

The person or link in the communication loop who receives information from a sender is the receiver. As stated above, this person, along with the sender, causes more communication problems than any of the other links in the loop. When possible, the sender should tailor messages to the needs and sensitivities of the receiver.

Obviously, a receiver who is the recipient of information in the communication loop, becomes a sender when that information acts as a stimulation causing him to go to his information bin and send additional information. And so the loop is continued. Also, when feedback from a receiver occurs, the sender now becomes a receiver and the process of the communication loop continues following the pattern:

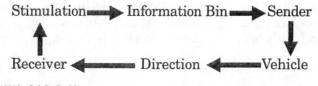

OBSTRUCTIONS TO EFFECTIVE COMMUNICATION

As illustrated, the communication loop is made up of six links, much like the links of a chain. If each individual link functions well, then the loop also functions well. But if any of the links breaks, then the same happens to the loop.

Listening Failure

The most frequent obstruction to communication is failing to listen. Most of the time it is due to "polite listening." This occurs often when the sender is the superior, and the receiver is the subordinate. Not wishing to seem incompetent or imply that the boss is not communicating clearly, the subordinate acts as if he understands, whereas in actuality he is engaging in polite listening. "White collar workers, on the average, devote at least 40% of their work day to listening. Apparently 40% of their salary is paid to them for listening. Yet tests of listening comprehension have shown that, without training, these employees listen at only 25% efficiency."[2]

Prejudice and Bias

Prejudice and bias affect both senders and receivers. Preconceived notions about participants will influence how and what is communicated and received. For example, the information bin which a sender uses to develop the details of his communication is impacted by prejudice and bias. If a receiver's appearance produces a bias on the part of the sender, then this could cause the sender to improperly access or totally avoid his information bin. For example, a sender may feel that a poorly-dressed person is not capable of understanding what is being communicated and may leave out pertinent information, which in turn weakens the communication.

Prejudice and bias can also cause an over-rating of the other person(s) so that too much is expected from them. This also blocks communication, since not enough detail is included in the communication. The sender expects too much from the receiver, falsely believing that the receiver is so competent and well-versed in the matter that he already understands the issues and requires few details.

Status Intimidation

When rank or position in the organization creates gaps between senders and receivers which cannot be bridged, status intimidation occurs. More attention is given to the position of the person than to the message. Since downward communication will travel more easily than upward communication, highly positioned members may be able to send information down to subordinates, but they may fail to receive accurate information in return. The subordinates become intimidated and fearful of making mistakes. They try too hard to listen as a receiver or to transmit as a sender. The natural process of communication becomes unnatural, causing participants to become overly cautious about what they say or what they hear.

Status intimidation will also negatively impact upward communication. If the superior does not value the information sent from subordinates, he is not acting as a true receiver, and the communication loop will be blocked. In addition, once subordinates become aware of their superior's opinion, all communication from below will soon disappear.

Imprecise Language

Imprecise written or verbal language, or imprecise physical signs affect the choice of vehicle and block communication.

Consider the following:
Officer Egos is verbally reporting to Sergeant Rems the status of a missing child. Egos says, "I went to the playground and spoke to Ms. Harps, who saw the child before she ate her lunch."

The obvious question is, "Who ate whose lunch?"
Consider the following sign which was posted in a police station house:
"Officers are reminded that females visiting prisoners are prohibited from having children in the visiting area."
Clearly the intent of the sign was to prohibit the presence of children and not their births in the visiting area.

Finally, consider a boss who nods, intending to indicate he is listening to a subordinate. The subordinate, however, misinterprets the nod as approval.

Imprecise language refers to the improper use of words or signals. A sender must make certain that his statements are clear not only to him but also to the receiver.

Bad Timing

Bad timing of communications also adversely affects senders and receivers, and thus creates communication obstructions.

Consider the following:

Lieutenant Egos responds to a situation where uniformed Officer Ginty has just convinced a barricaded person holding a hostage to release the hostage and surrender. Lieutenant Egos notices that Ginty is wearing an unauthorized uniform tie clasp. Egos's only comment to Ginty is to advise him about the uniform rule infraction. Officer Ginty shakes his head in disbelief while taking away the handcuffed suspect.

In our admittedly extreme example, is Lieutenant Egos wrong to advise Ginty about a uniform infraction? No, that is part of the lieutenant's job. But it is not the right place or time. This will not only impact on the message but may forever impact on any communication between Egos and Ginty. If at all possible, communication should be postponed if senders or receivers are temporarily distracted or otherwise not prepared to communicate.

Personal Attitudes and Perceptions

A receiver may try to avoid anything that blocks his personal goals. Therefore, any communication that he perceives as interfering with these goals will not be received.

Consider the following:

Officer Egos strives to become a civilian clothes investigator. After several years of above average performance with the uniform division, he goes before the selection board which identifies candidates for investigator positions. A few days after

94

being screened by the board, Egos is told by his commanding officer that he impressed the board, and its recommendation is that Egos spend a little more time on patrol and develop more experience. They strongly recommend that he reapply in a year.

Because he is not immediately being accepted as an investigator, he perceives the recommendations of the board as negative when in reality they were positive. His attitude and perceptions interfered with his role as a receiver. Likewise, a sender who has an aversion to discussing certain subjects will not effectively communicate them.

Consider the following:

Captain Egos is uncomfortable discussing employee performance evaluations with subordinates. In discussing Officer Ginty's evaluation, which indicates that Ginty's performance barely meets agency standards, Egos, unwilling to confront the issue, tells Ginty how hard it is to accurately rate subordinates and that he perceives all evaluation forms as flawed. After some vague comments about the evaluation, the captain asks Ginty if he has any questions. Ginty shakes his head no and leaves the meeting no more informed than when he arrived.

In this example, the captain's personal attitude towards evaluations blocked his sending accurate information. Ginty never learned where he might improve, or even that he should improve. The officer went away as uninformed, if not more uninformed than when he arrived.

Selective Listening

Consider a variation of the above example. The captain describes to Ginty the ten dimensions in which he was rated, in nine of which he barely met the standard rating and in one of which he received an outstanding rating. The captain spends most of the time discussing the nine dimensions in which Ginty performed poorly. When asked about the meeting later, Ginty states, "The skipper really liked my performance. All he talked about was that dimension in which I was rated as outstanding." People like to hear what pleases them, and they tend to block out that which they do not like. This creates a communication block.

Sifting

Sometimes referred to as filtering, sifting is the process whereby a sender has received information along the loop, but sifts it before sending it along. Sifting occurs most often in upward communication, because subordinates believe their superiors do not want to hear certain information. Subordinates learn what superiors desire to hear. Hence, they become adept not only at avoiding the unpleasant, but also at stressing the positive. "Though the individual subordinate may consciously be entirely sincere and accountable, his personal anxieties, hostilities, aspirations, and system of beliefs and values almost inevitably shape and color his interpretation and acceptance of what he has learned and is expected to transmit."[3]

Consider the following:

Sergeant Egos is at the scene of a successful search warrant execution which has resulted in the confiscation of several kilos of heroin. However, during the raid, two of his officers improperly leave their portable radios unattended, and the portable radios are stolen. When reporting the incident to his commanding officer, the sergeant mentions only that several kilos of heroin were confiscated but says nothing about the missing radios. He has engaged in sifting. He has avoided passing on disagreeable information to his superior.

However, sifting also occurs in downward communications.

Consider the following:

Captain Egos knows that there will be layoffs in the department. The plan is to transfer all officers performing clerical and administrative duties to street patrol to make up for any pending reductions there. Egos is supposed to inform his subordinates that transfers are being made in an effort to deal with vacancies which are anticipated from the pending layoffs. Instead, Egos, wishing to spare his subordinates unpleasant news, tells them only that transfers are being made.

The captain has sifted out the part about pending layoffs. "Management, when considering issues of basic interest to employees—such as strikes, benefits, layoffs— sometimes takes the view that 'if we ignore it, maybe it will go away.' But

96

it will not go away."[4]   The result is that rumors distort the facts. Sifting is not a good practice for upward or downward communication.

The Critical Boss

Consider the following:

Sergeant Egos notes, "When Officer Ginty was first assigned to the unit, he used to participate in all our discussions openly, and when asked, he freely gave his opinion. But lately whenever I ask his opinion, he double- talks me. Trying to get him to commit on any issue is like trying to nail jelly to the wall. As his boss, I can't understand how he got like this. Especially since when he first got here I gave him advice and recommendations on all the ideas he came up with, you know, to make them better."

When a boss constantly critiques everything a subordinate says, subordinates tend to become noncommittal and leave themselves an "out" in everything they say. Unwilling to subject everything they say to evaluation, subordinates soon say little or nothing. As a result, communication will not only be obstructed, but stopped.

Premature Conclusions

Consider the following:

Officer Rems is on parade duty. He is told by Sergeant Egos that the crowd control barriers must be kept on the sidewalk pavement and not in the street. Egos then continues on patrol and leaves Rems on post. As the crowd begins to grow, Captain Ginty comes on the scene. Ginty tells Rems to give the crowd a little more room and place the barriers in the street, off the pavement. Rems explains to Captain Ginty that Sergeant Egos had instructed him not to do that. The captain tells him that it's O.K. and that if anyone asks, he is to tell them that it was done to accommodate the expanding crowd and that it was done on the captain's authority. Rems complies and moves the barriers as the captain leaves. Sergeant Egos returns and asks why the barriers have been moved. Rems starts to explain that the crowd has expanded, but Egos never lets him finish. Egos prematurely concludes that Rems moved the barriers on his own and tells

Rems he doesn't want to hear a word more and to immediately move the barriers back. Sergeant Egos says he cannot stand an officer who doesn't understand authority. Rems says no more and begins to move the barriers back. He smiles to himself because out of the corner of his eye he sees that the captain is walking hurriedly back toward the scene and calling out to the sergeant.

When a receiver engages in premature conclusions, a blockage of communication occurs. As in the example above, once the sergeant made a premature conclusion before allowing Rems, the sender, to complete his communication, further communication was blocked. This error is committed mainly by supervisors when acting as receivers of information from subordinates. They feel that they know what is going to be communicated even before the facts are made available.

Bottlenecks

Bottlenecks refer to the transmission of too much information. In the case of a receiver, too many communications are being directed at that person. Or, a sender may be transmitting too many messages. This person, like the receiver, may simply not be able to handle the transmission of all these messages. Whether the receiver or the sender is the bottleneck, an obstruction of communication will occur.

Static

People do not communicate in a sterile environment. They speak, listen, write, read, and both make and interpret physical signals in a world of distractions. These distractions tend to obstruct communication. A supervisor who interviews an applicant while also answering phone calls is blocking communication. He cannot receive information transmissions from the applicant, who will withdraw from the communication loop, thus further blocking communication. Loud machinery, lack of privacy, and even bad lighting can create what can be called static noise. It is anything in the surrounding environment that interferes with sending and receiving information. When it occurs, eliminate it from the environment or move to a more suitable environment.

PRINCIPLES OF EFFECTIVE COMMUNICATION

A supervisor's ability to communicate can be improved. While communication blocks will always exist, they can be reduced if certain principles are followed.

Know Your Objectives

Prior to communicating, the sender should clarify in his own mind what he wants to communicate by identifying the stimulation that initiated the communication he is about to transmit. This accomplishes two things. First, it forces the sender to seek out facts, possibly from his information bin, which should clarify why he is communicating and what he will be communicating. Secondly, it will clarify the identity of his receiver.

Choose Your Language

Once the objectives have been clarified, then the language and overall approach to the message should become evident. Should the message be an ultimatum, or should it be a polite request? Whatever the purpose is, the language and tone should be appropriate.

Consider the Environment

Consider where the communication is taking place. Is the environment appropriate, or should the communication be postponed or moved elsewhere?

Consider the following:
Sergeant Egos is to notify Officer Ginty that a disciplinary panel has found him in violation of regulations and will penalize him two days vacation. Leaving the busy station for the evening, the sergeant sees Ginty, who has just made an arrest for a serious felony. Egos yells to him to see him tomorrow about the disciplinary panel's decision.

What should Ginty understand? Is he in trouble, or because the sergeant is not taking the time to tell him the finding, is it not a serious matter? After all, Sergeant Egos apparently had no problem letting everybody in the station know what was going on. On the other hand, if it was nothing important, why didn't the sergeant let him know? Clearly the environment should be considered before communicating. If the environment, either the place or time, does not fit the message, change the environment if all possible.

Rehearse

If practical, ask others if what you are going to communicate is appropriate and clear. They can help you with your choice of words as well as with your tone of voice.

Consider the following:

Captain Rems wishes to announce a change in his unit's policy regarding vacation selections at Christmas. Before communicating the new policy to the members of his unit, he calls the union delegate and communicates the policy to him.

The captain is not getting permission, only assistance. He not only gets an additional view on the matter but also may get union support for the policy from the union delegate who has been advised of the new policy. As a result the policy may be more readily accepted.

Know Your Spoken and Unspoken Message

Consider the following:

A prisoner temporarily detained in an unauthorized area adjacent to a locker room was left alone and somehow got into an off-duty officer's locker and took a revolver. The prisoner then attempted to escape, but failed. During the attempt, the prisoner wounded an officer. Investigation later revealed that the locker had been left unlocked.

At roll call a few days after the incident, Sergeant Rems states, "Item One—Prisoners shall not be detained in any part of the station house other than one that has been specifically designated for detention. Item Two—the officer responsible for

100

any locker found unlocked while unattended shall receive disciplinary action." Sergeant Rems then looks around the room and with a clenched jaw says, "There will be compliance here, people."

In this instance, based on recent events, Sergeant Rems must know that he may be speaking out loud about detention locations and unlocked lockers, but the unspoken words are about a prisoner almost escaping and an innocent officer getting injured as a result. Without actually saying it, Rems is stating that the carelessness of one officer can cause serious injury to another officer. "One study of nonverbal communication has suggested that as much as 55% of the content of a message is transmitted via facial expression and body posture and that another 38% derives from inflection and tone. The words themselves account for only 7% of the content of the message."[5] A good communicator must always be sensitive to what he's saying both verbally and nonverbally.

Role Play

The sender should put himself in the position of the receiver and ask himself how he would feel if he were to receive his message. "Language uses words to convey ideas, facts, and feelings. Sometimes, semantic problems arise in the interpretation of words, because their meanings are not in the words, but in the minds of the people who receive them."[6] By empathizing, the sender can foresee difficulties that the receiver might have with the message. The sender can predict objections that the receiver might have and be better prepared to deal with them. Also by placing himself in the role of the receiver, the sender can identify benefits to the receiver and point them out.

Feedback

If true communication took place, then the receiver understood what the sender transmitted. The way to establish that understanding has taken place is through feedback from the receiver. As stated earlier, it is a mutual responsibility between the sender and receiver to establish that understanding has taken place. "Two-way communication allows the receiver to ask questions, request clarification, and express opinions that let the sender know whether he or she has been understood. In general, the more complicated the message, the more useful two-way communication is."[7] Without feedback showing that understanding has taken place there is no communication. Feedback can be directly solicited by the sender or it may lie in the actions of the receiver. Feedback is the best way for a supervisor to judge how he is communicating.

Hypocrisy

A sender must act in conformance with what he is communicating. He cannot say one thing and then do something else. If a supervisor announces a policy for his unit, it must apply to all members of the unit and most importantly to him. Nothing will destroy morale faster than a superior who has different rules for himself than for his subordinates.

Don't Overcommunicate

If there is a need to communicate, then do so. Do not communicate just for the sake of communicating. The supervisor who needlessly communicates soon bores his subordinates, and they start to see his messages as frivolous. Another danger of overcommunicating is inconsistent information. So much is put forward that subordinates begin to find inconsistencies in what is being transmitted.

Listen

To communicate well, the sender should listen. He should listen not only to what he and the receiver are saying, but also to what he and the receiver are not saying.

EFFECTIVE FORMAL ORAL COMMUNICATION

Supervisors are often called upon to communicate, or formally present, information orally. Most managers spend between 50% and 90% of their time talking to people.[8] Audiences differ in number and makeup. When preparing material to present

102

orally, separate the presentation into opening remarks which introduce the subject, a description of the subject, and a conclusion which summarizes what has been explained.

A formal oral presentation is usually based on background information, such as a new procedure. The presenter must be thoroughly familiar with such background material prior to making any such presentation. To "wing it" would be a mistake. Audiences are quite perceptive, and a presenter attempting to do this will soon be unmasked.

The job of the presenter is to select facts and details and present them to the audience. Dictating which facts and details to pick out are three factors: the purpose of the presentation, the audience, and the amount of time available.

The Purpose

What is the purpose of the presentation? It could be to introduce a new law for purposes of enforcement, or to explain the same law for purposes of compliance, same background material, but different purposes. It is the purpose of the presentation that determines which facts to select.

The Audience

A communicator must consider the people that comprise different audiences. Technically proficient groups require different facts and details than laymen. What is important to an audience comprised of members of the agency would obviously differ from what is important to an audience comprised of members of the community.

The Time

The amount of time will limit the facts and details that can be included. It will give the presenter a sense of how deeply he can delve into the subject. Is the presentation part of an all-day training session, or is it part of a ten-minute press conference?

Opening Remarks

During the introduction period, the presenter should introduce himself, if necessary. Obviously if the presenter works with the audience everyday, there is no need for an introduction. The opening remarks should also include an indication of what is going to be discussed and why it is going to be discussed. This all takes place while the presenter attempts to arouse and hold the attention and interest of the audience.

Description of the Subject

The body of a presentation should describe the subject, outlining the facts and details previously determined as significant, based on the purpose of the presentation, the audience, and the time available. The points should move in a logical sequential order. The level of the audience's understanding should determine the kind of language used. Repeating major points is a good way to help the audience identify and remember important details. Anecdotes which stray from the subject should be avoided. The presenter should stay on course and be succinct, not excessively verbose. If it is appropriate, graphs and other pictorial representations may be used to show why the subject is important to the audience.

The Conclusion

Concluding remarks should leave no doubt that the presenter is concluding. The major points should be recapped and the audience thanked for their time and attention. Any request for action and cooperation should be made at this time. If appropriate, questions should be entertained at this point. If the presenter does not know the answer to any pertinent questions, arrangements to get the answer should be made.

THE IMPORTANCE OF LISTENING

Consider the following:

Police Officer Ginty is promoted to sergeant. After his first six months on the job, he explains to a friend:

104

"You know, I couldn't wait to make sergeant after ten years of being a cop. For ten years I took orders and had to listen to everyone's complaints when I answered radio runs. I used to say to myself that when I made 'boss,' I would bark out so many orders that every day after work I would go home with a sore throat. But you know what happened?"

"No, what happened?" asks his friend.

"Well on my first tour as a supervisor, two cops approach me and ask if they could talk to me. They then proceed to complain about everything from how hard it is to get the cars washed to the rising crime rate in their sectors. After they finish with me, the commanding officer grabs me and pulls me into his office. He spends the next thirty minutes or so telling me how important it is to motivate the officers in the command and how glad he is that I've been assigned to his command cause he knows just by talking to me that I'll find a way to increase productivity around here. I leave his office and the union delegate tells me that he has heard only good things about me and that he has an earful to tell me about some working conditions in the command.

"Finally he finishes, and I get a chance to go on patrol. Now is the time I get to bark out some of those orders I have been saving up for the last ten years. No such luck. The head of the chamber of commerce sees me and flags me down. He takes about fifteen minutes of my tour telling me what's wrong with the traffic enforcement in the precinct. I no sooner finish with him then one of the senior sergeants in the precinct sees me and decides to give me a pep talk about how all the sergeants in the command stick together since we have such a tough job. The whole day I said about two words. Listen, listen, listen. That's all I seemed to do as a boss.

"Well I thought I could at least do something different off-duty. So I enrolled in a course at city college. The course is called 'Speech Communications.' I get to the class after a day of listening and what's the first thing the professor says? He says, 'At the heart of good communications is effective listening.' I couldn't believe it. But that was then and now is now. After only six months as a boss, the best way to describe myself is that 'I'm all ears.' "

As Sergeant Ginty learned, success as a communicator lies in his ability to listen. Listening can certainly be considered a skill that can be developed and improved.

The Principles of Listening

For listening to take place basically three things must occur:

1. the sender must physically utter sounds or give non-verbal signals which the receiver must interpret as words;
2. these words must be translated into meanings;
3. the receiver must synthesize the meanings of these individual words into an overall meaning or message.

Thus we have sounds becoming words, which have meanings, which are put together to create a message. This takes place while the receiver tries to understand the sender's point of view. Listening is not a complex task, but there are barriers to listening effectively.

BARRIERS TO EFFECTIVE LISTENING

a. Keeping a closed mind—believing you know what the sender will say before he says it, due to prejudices about the sender. "Try to put aside your preconceived ideas or bias on a topic...the speaker may have a new approach, a new concept, a new method of doing an old job that is worth putting into operation. Thus you must listen objectively."[9]

b. Allowing your thoughts to wander because you are able to think many times faster than the other person can speak.

c. Dominating a conversation—feeling that you can say what the sender wishes to say better than he can.

d. Getting sidetracked by personal feelings—blocking out the rest of a communication to dwell on possibly an opening remark which you found offensive or contrary to what you believe.

e. Allowing environmental distractions to interfere with what the sender is saying (e.g. slamming doors, honking horns, etc.).

f. Impatience with the sender's speaking style—listening to his imperfect speech patterns instead of what he is communicating.

g. Restricting the speaker's time—listening to the ticking of the clock instead of listening to what is being said. If you know there is not enough time to allow the sender to communicate, then it should be postponed until the appropriate amount of time is available.

h. Withholding pertinent questions—not asking questions to ensure that you heard what you think you heard. Do not make assumptions about what you think the sender means. If there is any doubt about what is meant, ask for clarification.

ISSUING ORDERS

Issuing orders is a special part of a supervisor's communication duties, because specific results must be obtained. Issuing orders is a process that has distinct parts. The supervisor gives the subordinate a specific direction, the subordinate must understand the direction, and finally the supervisor must make sure the direction was satisfactorily carried out. At any point during the process, problems can arise.

Types of Orders

Different situations call for different types of orders, as do the different personalities and abilities of subordinates. The type of order issued depends upon the circumstances of the situation and the abilities of the subordinate.

A Direct Command

A direct command should be issued to a worker who shows no initiative. Lazy or indifferent, this type of worker will do only what he is directly told to do. This type of order can also be used after a subordinate has been admonished repeatedly about the same error. For example, "Make only three copies. No more. No less." Direct commands are also used in emergency situations where time cannot be spent to explain actions, such as, "cover the back, we have the suspect trapped."

A Tacit Order

Consider the following:

Sergeant Ginty meets two of his officers, Officers Rems and Egos. He tells each of them that he has detected a rise in motor vehicle accidents at specific locations on their respective posts. He further informs them that these accidents are happening during their shifts, and most seem to be caused by motorists failing to obey stop signs. He tells them that they should keep an eye on it and that the three of them should talk about it next week. Rems tells Egos that he's going to get over to where the accidents are happening and issue traffic summonses to motorists running stop signs. Egos answers, "I wonder who the sarge is going to get to clear up that condition on my post?"

The tacit order implies that something should be done and then usually leaves how it is to be done up to the subordinate. Tacit orders are for subordinates who have the ability, initiative and judgment to do a job once it is merely pointed out that something needs to be done. Such orders are not for lazy subordinates who do only what they are specifically told to do. Nor are tacit orders for inexperienced subordinates who have no idea what to do. Tacit orders are a good supervisory tool to develop a subordinate's initiative and confidence. It is a difficult order to follow up on since no specific direction is given. However, when follow-up indicates that nothing was done or the wrong action was taken, then a direct command is in order.

A Request Order

This type of order is useful in directing a sensitive or older employee. For example, "Would you survey your sector and see if any street lights are out?" Most orders can be given this way and such orders tend to gain a cooperative spirit of teamwork. Of course, if such an order is met with resistance, then a direct command should follow.

A Call for Volunteers

This type of order can properly be used by a supervisor when the task is dangerous or otherwise unpleasant. It should not be used to escape command responsibility nor in situations where

108

time is critical. It can be used to allow willing subordinates to increase their job satisfaction, though care must be taken not to take advantage of such subordinates by allowing unwilling subordinates to escape their share of the work.

Ensuring Understanding

As mentioned, part of the process of issuing orders is ensuring that the subordinate understands the order. When communicating orders, this is the boss's responsibility. To simply ask the subordinate if he understands is not enough. Subordinates not wishing to appear incompetent will say they understand even if they know they do not understand. Also a subordinate may truly believe that he understands when in fact he does not. Therefore, to ensure that orders are understood, it is recommended that the subordinate be required to "sing it back in his own key." That means to repeat the order back in his own words.

Pitfalls in Issuing Orders

The following are common errors made in issuing orders:

a. Improperly choosing one's words. If you want to say, "by next week," say, "by next week," don't say, "the first chance you get." The subordinate's interpretation of "the first chance you get" might be in six months.

b. Issuing orders on the run. An order should not be given in a haphazard manner. Even in emergency situations an order must be given in a manner which allows it to be understood.

c. Believing that the order has been understood when it has not. This is the most frequent error.

d. Failing to explain the reason for an order. In appropriate circumstances, the supervisor should explain why an order is necessary. This usually brings about acceptance of the order more readily and makes the subordinate feel more like a team member. This works especially well with a call for volunteers.

e. Failing to follow up on an order. After the order is given, the supervisor must make sure the order was satisfactorily carried out.

Following Up on Orders

Consider the following:

On January 5th, Captain Egos tells Officer Ginty to perform ten crime prevention surveys within the next month. He asks Ginty if he has any questions. Ginty says that he understands perfectly, repeating, "Ten within the next month. No problem, Captain."

On February 1st, Egos asks Ginty, "How many have you done? Are you finished? The thirty days are almost up." Ginty says, "Done? I just got started. In the beginning of January, you told me you wanted ten within the next month. So the next month is February, and I plan to do ten within this month, by the end of February."

Captain Egos improperly chose his words and was misunderstood. This could have been prevented if Egos had Ginty repeat the order in his own words. "A careful study indicated that in general there is less than 50% understanding between supervisor and subordinate about the nature of the job the latter is supposed to be doing."[10] It was correct however to follow-up on his order before what Egos considered the due date. Supervisors should keep a tickler file or calendar of due dates. If a supervisor does not follow up on orders, soon little or none of his orders will be carried out properly. Subordinates will feel that he is not interested in whether or not his orders were carried out. Also, periodic follow-up to orders acts as an early warning to detect problems that may arise so that adjustments can be made.

THE GRAPEVINE

Information moves through an organization via such formal circuits as annual reports and unit memos. As long as these formal circuits satisfy the employees' need to know and their normal curiosity, these circuits are sufficient. However, when there is a gap between a small amount of information available and a high level of curiosity, an informal circuit begins to grow. Such an informal circuit is known as "the grapevine." Through this informal circuit flows accurate, as well as

110

inaccurate, information. Though not consciously designed by management, the grapevine is frequently an extremely effective means of communication. "Being flexible and personal, it spreads information faster than most management communications systems operate. With the rapidity of a burning powder train, it filters out of the woodwork, past the manager's office, through the locker room, and along the corridors."[11] While the grapevine does have its purpose, it should not be seen by supervisors as a substitute for formal information circuits.

Using the Grapevine

A grapevine should not be used in place of a formal vehicle to disseminate information or issue orders, nor should a supervisor pretend it is non-existent. Many administrators think and act without giving adequate weight to the grapevine. Even worse, they try to ignore it. "The grapevine is a factor to be reckoned with in the affairs of management. The administrator should analyze it and should consciously try to influence it."[12] The best way a supervisor can use a grapevine is as an early alert system. By being aware of what is being spread, the supervisor can make sure that accurate information is disseminated through formal circuits.

Rumors

The rumors that travel along the grapevine exist because of three conditions:

1. The issue is important to both the sender and the receiver;
2. The issue is shrouded in uncertainty;
3. The agency has not used its formal information circuits to give out accurate information.

The best way to dispel a rumor is to provide the facts about the issue. At times this may prove problematic because the facts may be confidential or simply unknown. In such situations, a supervisor should consult his superiors about what facts he is entitled to know and what facts he is entitled to pass on to his subordinates. He should then pass on any accurate information he is permitted to pass on. Employees should not have their curiosity about agency matters satisfied by outside sources such as the media or local politicians. This will lead to a feeling among employees that the agency is holding out on them.

EFFECTIVE WRITTEN COMMUNICATIONS

A supervisor will constantly be judged and evaluated by how he writes. Harvard Business Review subscribers have rated the ability to communicate as the prime requisite of a promotable executive.[13] There will be a permanent record which will reflect on him, and it may be read not only by the person to whom it was sent but also by anyone who has the opportunity to see it. Since writing is a skill, it can be developed and improved by adhering to certain principles. These principles are embodied in the four "Have's":

Have Something To Say

If you don't have something to say, then there is no need to write. Writing is time consuming, but reading is also. If a communication is perceived as non-essential, the receiver (reader) will see the time spent in reading the communication as a waste of time and will resent both it and possibly future communications received from the same source.

Writing is really speaking on paper. Therefore, before writing there should be something that stimulates the sender to write. An effective writer has a clear indication that he has something to say. Knowing what is going to be said gives the communication purpose.

Have Someone To Say It To

The intended audience should be identified before a supervisor begins to write. Is it a single person, or a group? Identifying the target audience helps to establish the reading level of the reader and guides a writer in the level of writing. Identifying the receiver tells the writer how much detail to put into the communication. Writing to someone who has no knowledge of the subject matter calls for a different amount of details than when writing to someone who is thoroughly familiar with the subject

112

matter. "Then the task becomes one of selecting the correct language level and determining the relative amounts of technical, informative, or persuasive discussion to be included."[14]

Have a Reason To Say It in Writing

Communication should be in writing when a permanent record is required. It can also be used to inform large numbers of persons or when reporting to a superior who may wish to forward the report to his superior. If the message is complicated and lengthy, writing would be better. If time is critical, then writing may not be appropriate. Writing also affords the writer the opportunity to get credit for any ideas that might prove beneficial to the agency.

Have the Tools To Do It

In order to write, a sufficient grasp of the mechanics of writing, such as punctuation and spelling, and an adequate vocabulary are required. Regarding vocabulary, the rule is—the simpler the language, the better the writing. If the words are stilted, the intent and true meaning will be lost. The reader will become sidetracked in translating the meaning of individual words and the words will lose their collective meaning.

Sufficient facts are also required. If conclusions are to be drawn, then facts must be obtained. Research may be necessary. An outline will help to determine what facts may be needed. When all the facts are gathered, a rough draft following the outline should be written. The draft should have an opening paragraph which tells the reader what will follow and why—that is, what is the purpose of the communication. The next paragraphs should logically flow from the opening paragraph and from each other. It is better to have several short paragraphs than just a few long ones. "The importance of 'paragraph construction' is often overlooked in business communication, but few things are more certain to make the heart sink than the sight of page after page of unbroken type."[15] The final paragraph should summarize what has been said and indicate what, if anything, is expected of the reader. After refining the draft, a final copy can be written and signed.

BARRIERS TO EFFECTIVE WRITING

Effective writing can be accomplished by recognizing and dealing with the following barriers:

a. Inaccurate facts. Nothing detracts from a written communication more than erroneous information. A writer must make sure of the accuracy of all factual material. If there is any doubt, it must be resolved or left out.

b. Unclear sentences. Written communication needs more clarity than spoken communication since the author is not present to clarify anything. Concise, clear sentences in which a reader does not lose the meaning are better than overly lengthy and confusing constructions.

c. Overloading paragraphs. It is better to increase the number of paragraphs than to try to force too much into each one.

d. Confusing opening paragraph. By the end of the opening paragraph a reader should know what the communication will be about and what the purpose is.

e. Poor grammar, spelling, and punctuation. This is often more a result of carelessness and an unwillingness to proofread than a lack of knowledge.

f. Improper use of words. For example, "I want to appraise you," instead of "apprise." The rule is if there is any doubt concerning the meaning of a word, use a simpler word. Remember, good writing is that which is easily understood. It is not a vocabulary test.

g. The wrong purpose. This occurs when a report is written in response to a superior's direction or some type of a request or complaint. For example, a supervisor receives a complaint about the appearance of an officer who was issuing parking summonses. The supervisor responds by explaining the need for parking summonses but never addresses the real complaint, namely the appearance of the officer.

h. Failing to support conclusions with facts. If a supervisor concludes that he requires an increase in personnel, he must

114

support this conclusion with facts. Newly appointed supervisors tend to have their writing efforts blocked by this barrier more than seasoned, experienced supervisors.

TEST YOUR UNDERSTANDING

1. For communication to occur, what three things must take place?

2. What is meant by communication being a two-way street?

3. Whose job is it to ensure that communication occurs?

4. What are the links of the communication loop?

5. Name and explain the obstructions to the communication process.

6. What are the principles of effective communications? Give examples and explain.

7. What is the importance of background information in oral presentations?

8. What are the three parts of the principles of listening?

9. Identify the barriers to listening.

10. Why is the issuance of orders an important part of a supervisor's job?

11. Name the various kinds of orders and give an example when each might best be used.

12. Identify errors commonly made when issuing orders.

13. Why is follow-up to an order important? Explain.

14. Define the grapevine.

15. How can a supervisor use the grapevine?

16. Explain how rumors travel along the grapevine and how they are able to exist.

17. What are four principles of effective written communications?

18. What are the barriers to effective writing?

FOOTNOTES

1. George Strauss and Leonard R. Sayles, *Personnel:The Human Problems of Management,* 3rd ed. (New Jersey: Prentice-Hall, Inc., 1972), p. 218.

2. "Listening Is a Ten-Part Skill." Copyright 1957 by Nation's Business. The Chamber of Commerce of the United States from *Successful Management* by Ralph G. Nichols.

3. Robert N. McMurry, *Conflicts in Human Values.* Harvard Business Review. May-June 1963, p. 130.

4. Norman B. Sigband, *Communication for Management and Business,* 2nd ed. (Glenview, IL: Scott, Foresman and Company, 1976), p. 30.

5. Albert Mehrabian, *Non-Verbal Communication.* (Chicago, IL: Aldine, 1972), p. 182.

6. S.I. Hayakawa, *How Words Change Our Lives.* (Bedford, NH: Curtis Publishing Company, 1982), p. 206.

7. Leonard R. Sayles and George Strauss, *Human Behavior in Organizations.* (Englewood Cliffs, NJ: Prentice-Hall, 1966), p. 238.

8. Henry Mintzberg, *The Nature of Managerial Word.* (New York: Harper and Row, 1973), p. 47.

9. Norman B. Sigband, p. 54.

10. Reported in A.S. Hatch, "Improving Boss-Man and Man-Boss Communication." The Journal of Business Communication, October 1966.

11. Keith Davis, *Human Relations In Business.* (New York: McGraw-Hill, 1957), p. 244.

12. Keith Davis, "Management Communication and the Grapevine." Harvard Business Review, Sept.-Oct. 1953, p. 49.

13. C. Wilson Randle, "How to Identify Promotable Executives." Harvard Business Review, (May-June 1956), p. 122.

14. Norman B. Sigband, p. 344.

15. John Fielden, "What Do You Mean I Can't Write." Harvard Business Review, (May-June 1964), p. 146.

117

SUGGESTED READINGS

Baskin, Otis W. and Craig E. Aronoff.
Interpersonal Communication in Organization.
Santa Monica, CA: Goodyear, 1980.

Hayakawa, S.I.
How Words Change Our Lives.
Curtis Publishing Company.

Mehrabian, Albert.
Non-Verbal Communication.
Chicago, IL: Aldine, 1972.

Mintzberg, Henry T.
The Nature of Managerial Work.
New York: Harper and Row, 1973.

Mitchell, Terrence R.
People in Organizations, 2nd ed.
New York: McGraw-Hill, 1982.

Vardaman and Vardaman.
Communications in Modern Organizations.
New York: John Wiley and Sons, 1973.

Whyte, Jr., William H.
Is Anybody Listening?
New York: Simon and Schuster, 1952.

CHAPTER 6
THE SUPERVISOR AS AN INTERVIEWER

INTERVIEWING DEFINED

The following questions and their answers define an interview:

a.	Who is required?	More than one person
b.	What takes place?	A communication exchange
c.	What is the purpose?	To get or give information or cause an impact on views or future actions
d.	How is it done?	By a combination of verbal and non-verbal communication
e.	Where is it done?	In either a formal or informal setting

Let us examine these more closely.

More Than One Person

To state the obvious, someone cannot interview himself. An interview is an exchange of information between participants. At times an interview may involve more than two people. For instance, a supervisor might seek information informally from two officers during a coffee break. In another instance, two supervisors might, in the same informal setting, be giving information to one officer concerning the formation of a new unit to which the supervisors will be assigned for which the supervisors are seeking volunteers.

A Communication Exchange

An interview should not be a one-way flow of information with the interviewer asking questions and the interviewee answering. The interviewer should also give information. Remember, it is an interview, not an interrogation. In an interrogation someone asks questions only and someone answers; the interrogator gives little or no information. Our goal is an interview in which "each party speaks and listens from time to time.

If one party does all of the speaking and the other all of the listening, no interview has taken place."[1]

Getting/Giving Information - Causing Impacts on Views/Future Actions

The intrinsic purpose of an interview is as we have indicated not only to get information but also to give information. Interviews may impact on the views of those involved in the interview either the subject of the interview or the interviewer. For example, a supervisor is interviewing an employee who is asking for a transfer from the supervisor's unit. The employee's reasons for a transfer could impact on the supervisor's view of his own unit and give him valuable insight.

An interview can also impact on the future actions of either an interviewer or an interviewee or both. For example, the interviewer could decide to promote someone instead of transferring him. Or, an interviewee could decide to ask for a transfer or accept a change in hours.

Verbal and Non-Verbal Communication

In interviews, information is transmitted both verbally and non-verbally. Non-verbal communication, plays a large role in interviews. Understanding what is being communicated by body language is as important as understanding what is being said verbally. It is also important to recognize how things are said. "One should not only focus on what a person says to you (content) but also on the way he says it (process)."[2] An insightful interviewer will be attuned to the many levels of communication going on in any conversation.

Formal or Informal Setting

The answer to "Where can an interview take place?" is anywhere, and that includes formal and informal settings. Certain interviews should take place in a formal setting at a specific, predetermined time. But many interviews need no formal setting and are held impromptu in the field or in the lunch room. Where an interview should be conducted is more often than not a function of, and depends on, the purpose of the interview.

In summary, an interview is a communication exchange, done verbally and non-verbally, between at least two participants for the purpose of getting or giving information or causing an impact on the views or future actions of the participants.

GOALS OF INTERVIEWING

A successful supervisor knows the job, his subordinates and most importantly, knows himself. This combination provides him with a formula for successful supervising. Although each of these areas of knowledge is different, they do have something in common. They require information. The best way to maintain a continuous flow of information is to talk with and listen to subordinates. Good interviews provide this flow of information. The goals of interviewing for a supervisor are to assist him in knowing his job, his subordinates and himself.

Knowing the Job

Consider the following:

Sergeant Rems is interviewing Officer Ginty about a motor vehicle accident Ginty had in a department radio car. Ginty says the accident was not his fault. He was hit from the rear as he rolled up to a stop at a stop sign. Rems asks Ginty what, if anything, could have been done to avoid the accident. Ginty believes that the bumpers and other chrome trim on the rear of the radio cars are extremely shiny and the excessive reflections are interfering with the vision of motorists driving behind the radio cars. He suggested that the chrome should be made with a duller finish.

After the interview, Sergeant Rems examined other accidents involving radio cars and found a significant number involving rear collisions. He also looked at the rear of some of the radio cars and found that Officer Ginty was right. He then forwarded the suggestion which Ginty had recommended. Newly acquired radio cars are now equipped with chrome bearing a dull finish.

The sergeant's desire to know more about the accident led to a better understanding of what field officers were facing; in turn, an improvement was made for the officers, the department and the community.

Knowing Subordinates

Interviews can provide a supervisor with insight into his subordinates.

Consider the following:

Officer Ginty's performance has fallen off lately. His uniforms have gotten sloppy, and his shoes are never shined anymore. Suspecting that Ginty's attitude had become noncaring and indifferent, Lieutenant Rems called him into his office and informed him that his performance and appearance are not acceptable and that he believes that Ginty has lost interest in his work.

Ginty, somewhat embarrassed, says he is as interested as ever in his job but that, lately, he has been going through a difficult time. Ginty's ailing older brother has come to live with him, and Ginty is spending all his spare time taking care of him. He has barely enough time to eat and sleep, let alone to press his uniform and shine his shoes. And when he gets to work, he is tired and finds it difficult to muster his old enthusiasm for the job, even though he is still proud of being a cop.

Lieutenant Rems can now offer assistance to Ginty, something he could not have properly done had he not inquired about Ginty and his situation.

Knowing Yourself

"The wise maxim of the ancient Greeks, 'Know Thyself,' applies especially to interviews."[3] A supervisor needs to be ready to learn from his subordinates.

Consider the following:

Sergeant Rems explains in a performance evaluation to Officer Ginty. that he has rated Ginty below standards in his "Ability To Follow Directions". The sergeant claims that on

122

more than one occasion, what Ginty had done was nothing like what he had directed him to do. Ginty says that he feels that the real cause is vague directions. Ginty says that most of the officers see the Sergeant as a dedicated supervisor. However, they feel that his directions are often unclear and that most officers are reluctant to approach him to ask for clarifications. If what Officer Ginty is saying is accurate, then Rems can learn quite a bit about himself, improving his performance where needed.

CATEGORIES OF INTERVIEWS

There are two categories of interviews, each with its own distinct approach to giving and taking information: the direct interview and the indirect interview. The direct interview is both planned and controlled by the interviewer, while the indirect interview is planned by the interviewer but controlled by the person being interviewed, the interviewee.

Comparison of the Direct and Indirect Interview

In the direct interview, the interviewer writes the questions down in advance of the interview and rarely deviates from the questions which have been selected. He decides what information is to be gathered based on what he, the interviewer, believes is important and essential information. The questions are quite specific and elicit factual answers rather than opinions. "This technique enables the amassing of a large body of factual data in a short period, but falls short in getting at the candidate's generalized and integrated attitudes, traits, abilities, and habits."[4] For example, it would be appropriate to ask in a direct interview, "What time did you leave the station house to deliver the fingerprints to the police lab?" A direct interview would not ask, "Why were you late in delivering the fingerprints from the station house to the police lab?"

As rigid as a direct interview may sound, there is room for an interviewer to give information to the interviewee.

In an indirect interview the interviewer may also record the questions which are planned to be asked. They are written down in advance but are not as rigid as those asked in a direct interview. They are more open ended, intended to seek out opinions and attitudes. Example: "What do you like most/least about the new accident form?" The object is to get the interviewee to talk about his views, likes and dislikes and even goals.

In the indirect interview, the questions do not have to be asked in the exact order as planned. Instead, the responses of the interviewee should dictate the direction of the interview. It is incumbent on the interviewer, however, to ensure that he does not accidentally overlook an important question he has prepared to ask. When people are given the opportunity to express themselves they tend to talk more freely. And when people talk openly and freely, they tend to believe they have not said enough and, therefore, say even more than is required to answer a question. This gives the interviewer a chance to see more of what a person is like.

Summary of Key Distinctions Between Direct and Indirect Interviews

Direct Interview	Indirect Interview
a. Structured and little flexibility	a. Less structured and more flexible
b. Specific questions are prepared by the interviewer in advance but are not open-ended	b. Questions may be prepared in advance and are open-ended
c. Questions are asked in a predetermined order	c. Questions are not necessarily asked in a predetermined order
d. Not interested in interviewee's opinion	d. Interested in opinion of interviewee

THE MOST COMMON TYPES OF INTERVIEWS

We have indicated that an interview involves a communication exchange, and that its purpose is to get or give information or cause an impact on views or future actions. We also mentioned that the general goals of an interview for a supervisor are to assist him in knowing his job, his subordinates and himself. While all three goals of interviewing can be served by any one of the types of interviews we will be addressing in this chapter, certain interview types seem to lend themselves more toward one goal than another.

The Chatting Interview

This interview is extremely informal, as its name indicates, "a chat". It can provide the free and open exchange of a great deal of information. This type of interview needs no formal location nor formal reason to take place. During a chatting interview, a supervisor can reveal to his subordinates insights into what he expects from them. Consequently subordinates can respond and the interaction can lead to formulating more realistic standards that can benefit both parties.

Consider the following:

While having a cup of coffee with Officer Ginty, Sergeant Rems asks him what he thinks about the captain's mandate that each officer on patrol visit any narcotics prone locations on his post at least once during the third, fifth and seventh hours during each eight-hour shift. Ginty responds, "Do you really want to know, Sarge?" Rems assures him of his interest. Ginty then makes two points, "First, it will take the drug dealers less than a week to figure out when the cops are coming to make their visits. Therefore the times of the visits should be left to the individual officers. Second, by mandating a specific number of visits, some officers will figure that if they make three visits they've done enough in enforcing of narcotics laws."

The sergeant attempted to gain feedback. Ginty, once satisfied that the sergeant was approachable, gave his opinion concerning policy from the perspective of one who has to do the job. Hence through a chatting interview, Sergeant Rems was able to get a view from someone on the job. Great care should be taken by the supervisor during a chatting interview to avoid misinterpretation of his comments. This could result in the creation of rumors and distrust.

If Ginty had not understood that the sergeant was honestly soliciting his opinion, he might have construed what the sergeant was saying as nothing more than selling the captain's mandate. The supervisor must listen and clearly understand what the subordinate is saying and how he is responding.

Chatting interviews present a great opportunity for a supervisor to offer his ear for problems that a subordinate may be experiencing. The boss should make it clear that he is available to help a subordinate help himself address issues that may be affecting the subordinate's performance. The best way to do that is for the boss to deliver the message that he has an "open door policy" and that he can be approached by the subordinate.

The Performance Interview

Generally, this interview aids a supervisor to better know his subordinates. On occasion, however, it can help to gain insight into one's own self and supervisory style through the responses of subordinates during such interviews.

Formally or Informally

When held formally, it takes the form of an evaluation interview (which will be discussed in greater detail in the section of the text dealing with performance evaluations). When conducted informally, it is similar to a chatting interview but has a more specific goal: to give the employee guidance and constructive criticism about his performance. "The appraisal interview is primarily a teaching device. The objective is to help the employee help himself by persuading him to recognize and correct his deficiencies."[5] It can be a follow-up to a previous performance interview or it can be used to initially advise a subordinate about a facet, either positive or negative, of his performance.

Facts First

It is extremely vital that the boss have the facts before beginning any performance discussion. This calls for the boss to look into the background of the subordinate and any other data which may hold information concerning the subordinate's performance. If any criticism of performance is to be delivered to the subordinate, it must contain documentation. "There is nothing more exasperating to a person than to be criticized in general terms or believe that he is the victim of inaccurate information or that his superior has judged him on hearsay evidence."[6]

Calmly Take Your Time

A performance interview must be held in an atmosphere of calmness. It cannot be hurried along for two reasons. First, the subordinate will feel that the interview was merely for the record and was not really important. Second, it is offensive to the subordinate that someone would hurriedly inform him of his performance. If the hastened remarks are positive, then he will feel that his good performance was not given enough recognition. If the hastened remarks concern faulty performance, then the subordinate will not be motivated enough to change by what he sees is "a quick and light dusting" of what he supposedly is not doing correctly. If the subordinate wishes to be heard on an issue, enough time should be allotted. However, the supervisor should never debate issues. He should, instead, listen and be able to firmly and accurately document what he is saying with facts. The interview is successful if the subordinate goes away with a clearer picture of how he is performing and how he can improve. Follow-up interviews should be conducted to determine if required changes have been made or if positive performance continues.

The Subordinate's Grievance Interview

In this interview (discussed in greater detail elsewhere in the text), a subordinate comes to the boss with a complaint about the work environment. Whether real or imagined it is real to the subordinate and so it should be treated as real and important during the interview.

What to Do

After being made aware of a grievance, a supervisor should conduct the interview as soon as possible, in a private setting without interruptions. The subordinate should be allowed to tell his story while the boss takes notes. Many supervisors find it helpful to have the subordinate tell it twice to make sure they understand the details and also ensure that the subordinate has included all the details. It is also helpful for the boss to repeat the grievance in his own words so that both he and the subordinate agree on the facts. If the grievance can be remedied on the spot, it should be immediately addressed. If a decision is made, the reasons should be explained. If a decision is postponed, the subordinate should be informed when the boss will get back to him. Sometimes a grievance lacks factual basis, a person may be just reacting or overacting to something in the work environment. A supervisor must tactfully determine if the person with the complaint will be satisfied with more information or not.

Consider the following:

Officer Ginty approaches the watch commander, Lieutenant Rems and tells him that he thinks the way overtime assignments are meted out is unfair. Since Rems keeps meticulous records on accrual of overtime he is aware of the issue. Each time an overtime assignment arises, Rems personally offers it to a member of the shift in strict sequential order. Whenever an officer refuses or accepts an overtime assignment, a record is made of the offer and the resulting acceptance or refusal. Rems also is aware that Ginty has turned down overtime assignments on three occasions within the last six months. However, Lieutenant Rems patiently listens to Ginty's grievance and after making sure he has all the facts, the Lieutenant tells Ginty that he can understand why Ginty might feel that way, but he'd like to review some of the overtime records together with Ginty in an effort to ensure that Ginty is being treated fairly. Officer Ginty replies that he would like to see the records.

Lieutenant Rems is positive that Ginty's grievance is unfounded. However, he does not immediately confront Ginty with the facts. Instead, he allows Ginty the opportunity to air his grievances and to review the facts and thereby possibly see his claim in another perspective. Very often when this is done, a subordinate will see that his grievance is not founded and will react positively to the supervisor's attempt to deal with the issue. Whatever the final outcome, after the matter has been resolved, the boss should in the near future follow up by asking the subordinate if any recurrence of the issue has taken place.

The Assignment Interview

This interview assists a supervisor in learning about and assessing a subordinate who is requesting assignment to the supervisor's unit. Whereas records exists about such candidates, in terms of their records of past assignments and evaluations within the agency, clues and hints of their attitude and opinions toward work-related matters may be obtained during such interviews.

Kind of Questions

In such an interview open-ended questions which encourage free and open conversation should be used. The kinds of questions which can be answered by a simple yes or no should be avoided. It is better to formulate questions which provide insight into the subordinate's background, attitudes and goals.

How Much Time To Use

The benefit of assignment interviews is not recognized by most interviewers. As a result the greatest hindrance to successful assignment interviews is the amount of time supervisors are willing to dedicate to such interviews. Anything less than one-half hour in duration will rarely succeed. In addition, these interviews should be conducted in a private and comfortable atmosphere. The pace should be easy and allow appropriate answers about the unit to which he is applying.

The Overshadowing Effect

Supervisors must guard against making a decision based on only one characteristic of the applicant. For example, if an applicant is especially neatly attired and speaks well, that does not necessarily mean that he will make the best burglary detective. This "overshadowing" or "halo" effect must be closely guarded against so that a true appraisal of the subordinate who is applying may be made.

PREPARATION FOR AN INTERVIEW

Sometimes an interview occurs spontaneously, but, whenever possible, it is best to prepare for an interview. "Preparation provides a base from which to ask and respond to relevant questions. The more complete the preparation for an interview, the greater the quantity and quality of information you receive."[7]

The objective(s) of the interview should be as clear as possible to the interviewer. A checklist of important points to cover must be prepared by the interviewer. This checklist will serve as a guide to the formulation of questions that should be asked.

In order to refine the questions, the background of the interviewee should be reviewed: past assignments, performance records and other personal history information.

A location and time must be decided upon. Advance notice of the interview and its exact location should be given to the interviewee. In appropriate circumstances, the interviewee should be told approximately how long it is envisioned that the interview will take. The supervisor must set aside enough time from his schedule to prepare for and to conduct the interview.

CONDUCTING THE INTERVIEW

For ease of understanding the actual conducting of the interview has three components: (a) the opening, (b) the questions and answers, and (c) the sum up.

The Opening

The interviewer should introduce himself to the interviewee. It is appropriate for a supervisor to stand up, welcome the interviewee and shake hands. This is not an investigation; it is an interview The atmosphere should be friendly and positive. Opening with a positive statement about the interviewee can help create a positive atmosphere. For example, "I see that you have made several burglary arrests in the last two months. That's really good work." To jump right into the interview without any greeting or opening recognition doesn't put the interviewee at ease.

The reason for the interview should be clearly stated. "It is not enough for the interviewer to be aware of his objective. He must transmit this information to the interviewee. Once armed with the information the interviewee has more insight into the direction to be taken by the interviewer and he can then organize his responses accordingly."[8] At the outset, the skilled interviewer should advise the interviewee to contribute freely and ask questions if something is unclear.

Questions and Answers

The interviewer should use his previously prepared notes to guide him in the actual questioning of the interviewee. During the question and answer stage, it is important to maintain eye contact with the interviewee. This accomplishes a few things. First, it makes the questions more personal and the interviewer more personable. Second, it tells the interviewee that the interviewer is interested in what he has to say. Third, it allows the interviewer to observe non-verbal responses.

If any directions are to be given during the interview they should be specific and not vague and general. If a decisive course of action is agreed upon, then it must be clearly stated and clearly understood by all concerned. If anything is agreed upon to be done or delegations made, then controls must be put in place to accomplish them. The interviewer must keenly observe all verbal and non-verbal communication and gather as much information as possible.

The Sum Up

Review what has taken place and specify what has been agreed to be done, who will do it and when shall it be done. Ask if there is anything that he would like to say before they conclude. If so, address it before he or she leaves the interview. The interviewee should be thanked for his time and informed when he can expect to hear from the interviewer if future contact is required.

INTERVIEW LISTENING

Effective listening is listening in a way that invites and encourages a subject to open up and talk freely. If you are good at listening, you have an excellent chance of becoming a good interviewer. What will be required is patience and insight. This insight will certainly allow a supervisor to hear what the subordinate is saying but it will do more. It will allow the supervisor to see "how" it is said by the interviewee. "If you are to begin to analyze what is going on in an interview, you must listen, not only with your ear, but also with your eye."[9]

There can be no understanding without listening. If the goals of interviewing are to learn more about the job, the subordinates or oneself, then the goal(s) cannot be reached without listening. Listening is a difficult task, especially for law enforcement supervisors who are conditioned to come upon an emergency, take charge, and immediately dictate what must be done. In so many instances, the boss's job is to tell people what to do, to impose views on others. However, in interview listening, it is different. It is trying to understand the subordinate's views.

Active vs. Passive Listening

Listening during an interview is anything but passive. It is an active and continuous process. Listening is difficult because a listener is able to think many times faster than a speaker can speak. This causes the mind to "take a walk down wandering lane" and stop listening while the speaker is still speaking. An interviewer should listen constantly and actively. He achieves this when he is able to understand what is being said and what's behind it.

Consider the following:

In the beginning of the year, Sergeant Rems mentioned to Officer Ginty that Ginty's arrest activity was below standards, and he should attempt to improve it. It is now several months later, and the sergeant is again interviewing Ginty concerning his performance. Ginty says, "Don't you think my arrest activity has gotten better since the last time you spoke to me about it?"

Rems answers, "Seems to me that you feel your activity has improved since the last time we spoke."

Note that Sergeant Rems listened to what Ginty had to say and then made the kind of comment that would cause Ginty to talk some more about the issue. Rems's intent was to get Ginty to talk openly so that Rems could get a deeper understanding of how Ginty felt. The boss who is easy to talk to is so because he tries to get a handle on what is being said. He creates a fertile field for his understanding by getting the subordinate to talk.

Getting the Interviewee To Talk

Most people like to talk. A skilled interviewer recognizes this and also recognizes how important listening is. However, to ensure that the subordinate being interviewed does talk openly and freely, certain tactics can be used. For instance, he can use reinforcing remarks such as, "I see" to continue the interviewee talking. Also he can use questioning techniques such as "echoing" and "boundering."

Echoing is a type of question which takes the last few words stated and uses them to ask a question.

Consider the following:

A subordinate says, "They don't treat us like they use to." The interviewer answers with the question, "Like they used to?" Echoing is intended to elicit more information.

Boundering is a questioning technique used by an interviewer to prevent the interviewee from straying from the subject matter being discussed.

Consider the following:

In an interview concerning a grievance about vacation policies, the interviewee remarks, "You know how the vacation and the rest of the precinct policies are."

The interviewer responds, "How is the vacation policy?"

He has attempted to keep the interviewee from straying away from the subject of the interview.

Documenting the Results of an Interview

The results of an interview should be documented. At times, a permanent record of the event is required. When done properly, documentation should include what was discussed, when and where, who participated and what was the result. The documentation serves as a reminder of such action steps and assignments.

It becomes a thorny issue as to whether notes should be taken during an interview. Some argue that if notes are not taken until the interview is completed, then important details can be forgotten. Others argue that to take notes during an interview is bad because it will unnecessarily inhibit the interviewee from freely discussing issues. We believe, however, that it is a good idea for a supervisor to document any interviews. If an interviewer announces that he will be taking notes during the interview and the reason why (e.g. to make sure what is agreed upon actually happens), any apprehension should be removed.

INTERVIEW FOLLOW-UP

An interview is of no consequence no matter how expertly it has been conducted nor how much information has been collected unless the goals which were targeted are reached. It is the supervisor's job to see that the goals are reached and that what was agreed upon happens.

Consider the following:

Officer Ginty approaches Sergeant Rems and tells him he feels he does not get choice assignments. He feels that he has been in the command for a good while and has done a good job. He wonders why he can't be considered for one of the civilian clothes precinct anti-crime units. He tells Rems that he thinks it's because he is not one of the boys and does not socialize with other members of the command while off duty. Rems takes down Ginty's complaint and tells him to get a synopsis of his arrest activity, and then he'll look into it.

In this instance, the sergeant should have specifically told Ginty when he should get the information to him and when Ginty

© 1995 by J. & B. Gould
Printed in the U.S.A. Ms

could then expect an answer from him. Merely telling Ginty that he would look into it is just one part of the sergeant's job. It is the interviewer's job to follow up on those things which were discussed during the interview and to set specific expected results and dates. In addition, after the subject of the interview is resolved, a supervisor should again check on the situation which brought about the original interview to see if the matter has been satisfactorily addressed and is not an unresolved issue.

BARRIERS TO EFFECTIVE INTERVIEWING

The interview process can be difficult. A great deal of this difficulty is due to barriers which block effective interviewing. It is essential to recognize and be familiar with these barriers in order to avoid them when possible:

a. The parties involved in the interview are not physically prepared for the interview. The interviewer or interviewee are too mentally or physically tired to properly participate in the interview. To be interviewed or conduct an interview after working a 12 midnight to 8 a.m. shift is probably not the best time for an interview. In such cases the interview should be postponed to a more conducive time.

b. Speech sifting or filtering. This happens when a participant in the interview does not say what he genuinely means. Instead, he says what he thinks he is expected to say. "It is...difficult for the respondent to accept his superior in the interviewer role and to ignore, even for the brief period of the interview, the status and power differences which exist between them. He must protect himself against the possibility of administrative action on the part of the interviewer when he resumes his supervisory role."[10] Without a doubt this is the most common block to effective interviewing.

c. Insufficient preparation on the part of the interviewer. He fails to gather available background material on the person to be interviewed and the issues involved.

d. A belief on the part of the participants in the interview that they know what is going to be said by any one of the participants before he actually says it. Based on external factors such as previous encounters with the person talking, they believe they can predict what is going to be said and stop listening to what is actually being said.

e. Daydreaming. Because a person can think several times faster than he can speak, the listener in the interview stops listening and allows thoughts other than those connected with the interview to creep into his mind, thus turning off any real listening to what the speaker in the interview is saying.

f. Listening with one's mouth. Most people want to talk more than they want to listen. However, there can be no real interview unless real listening takes place.

g. Permitting outside distractions to interfere with the interview. A good example of this is the ringing telephone which continues to be answered by one of the participants during the interview.

h. Going in to an interview with a mind set which refuses to entertain any thoughts which are foreign to what is believed to be correct. This prevents participants in the interview from dealing with the issues involved through any fresh and innovative approach.

i. Not asking questions about unclear issues. Instead, erroneous assumptions are made about what certain statements made actually mean.

j. Failing to take into consideration the non-verbal statements made by a participant. Here verbal statements are taken literally, and any real behind the scene meaning is ignored.

Consider the following:

Officer Ginty is being informed during a performance interview that he will be reassigned to embassy duty which calls for him to work at a fixed post, in uniform, in front of an embassy. His duties pretty much limit any mobility since he must stay at a police booth. To this Ginty looks straight ahead and unemotionally responds in a monotone voice, "Whatever you say, boss."

Verbally, Ginty is accepting his assignment. But his non-verbal communication is another message.

k. Fragile feelings. When one participant makes a statement to which the other participant takes exception, justifiably or unjustifiably, anything else said for the remainder of the interview falls upon deaf ears.

TEST YOUR UNDERSTANDING

1. Define interviewing.

2. What are the goals of interviewing? Give examples.

3. What are the two major categories of interviews? Explain the differences between them.

4. Name several types of interviews and give examples.

5. What is the "overshadowing effect?"

6. Specifically explain the importance of preparing for an interview.

7. Name and explain the components of an interview.

8. Should an interviewer listen actively or passively? Explain your answer.

9. Explain "echoing" and "boundering" as questioning techniques.

10. Explain why documentation of an interview is important.

11. Is follow-up to an interview important? Give reasons to support your answer.

12. Name and explain the barriers to effective interviewing.

© 1995 by J. & B. Gould
Printed in the U.S.A.   Ms

FOOTNOTES

1. Charles J. Stewart and William B. Cash, Jr., *Interviewing Principles and Practices,* 4th ed. (Dubuque, IA: William C. Brown Publishers, 1985), p. 9.

2. Lawrence R. O'Leary, *Interviewing for the Decisionmaker.* (Chicago, IL: Nelson-Hall, 1976), p. 23.

3. Annette Garrett, *Interviewing - Its Principles and Methods.* (New York: Family Service Association of America, 1972), p. 7.

4. Theodore Hariton, *Interview - The Executive's Guide to Selecting the Right Personnel.* (New York: Hastings House Publishers, 1970), p. 36.

5. James M. Black, *How To Get Results From Interviewing.* (New York: McGraw-Hill Book Company, 1970), p. 79.

6. Ibid., p. 82.

7. Richard Fischer Olson, *Managing The Interview - A Self-Teaching Guide.* (New York: John Wiley and Sons, Inc., 1980), p. 37.

8. James M. Lahiff, "Interviewing For Results." from *Readings In Interpersonal Communications* by Huseman, Logue, and Freshley, eds., 1973, pp. 396-397.

9. Cal W. Downs, G. Paul Smeyak, and Ernest Martin, *Professional Interviewing.* (New York: Harper and Row Publishers, 1980), p. 84.

10. Robert L. Kahn and Charles F. Cannell, *The Dynamics of Interviewing - Theory, Technique, and Cases.* (New York: John Wiley and Sons, Inc., 1957), p. 317.

SUGGESTED READINGS

Beatty, R.H.
The Five-Minute Interview.
New York: Wiley, 1986

DeVito, Joseph A.
The Inter-Personal Communication Book.
New York: Harper and Row, 1983

Krannich, Caryl Rae and Ronald L. Krannich.
Interview For Success.
Woodbridge, VA: Impact Publications, 1990

Stewart, John
Bridges Not Walls - A Book About Interpersonal Communication.
Boston, MA: Addison-Wesley, 1982

Vlk, Suzee.
Interviews That Get Results.
New York: Simon and Schuster, 1984

CHAPTER 7
THE SUPERVISOR AS AN EVALUATOR OF PERFORMANCE

It is an established and accepted fact that personnel represent the most expensive resource of a law enforcement agency. An agency's personnel complement is also its most important resource, more important than any computer able to search for single fingerprints or than any laboratory tool able to identify DNA samples. It would seem logical then that law enforcement agencies would welcome the opportunity to identify and assess through personnel evaluations the abilities and performance of their most important and expensive resource, their work force. Unfortunately this is not always the case. Bosses do not like performing personnel evaluations, and subordinates often resent being evaluated. Supervisors complain, "Nobody ever reads these things. All they care about is that they're done on time." On the other side, subordinates say, "I know I'm doing my job. Why do they have to put me through this?" An understanding of evaluations, their purpose and benefits can help everyone involved have a better attitude toward evaluations.

GOALS OF PERFORMANCE EVALUATIONS

Regardless of what they are titled, all performance evaluations to varying degrees seek to accomplish these goals:

a. To provide an accurate measure of what the employee is doing. The history of law enforcement shows us that the measurement of officers was largely based upon numbers of arrests. Little recognition was given to an officer who operated well in serving the public with service related duties. With accurate performance evaluations, the agency is able to identify, recognize and measure the actual performance of each employee. Such an evaluation should be able to tell what and how well each employee is doing regardless of his duties.

b. To help the supervisor know his subordinate. Requiring a supervisor to stop and examine what and how well each specific employee is doing will result in the supervisor getting to know his subordinates better. This in turn will improve an already existing work relationship between the supervisor and the subordinate.

c. To identify the strengths and weaknesses of an employee. This allows the supervisor to credit a subordinate with proper recognition for those things he is doing well and allows the subordinate to improve in those areas where the subordinate may not be performing well.

d. To provide a plan for the future improvement of employees. If an employee is identified through performance evaluation as not doing well, then a plan can be created by the supervisor for the improvement of the subordinate's future performance. If a subordinate's level of performance is high, then a plan can be created to improve the present high level performance even more.

e. To provide lookback. Evaluations help an agency to "lookback" and determine if the standards it is using to hire employees are getting it the kind of employees wanted in the agency.

f. To get rid of the dead wood. As difficult as it is claimed to be by law enforcement agencies, discharging employees who are not performing adequately despite all efforts to assist them becomes impossible without a well-constructed, well-run, and well-documented evaluation process.

PREREQUISITES FOR AN EVALUATOR

Job Knowledge

Before a supervisor can rate a subordinate, the supervisor must know the job of the subordinate. That does not mean that the supervisor must be totally skilled in the subordinate's job, but the supervisor must be sufficiently aware of the subordinate's job responsibilities. It is difficult for a supervisor to satisfactorily explain that based on his current evaluation, an employee must improve his performance if the supervisor knows little or nothing about that job. The chances of such an assessment by the supervisor being accurate are remote and, even if accurate, the chances of the subordinate accepting such an evaluation are even more remote.

Training in the Performance Evaluation Process

"Regardless of whether evaluations are obtained from multiple appraisers or from only the employee's immediate superior, all raters should be trained to reduce errors of judgment that occur when one person evaluates another. This training is necessary because to the degree a performance appraisal is biased, distorted, or inaccurate, the probability of stimulating the productivity of the employee is greatly decreased."[1] The supervisor should be comfortable with the format used by the agency in the evaluation process.

Observation of the Subordinate's Performance

Consider the following:

Officer Ginty has just been informed of his evaluation results prepared by Sergeant Egos. Later, when the shift is over, Ginty is in the locker room preparing to go home. He remarks to another officer, "I just got my yearly evaluation. I'm doing great according to Sergeant Egos, who just got promoted and assigned here. This is only the third time I've ever seen this guy in my life. I first saw him three weeks ago when he arrived here. I saw him again two days ago when he pulled up to a job the cops in the sector adjacent to mine were handling. And I just saw him twenty minutes ago. He tells me that I'm doing a real good job, but that my ability to get along with the community could improve a little. He bases his criticism on a letter from someone to whom I gave a traffic summons. The guy complained that he should not have been given a summons by me because although he did go through a stop sign, there was nobody coming. Doesn't he know I'm the traffic conditions man? Anytime there's a rash of accidents in a particular location, I'm sent to the area to try to reduce the accidents by issuing summonses. I give lots of summons each month. Now that will make me real popular in the community. He has never seen me work and knows nothing about what I do. How is he supposed to rate me and how am I supposed to accept what he says? The whole thing isn't on the level."

The actual performance of the subordinate must be observed by the supervisor before any real and accurate assessment of performance can be made. The amount of contact that a supervisor has with a subordinate should be sufficient to provide the supervisor with first-hand knowledge of the subordinate's performance. Without such knowledge the chances of the evaluation to be accurate are slim, and it would not be accepted by the employee. A subordinate cannot be rated on hearsay.

Use of Commonly Understood Standards

Before an evaluation both the supervisor and the subordinate should clearly understand what dimensions are being rated and what standards are being used. For instance, if a subordinate's decision-making ability is being assessed, then both parties should be aware of the standards of evaluation. For instance:

a. Does the subject get all possible information before making his decisions?

b. Do the decisions made comply with agency policy?

c. Do the decisions made take into consideration the needs and concerns of the community?

d. Can the subject appropriately prioritize his duties?

The supervisor should strive to make known to the subordinate who is to be rated what is being measured and how it will be measured. If all parties concerned can see the objective standards used for measuring abilities then the process becomes less subjective.

Ability to Communicate the Results of a Performance Evaluation

The evaluation process is not a covert operation. It is not to be considered a secret. Keeping the ratee informed is the most important step in gaining acceptance of and compliance with the agency's personnel evaluation system. If an evaluator cannot properly inform and motivate a ratee while communicating the results of the evaluation, then the entire evaluation defeats its purpose.

An Objective Disposition

There are no performance evaluations systems that are completely free of subjectivity. After all, an evaluation is one person judging another person. However, a supervisor must strive to be as objective as possible. One way to do this is to be able to clearly articulate the facts justifying why he took a particular position and thus arrived at a particular rating. The evaluator should pretend he is being asked to explain how he has arrived at the evaluation. In this way he will be able to articulate the facts and satisfactorily explain how he has arrived at his conclusions.

The supervisor should be aware of his own disposition and not allow it to get in the way of objectively rating his subordinates. Evaluations should not be conducted nor their results reviewed if the supervisor is preoccupied with other matters which might impact negatively on his ability to be objective.

LEGAL ASPECTS OF PERFORMANCE EVALUATIONS

Agencies conducting performance evaluations must comply with appropriate statutes at the federal, state and local levels. Such laws are geared to protect personnel from such things as age discrimination, civil rights discrimination, and unlawful compensation practices. "More often than many of us care to admit, factors such as an employee's race, sex, or age may lie behind negative comments couched in objective terms. In recognition of this fact, legislative acts and court decisions have subjected performance appraisals to close scrutiny and rigid requirements to eliminate discrimination."[2]

Each agency therefore is bound to comply with those statutes within its geographical area. "Violation of federal laws regarding performance appraisal can easily cost an organization several million dollars for legal fees, court costs, damages, and back pay, not to mention the drain on an organization's time and personnel in preparing for a case."[3] What is contained below is not an enumeration of performance evaluations laws but some guidelines to help an agency deal with the legal aspects of performance evaluations.

Rater Training

An evaluator must be trained. He must be aware of the nature of evaluations, what their purpose really is and how they can be used to benefit all concerned. He must be made aware of the common errors made by raters so that he can avoid them. He must be taught how to conduct a review of the evaluation with the ratee. If it can be shown that a rater was not properly trained then the validity of the agency's formal performance evaluation system can be challenged.

Oral or Written?

A performance evaluation system should utilize written forms. "From everything said so far, it should be obvious that informal oral evaluations do not meet the requirements of a formal performance appraisal of on-the-job behavior. There can be no appraisal system worthy of the name that is not written and not recorded." [4] This involves what are sometimes called "Critical Incident Recordings," which refer to incidents where the subject of the evaluation performs either very well or very poorly in a particular work situation. "There is no contradiction between urging the manager to observe employees at work informally and furnishing them with constructive feedback on the scene, and advocating a formal system. The informal and formal should be mutually supportive." [5] Written evaluations lessen the chance of misunderstandings, provide documentation for supervisory action and act as a blueprint for plans to improve a ratee's future performance. They also aid in transition when a new supervisor is assigned, or the ratee is transferred to a new command. Written evaluations provide a permanent picture of an employee's performance which can and should be used when the agency interacts with the employee.

Individualized Formats

There should be different formats for the different titles or positions which exist in the agency. Obviously the job of the unit commander is different from the job of the newly hired entry level clerk. The same form could not possibly capture and measure the different duties of each title.

146

Agency-Wide Involvement

The whole agency must be aware of and committed to the performance evaluation system. It cannot work if only certain units or certain supervisors take it seriously. Support for such a system must come from the top, if it is to be supported at the bottom. If the individual members of the agency are to believe in the evaluation system, they must be informed about it, understand it, and see it in action. This means that the merit increases, promotions, and choice assignments should be closely tied to performance evaluations so that the evaluations will be seen as a valid and worthwhile effort.

Continuous or Continual Evaluations

Should performance evaluations be conducted continuously or continually? The answer is both. This means that a supervisor should be continuously, in an unbroken effort, monitoring the work effort of his subordinates. The supervisor skilled in evaluating employees should keep a record of these contacts with subordinates and use them to form the basis of his preparation for the formal evaluation. "The roots of the formal appraisal situation should be in the day-to-day, week-to-week, and month-to-month interface between the manager and the subordinate based upon the conduct of assigned tasks."[6] The formal evaluation form should be done periodically or continually at least once a year.

Specification of What Is To Be Evaluated

The behaviors or work actions to be used as the basis of the evaluation must be job-related, specific and well-defined. Personal traits which have no bearing on performance should not find their way onto an evaluation form.

Evaluation Interview

An employee should be shown his completed evaluation form and be required to sign and date it in the presence of the evaluator, who also signs and dates it. There should be a caption on the form requiring the rater's supervisor to review the form to ensure it is properly prepared and it should include a place for his comments. The evaluation review is the most distasteful part of the evaluation process for the rater, especially when dealing with poor performers.

Appeal Procedure

The evaluation system should provide for an appeal if the ratee believes he has not been properly rated. The review of the appeal should be conducted by the supervisor of the rater. "He [the rater] will probably strengthen relationships as well as show himself as desiring to be honest and helpful if he allows this appeal. He should make the arrangements in such a way that he is not shifting his responsibilities to his boss but rather is allowing for an impartial re-examination of the evidence on both sides."[7] The ratee should be advised in writing of the finding of the reviewer of the appeal. There needs to be guarantees that an employee appealing an evaluation will not suffer recourse from the agency.

Constantly Reviewed

Staff experts should review completed performance evaluations from time to time to ensure that agency policies are being followed. There should be feedback and evaluation of the evaluation system itself in an effort to insure that the process meets the changing agency needs and legal mandates.

Periodic Review by Legal Advisors

The agency's legal staff would be wise to periodically confer with federal, state and local Equal Employment Opportunity (EEO) agencies. This should establish valuable lines of communication with the EEO agencies concerned and keep the agency's evaluation system current with changing laws.

PERFORMANCE STANDARDS

As we have mentioned earlier, a performance evaluation calls for one person to make a judgment about another person. Any such evaluation cannot be completely objective. We all have subjective preferences. In an attempt to deal with this, raters must have a clear

148

understanding of the individual standard they will use in measuring each of the dimensions which appear on a performance evaluation form.

Outputs vs. Behaviors

In law enforcement there is both "what you do" and "how you do it." This creates a problem in evaluating law enforcement personnel. Some of the dimensions seek to measure outputs or what is being accomplished, such as the number of accidents handled. Other dimensions seek to measure behaviors or how the job was done, such as the empathy exhibited by an officer while performing duties at the accident scene. This latter aspect of job performance is harder to quantify. Therefore it must first be decided what will be measured, then standards must be set for each dimension. It must be clear how attitudes, disposition and qualities will be measured.

Measuring Performance Levels

Agency policy will determine what constitutes above standard, below standard and extremely poor rating levels. However, a supervisor plays a large role in the standards he sets for each of his subordinates. What he demands from his subordinates will set the benchmark for what they do and how they will be evaluated. When measuring outputs in dimensions, such as how many aided cases were handled, a quantifiable standard might suffice. However standards of performance become a little more elusive when measuring a trait such as stability or flexibility. In such instances, it is recommended that the rater develop (if the agency has not already done so) a series of questions about the ratee's stability.

Consider the following:

Suppose there are four gradations on an evaluation form: superior, fair, unsatisfactory, and well-below standards. To evaluate the quality of stability, the following questions and number ratings would help:

Does the subject maintain composure in stressful incidents?	1/ 2/ 3/ 4
Does the subject adapt to changing situations?	1/ 2/ 3/ 4
What is the subject's reaction to unforeseen circumstances?	1/ 2/ 3/ 4

The number four represents a superior rating; while the number one represents a below-standards rating. After averaging the numbers, the rater can now determine the overall rating.

This is just one way to set performance standards. What is most important is that whatever procedure is used, the same procedure should be used for all subordinates.

No matter what performance standards are used, they will have an impact on the level of performance of the agency. Employees will be quick to recognize what is considered as superior effort and will target it for their level of performance. Performance standards determine what employees will actually do, so their standards should be chosen carefully.

FORMAL EVALUATION SYSTEMS

There are a variety of formal evaluation systems. Although the choice of one system over another is usually made by top-level policy makers, a law enforcement manager/supervisor should be conversant with some of the more common systems and how they operate:

The Model Employee Method

This method sets out by defining the "model employee" who has the optimal attributes for a particular job position. The rater evaluates subordinates by measuring them in comparison with this model employee. This method presents some difficulty in agencies with a large number of raters since each rater will have his own mental picture of a model employee, and thus subjectivity is greatly increased.

150

Top to Bottom Method

Here the rater merely places ratees in rank order. This is also known as a forced distribution method. If the rater has ten members assigned to his squad, he indicates his highest rated subordinate as one, the next best as two, and so on. This method sometimes creates antagonism and resentment on the part of those who are doing a job good enough to be considered superior in any other unit of the agency, but under these circumstances, they might find themselves rated twenty of twenty. Also, more than in any other evaluation method, seniority seems to play an inordinate role in getting a high rating or ranking. The worst characteristic of this type of evaluation system is that the rater is often asked to place subordinates who are performing different duties in rank order. This type of evaluation system works best when everyone who is rated under the system performs the same duties.

We do not recommend either the model employee or top to bottom methods. The problem which arises with both the model employee and top to bottom methods is that the rater is comparing the performance of one subordinate with the performance of another. Instead the performance of a subordinate should be measured against clearly defined agency standards.

Forced Choice Method

Here a rater is required to select one statement that best describes the ratee with regard to the dimension listed. For instance, in the dimension of work analysis, the rater might typically be forced to choose one of the following:

a. Consistently produces extremely high quantity and quality of work.
b. Produces an acceptable amount of work whose quality meets agency standards.
c. Must be prodded to meet minimum standards of quality and quantity of work.
d. Constantly fails to meet agency standards regarding quality and quantity of work despite admonishments.

Forced Choice Diagnostic

A variation of the forced choice method, here a rater selects statements which he feels describe the ratee. The statements do not reveal any value of worth. Each statement has, however, through various inputs, previously been determined to indicate worth from very favorable to not favorable at all. The rater, however, is not aware of the worth of these statements. He simply chooses statements he feels describes the ratee's performance. After he has selected his choices, they are tabulated by a central source and an overall rating is given to the ratee.

The Critical Incident Method

This method requires great input from the rater. The rater must make comments about the performance of the ratee occurring during positive and negative incidents the rater personally observed. It calls for the rater to have had a great deal of contact with the ratee throughout the rating period. The rater actually writes his comments in paragraph format on the evaluation form. This method does give a rater some flexibility concerning the comments he wishes to make, but it requires him to have extensive contact with the ratee and observe him often.

An example of a critical incident entry:

Communication Skills: During the electrical blackout of the town, subject was able to listen with empathy to others who were under extreme stress and was still able to extract pertinent information. These actions and resulting information were extremely valuable in preventing vandalism in the business district of Main Street.

Critical incident entries should be specific. In a few short words, the rater is able to specifically indicate how the incident was critical and describe the positive or negative actions of the ratee.

Staff Specialist Method

In this method the rater is interviewed by personnel specialists about his subordinates. The rater merely answers yes or no to questions which are prepared in advance by the personnel specialists. It calls for the rater to be extremely knowledgeable about his subordinates since the rater is not privy to the specialist's questions before the interview. After the interview, an evaluation is prepared by the personnel specialists. The evaluation is then sent to the rater who, if he agrees, signs the evaluation indicating its accuracy. If he does not agree, he puts his objections in writing and submits them to the personnel specialists With this type of evaluation method however, raters rarely object and tend to accept the evaluation prepared by the specialists. This method was originally developed to assist supervisors with the unpleasant task of evaluating subordinates.

Making the Right Choice

Each method has its advantages and disadvantages, and each individual agency must decide for itself which formal evaluation system or combination of them it wishes to use.

DOCUMENTATION

Throughout this chapter we have stressed the importance of documentation, here are some reasons for careful documentation.

Facts - Not Impressions

Consider the following:

Sergeant Rems is a patrol sergeant with twelve officers assigned to his squad. Each January he is responsible for preparing annual performance evaluation reports for each of these officers. He is conscientious about these reports and is aware that they become part of an officer's permanent personnel file.

Rems has devised a procedure where throughout the year while working side-by-side with the officers, he makes notations on a card about the level of work done by the officers. The cards are a valuable reference for his evaluations. Before he began using this method, Rems found that the more he had to rely on his memory, the more he found himself relying on general impressions of the officers involved rather than on factual information. Resolved to not have this happen year after year, Rems now witnesses first-hand their arrests, responses to calls for service and reporting actions, and he records his personal notes and observations of their performance.

In order to base an evaluation on facts, a rater must have exactly that, the facts. They must be gathered by him through first-hand observations and not through hearsay. "Keep a daily written record of each employee's specific achievements and contributions. Tell it the way you see it every day. Make it a habit to share your comments with subordinates. Subordinates generally appreciate honesty and, like you, they don't appreciate surprises."[8]   Doing this allows the evaluations the supervisor prepares to be based on facts and not on the rater's memory and general impressions.

Nip Things in the Bud

If a rater keeps ongoing documentation, he can detect patterns in the subordinate's performance which may indicate a need for immediate remedial action. When required, remedial action can better the employee's chances of improving his performance and getting a favorable evaluation for the current evaluation period. This way he does not have to wait until evaluation time and possibly suffer an unfavorable evaluation.

Provides Backup

At an evaluation interview it may be necessary to show areas where performance can be improved. While the rater should not enter into a debate over such issues, comments can be backed up and supported if he can provide documentation. Such documentation can also be used to support and validate positive rewards such as merit increases, choice assignments and even promotions.

Documentation also allows a rater to respond to an appeal which a ratee may make concerning the evaluation. Should the

154

situation ever reach the point where termination is considered, documentation of any substandard evaluation will be an absolute must both from a managerial and legal standpoint.

THE MARGINAL EMPLOYEE

Probably no one is better equipped to deal with the marginal or borderline employee than the person who rates his performance.

Consider the following:
Sergeant Rems is Officer Egos's immediate supervisor and evaluator. Rems has given him a satisfactory evaluation for the last two years, but Rems believes Egos can do better. Rems sees Egos as doing just enough to get by and never doing more than the absolute minimum. While Egos hasn't done anything serious enough to be brought up on charges or to warrant termination, his performance is a topic of conversation among the other officers. The consensus of the other officers is "Why should we push so hard? Egos slides along and nobody bothers him."

It is Sergeant Rems's duty to deal with the situation. If he does not, the productivity and morale of the other officers on the shift will eventually decline. Among Rems's possible options are: to ignore the situation, to try to transfer this marginal employee to another assignment, to start to document a case to have Egos terminated, or to work with Egos to bring him from being a borderline or marginal employee to a superior worker. The latter is the option Rems should follow, that is, to try to raise the level of Egos's performance. If as we have recommended, Rems has been documenting Egos's performance, then Rems can point out specific ways that Egos's performance can be improved. The improvement should be planned and attempted in increments with specific milestones in mind.

The point here is that it is with the rater, through the evaluation of a marginal employee, where any plans to change this type of employee must begin. If such efforts are taken up at any other place in the agency, then serious questions must be raised about the effectiveness of the agency's performance evaluation system.

WRITTEN NOTIFICATIONS OF PERFORMANCE EVALUATIONS

Some agencies notify their employees of their performance evaluations simply by sending them a copy of the evaluation. This works poorly when an employee's performance requires improvement. Such a system does not provide for any exchange of information. After all, the employee receiving a substandard evaluation may have significant information which may shed light on his performance as well as the overall performance of the unit. A procedure which does not provide for face-to-face communication between a rater and ratee does little to establish any plans for the future improvement of the performance of the substandard employee. It also does not provide enough recognition for the well-above standards employee.

THE EVALUATION INTERVIEW

An evaluation interview is the discussion between the rater and the ratee concerning the judgments that have been made about the ratee and the setting of goals with specific future milestones. The supervisor who has rated the subordinate and now must conduct an evaluation interview would do well to divide the evaluation interview into two parts. The first part is preparing for the interview; the second part is conducting of the interview.

Preparation for the Evaluation Interview

Without adequate preparation prior to an interview, the process will be self-defeating. If the interview does not accomplish its purpose then the actual evaluation is wasted time, as were any supervisory observations which were made. The entire evaluation system is of little value to the agency. This is why preparation for the evaluation interview is so important.

The preparation for an evaluation interview should be complete and painstakingly undertaken. The rater should prepare a checklist of actions to be taken prior to the actual interview.

© 1995 by J. & B. Gould
Printed in the U.S.A.   Ms

A sample checklist might include:

a. Has an appropriate time for the interview been selected? Schedules, timing, and needs should be considered. For example, 8 A.M. after a rater and ratee have worked a midnight shift is probably not the best time for an evaluation interview.

b. Has an appropriate place for the interview been selected? Is the location one where privacy exists and there will be no interruptions, such as ringing telephones?

c. Has the ratee been notified? The ratee should be notified sufficiently in advance so that he too can prepare for the interview. "To make sure you are both on the same wavelength, tell the employee exactly how you plan to prepare for the meeting. Then suggest the employee do the same thing to prepare for the meeting - think about some things she thinks she's doing particularly well on the job and, after that, areas where she thinks she could stand to improve. By doing this, you'll make it clear what's going to happen during the interview, and you'll send an important message about the employee's role in the process."[9]

d. Has the purpose of the interview been clearly established? In other words, do both the rater and the ratee agree on what the purpose of the interview is? "Don't assume employees know what you mean when you say the purpose of the meeting is to review your performance."[10] Instead, say, for example:

"Next Tuesday at 10 A.M., we will be meeting to discuss your performance during the past year and also to set some goals for you based on your personal performance and the goals of the agency."

e. Can documentation be provided to substantiate criticism of the ratee's performance? Specific examples of both good and poor performance should be gathered and used to establish how the ratee's performance measured against agency standards. Controversial areas should be anticipated and appropriate comments prepared by the rater.

f. Has a list of goals been established for the ratee for the coming year? Assuming that the formal evaluations are conducted yearly then the ratee should be prepared to indicate clearly what goals will be expected of him during the next year. Any such goals should be accompanied by appropriate milestone dates. While these goals and milestones should be prepared by the rater in his preparation for the interview, they are not set in cement. At the interview the ratee should be invited to help shape these goals and milestones. As long as it is consistent with agency goals and geared to improve the agency.

g. Has follow-up to the interview been planned for? The rater must be prepared to engage in follow-up as dictated by the goals set forth during the interview. Such follow-up will be discussed later in this chapter.

Conducting the Evaluation Interview

This is the second part of the evaluation interview. When the interview is completed, it will be considered a success if it recognized good performance, corrected past poor performance, and set goals for improvement in the future.

Beginning the Interview

The rater should begin by establishing that the main purpose of the interview is to try to assist the ratee to improve his performance. The rater should make an effort to get the ratee talking. "The probability that an appraisal interview will accomplish its purposes is directly related to the amount of talking done by the subordinate. In interviews that show real promise of accomplishing their purposes, the supervisor speaks only about 10% of the total words in the interview. The least successful interviews show the supervisor dominating the conversation."[11] Here's a simple opening to get the ratee talking:

How do you feel you have been doing in your assignment since the last evaluation interview?

Whether the ratee's comments indicate that he believes he is doing well or not doing well, the rater should respond and, if possible, begin his evaluation with some positive comments about the ratee's performance. This is recommended before any negative comments on the part of the rater are made. By doing this the ratee is made to feel confident and can deal more easily with any negative criticism which may follow.

Negative Comments

Most raters have no problem discussing the performance evaluation of an outstanding subordinate, but these same raters cringe when asked to discuss a substandard performance. If there are negative comments, they should be short, to the point and assertive. They should be done with an eye towards emphasizing constructive criticism. The best way is to be specific and not try to dance around the issue. If the issue is, for instance, uniform appearance, then the rater should leave the ratee with the understanding that the ratee's uniform appearance does not meet agency standards and why.

For example:

"Officer Egos, when you come to work your uniforms do not meet the standards of the department. Your shoes are not shined, your pants are not pressed, and your ties are frequently stained. Anything that does not reflect favorably on the department or its members will not be tolerated."

It would not be correct for the rater to state:

"Officer Egos, when you come to work your uniforms could use a little help. See what you can do about it."

This is not specific enough and implies that the issue is not as important as it really is.

A Copy of the Report

The rater should give the ratee a copy of the evaluation report for the ratee to follow as the rater makes his comments. When the rater makes a negative comment he should be able to document the comment to validate what he has said. Make no mistake, however, this is not about lecturing a subordinate about what he has done wrong. It is just as much about recognizing his above average performance and even more about identifying ways to improve future performance.

Future Actions

An action plan, action steps, goals and milestones to measure future progress are the most important results of an evaluation interview. Both the rater and the ratee must agree on the steps to be taken. It is a good practice for the rater to have the ratee repeat back in his own words that which has been agreed upon.

The Conclusion

In concluding the interview, the rater should make an appropriate positive comment about the performance of the ratee and explain that he, the rater, will be following-up to ensure that the goals which have been set for future performance are met. The appeal procedure should be explained at this time and any questions relating to it answered. After both sign and date the evaluation form, the rater should also make it quite clear that his door is open and that he is available to assist the ratee in his efforts to achieve these goals.

FOLLOWING UP ON THE EVALUATION INTERVIEW

Supervisors conducting performance evaluation interviews who fail to follow up on what has been agreed to during the interview will soon find that little or nothing positive will result from evaluating subordinates. Such supervisors will be seen as all talk. Subordinates will see the evaluation as a perfunctory exercise which they have to go through once or twice or year. But if supervisors follow up to improve the future performance of ratees, then the evaluation system will be viewed as it should be, namely a self-improvement tool.

Based on what was said during the evaluation interview, the supervisor should periodically observe the actions of the ratee. For instance, if Officer Ginty has agreed to follow a certain procedure when preparing accident reports, Sergeant Rems, should check to see if Ginty is actually following the procedure. Rems should make a note as to Ginty's performance and retain such notations for use during formal evaluations. In this way employees will come to understand that the agency's evaluation system is comprised of many periodic observations which should be viewed as ways to improve their performance and not as threats to their security.

160

BARRIERS TO EFFECTIVE EVALUATIONS CREATED BY RATERS

Performance evaluations are not performed by machines. They are performed by imperfect people about imperfect people. Thus the chance for error is constant. Most errors committed by raters which set up the barriers to effective evaluations are caused by the approach or attitude of raters to the agency's evaluation system. The most sophisticated evaluation form cannot override errors introduced by the actions of raters. By recognition of some of the rater approaches or attitudes which often cause these evaluation errors, the manager/supervisor who is required to conduct performance evaluations of subordinates can take steps to avoid or rectify these approaches or attitudes and remove some of the barriers to effective evaluations.

Rater Leniency

The most common barrier is rater leniency. Supervisors rate subordinates too leniently for a variety of reasons. The most prevalent reason for leniency is the desire on the part of supervisors to obtain and/or retain the friendship of subordinates. They will do this in an attempt to avoid unpleasant encounters and often falsely reason that evaluations really do not mean anything anyway. "The manager who gives an unjustifiably flattering picture of an individual is just as misleading, just as unethical, and just as unfair to an employee as is a manager who gives an unjustifiably unflattering description."[12] Another reason for leniency is that supervisors do not want to open the door to criticism of their unit. If subordinates under their command are performing poorly, then it might be argued that they as supervisors are not doing their job. When they rate leniently, they actually undermine the evaluation system and prevent the evaluation from being used as a tool to develop the performance of the subordinate. Some supervisors will rationalize they do not want to hurt their subordinates by being the only ones rating objectively while other supervisors continue to rate their subordinates leniently. If leniency is to cease to be a barrier, all supervisors must make an effort to rate accurately and objectively.

The Overshadowing Effect

The overshadowing effect occurs when a rater allows a general impression of the ratee to be created based on one or two traits instead of basing his evaluation on the entire span of dimensions. For instance, Sergeant Egos is aware that Officer Collars makes more arrests than anyone in the department. Therefore, he rates him above standards in all categories, even though the officer is constantly late, has a poor uniform appearance and a disproportionate number of his arrests result in acquittals. Evaluations should be conducted trait by trait, dimension by dimension, and should be measured against clear standards.

Some refer to the overshadowing effect as the halo effect. The use of the word "halo" connotes that this barrier can be created when a subordinate is rated highly on the basis of one good trait. This is incorrect because this barrier is also created when a subordinate receives a poor evaluation because of one bad trait. For example, Sergeant Egos rates Officer Green poorly in all the dimensions of the evaluation because Green has poor uniform appearance. In reality, Green performs well-above standards in all other categories of his work. The overshadowing effect results when rating too high or too low overall based on a general impression created by one or two traits.

Middle Range Tendency

Also known as the central tendency error, the middle range tendency occurs when a rater rates everyone as average. No one is rated as outstanding or very poor. Extremes are avoided. This is apt to be the case when raters are not that familiar with the performance of the ratees. This will also occur when raters are required to justify by accurate documentation any outstanding or poor evaluations. Not wanting to provide such documentation, raters simply lump everyone together in some middle range. Obviously the good worker suffers here in that he does not receive the recognition he deserves. The agency also suffers since those employees who are not performing up to standards are not identified so that their performance can be improved.

Association of Traits

This barrier occurs when a rater combines two different traits and a high or low rating for one trait also results in the same high or low rating for another trait. For example, Officer Bailes is rated "well- above standards" in punctuality. Because of this his rater also rates him "well-above standards" in punctuality of reports. Actually Bailes is never on time with his reports. Raters seem to especially make such associations between traits which physically appear adjacent to each other on evaluation reports.

The Image Influence

Here the rater mentally says one of two things. "He looks like a cop, so he must be doing a terrific job and I will rate him accordingly. Or he looks like anything but a cop, so I must give him a poor evaluation." Either way the rater is incorrect. He is measuring the ratee based on some personally biased mental image he has of the position and not specifically on the individual traits which comprise the evaluation.

Lasting Memory Syndrome

This occurs when a rater remembers a positive or negative incident long after it is over but continues to use it as the basis for his evaluation of the ratee.

Consider the following:

Officer Lynn during a traffic stop arrests a felon who was wanted in six states. That is about all Lynn has ever done. However, his rater time after time rates him as excellent in all dimensions of his evaluation, despite the facts which indicate that Lynn is actually a below standard performer.

Officer Bailes once caused a mini riot while issuing a traffic summons. Each time he is rated he receives a poor evaluation even though his performance has improved to above average.

In both cases the rater has a lasting memory of the ratee usually based on one critical incident and unduly relies on that memory to rate the subject instead of reviewing the subject's performance in each dimension of the evaluation. This becomes even more of a problem when the critical incident has occurred just before the actual formal evaluation. The best way to combat this is to keep accurate and up-to-date performance records.

BARRIERS TO EFFECTIVE EVALUATIONS CREATED BY THE AGENCY

The following barriers are created by the policies and actions of various agencies utilizing a performance evaluation system.

Poor Training of Raters

Nothing contributes more to a barrier to effective performance evaluations than poor training of raters. Typically, raters are given an evaluation form and told to start evaluating. Often, at best, they are given a pamphlet to read. They should receive classroom training and be allowed to explore the evaluation system under the direct supervision of experienced raters.

During formal training sessions, raters should be taught the purpose of the system and be made familiar with the standards they will employ while conducting evaluations. If training is not conducted and the raters are not comfortable with the system and able to explain it, there is no way that those who will be rated can understand and support the system.

Perfunctory Attention

Just having raters go through the motions and not seriously dedicating any time or effort to the conducting of performance evaluations will soon become apparent to all members of the agency. If evaluations are seen as just another task to be performed without any regard to its quality, then it will be done with the only goal being to get them done and over with by a certain date. If such a policy exists in an agency, no possible benefit will derive from the evaluation system and the agency would be better off with no evaluation system.

Solely Punitive

If the policy of the agency is to use evaluations only for punitive actions, such as demotions and even separations, then the evaluations will be seen solely as a threat and considered the enemy. This creates an us-versus-them environment, a win-lose scenario, where management wins and subordinates lose. It can be expected that those who are to be rated will defend themselves by whatever actions possible. It is much better to create a win-win scenario. Evaluations should be used to recognize superior performance, rather than punish everything that is not superior.

Overly Complex

If the actual evaluation form is too complex, with complicated statistical scales and rating matrices, then raters will view the process as an unpleasant experience and will act accordingly. The evaluation form must be easy to read, follow, and interpret for the agency, the rater and the ratee, without such interpretation the system offers no benefits.

Lack of Performance Standards

If a law enforcement agency decides that its members should be rated on, for example, decision-making, the agency must also provide what constitutes good and bad decision making. Otherwise it has a "look nice" evaluation system which no one can validly use and will produce little more than a myriad of subjective opinions on what decision making or any other trait is.

Secret Evaluations

This occurs when evaluations are performed, but the results are not communicated. This defeats the purposes of a sound evaluation system, namely, improving poor performance while recognizing superior performance. "By presenting a thorough analysis, you'll be meeting a very important employee need—the need for candid, helpful feedback. In our view, all people crave feedback, and there's no reason to believe your employees are any different."[13] When a secret evaluation policy exists, fear and distrust among members of the agency will result and frustration will increase because employees want to know where they stand and how they are doing.

TEST YOUR UNDERSTANDING

1. Name and explain the goals of a performance evaluation system.

2. What are the prerequisites for a performance evaluator?

3. Describe the legal considerations of creating a performance evaluation system.

4. Explain the importance of performance standards in connection with the conducting of performance evaluations.

5. Name and explain several major formal evaluation systems.

6. Is documentation important when conducting performance evaluations? Explain your answer.

7. How should a marginal employee be dealt with?

8. How should a ratee be notified of his evaluation?

9. Name and describe the parts of an evaluation interview.

10. Prepare a sample checklist for a rater to use in preparing for an evaluation interview.

11. How should an evaluation interview be followed-up on by a rater?

12. Name and explain the barriers to effective evaluations created by raters.

13. Name and explain the barriers to effective evaluations created by individual agencies.

FOOTNOTES

1. Gary P. Latham and Kenneth N. Wexley, *Increasing Productivity Through Performance Appraisal.* (Reading, MA: Addison-Wesley Publishing Company, 1981), p. 91.

2. Ibid., p. 13.

3. Ibid., p. 13.

4. Thomas H. Patten, Jr., *A Manager's Guide To Performance Appraisal.* (New York: The Free Press, 1982), p. 53.

5. Ibid., p. 53.

6. Ibid., p. 46.

7. Marion S. Kellog, *What To Do About Performance Appraisal,* Revised Edition. (New York: AMACOM, 1975), p. 19.

8. David K. Lindo, *Supervision Can Be Easy!.* (New York: AMACOM, 1979), p. 101.

9. Dr. Peter Wylie and Dr. Mardy Grothe, *Problem Employees - How To Improve Their Performance,* 2nd ed. (Dover, NH: Upstart Publishing Co., Inc., 1991), p. 66.

10. Ibid., p. 66.

11. Robert G. Johnson, *The Appraisal Guide.* (New York: AMACOM, 1979), p. 72.

12. Kellog, p. 14.

13. Wylie and Grothe, p. 168.

SUGGESTED READINGS

Henderson, Richard.
Performance Appraisal: Theory to Practice.
Reston, VA: Reston Publishing Co., 1980.

King, Patricia.
Performance Planning and Appraisal.
New York: McGraw-Hill Book Company, 1984.

Kirkpatrick, Donald I.
How To Improve Performance Through Appraisal and Coaching.
New York: AMACOM, 1982.

Lopez, Felix M.
Evaluating Employee Performance.
Chicago, IL: Public Personnel Association, 1968.

Maier, N.R.F.
The Appraisal Interview.
New York: Wiley, 1958.

CHAPTER 8
THE SUPERVISOR AS A HUMAN RELATIONS SPECIALIST

THE HUMAN RELATIONS RESPONSIBILITY OF SUPERVISORS

According to one dictionary, a supervisor is a manager who oversees and directs the work-related activities of employees. Unfortunately, far too many supervisors limit their attention to just that, merely directing the work-related activities of their subordinates. This perception fails to emphasize the critical responsibility of a supervisor to counsel and otherwise show concern for their subordinates.

It is, therefore, important for a supervisor to concern himself not only with the best way for workers to do their jobs, but also with the accepted methods of developing and maintaining sound human relations with those workers. A supervisor's effectiveness is determined in large part by the quality of his interpersonal relationships. "Whether you are a top executive, a middle manager, a first line supervisor, ...your success depends largely on your ability to deal with other human beings."[1]   What's more, the burden of responsibility to build these relationships clearly rests upon the supervisor and not with the subordinates. There is, however, considerable debate over how this task should be approached. Maintaining good relationships has become an ever-changing challenge with the increasingly diverse work force and the complexity of minority communities needing service.

Balancing the Needs of the Agency with the Needs of Subordinates

Balance is a key concept in family, work and community. Competing demands continually threaten us to let one good thing go at the expense of another. But effectively balancing competing demands is the mark of mature leadership. It is wrong for supervisors to get so carried away with developing good human relations that they put this above achieving the goals of the organization. Supervisors who make this error often adopt the attitude that nothing is more important than the welfare of the workers. Consequently, they dread the thought of taking any action which would alienate or upset subordinates. They become permissive and put the needs of the workers ahead of the needs of the organization. This type of supervisor is no more efficient than the napoleonic type who doesn't care at all about the welfare of subordinates. "Over emphasis on trying to make people happy at work is neither useful for the organization nor helpful to the individual. A man does not need to be 'happy' to be effective. What is required is establishing a satisfactory balance between organizational effectiveness and personal satisfaction derived from doing a worthwhile job."[2]

The goal is balance between the needs of the organization and the needs of the employees. But, when such needs are in conflict, there is no question that the needs of the organization must prevail. The whole idea behind emphasizing the human relations aspect of supervision is motivated by a desire to achieve maximum production from workers while at the same time fostering as much employee satisfaction as possible. But, when necessary, supervisors must be forceful, they must be critical of subordinates, they must employ discipline, and they must be dissatisfied with below standard performance.

The Primary Human Relations Objective

The primary objective of sound human relations is to enable each subordinate to interact productively and comfortably with his peers and his supervisors. This must be accomplished one worker at a time. It is essential that supervisors get to know their subordinates as individuals and then supervise each individual so as to obtain maximum productivity. Supervisors should also stress the vital importance of mutual respect and cooperation in the work unit. The end result, therefore, should be a work force where each individual feels he is needed, welcomed, appreciated, and part of the cooperative effort of the unit.

GUIDELINES FOR BUILDING SOUND HUMAN RELATIONS

Although there are no set rules there are widely accepted guidelines for developing mutual respect and understanding in the work place.

172

Practice Empathy When Communicating

It is contrary to sound human relations to criticize another person's opinion simply because it is different from yours. Such criticism virtually guarantees that no further opinions will come from that person. Instead, supervisors should always attempt to empathize with subordinates. They should try to view situations from the subordinates' position. Empathy creates understanding. "The boundaries for understanding expand when empathy exists. When you practice empathy you listen non-evaluatively. You listen without arguing or passing judgment on what is being said at the time."[3]   This is not to say that empathy guarantees agreement. There will always be a certain amount of disagreement between workers and their supervisors. However, an empathetic approach to disagreement minimizes its negative impact.

Consider the following:

Sergeant Rems is interviewing Officer Ginty about a new program designed to assist the homeless. This dialogue follows:

Sergeant: Officer Ginty, I would like to go over the new department program to assist the homeless. Since there are many homeless people in your patrol area, I want to make sure you fully understand your new responsibilities.

Officer: Okay, Sarge, anything you say, but I just don't understand why we make such a fuss over the homeless. After all, they are homeless because they don't want to work to support a home. If they all just got a job, the problem would go away, and I wouldn't have to deal with all of the headaches they create for me, nor would I have to learn about this new program.

At this point, it is absolutely essential for the sergeant to attempt to modify the officer's attitude towards the homeless. But first, the sergeant should empathize with the officer by showing an understanding of the officer's point of view. Here's an example of how this could be done:

Sergeant: Officer Ginty, I can understand why you feel the way you do. The homeless in your area do cause you a lot of work. But, the majority of homeless are unwilling victims of unfortunate circumstances and are deserving of our help.

Remember, as police officers it is our sworn duty to protect and serve all members of our community. Now, let's review this new program.

The sergeant made his point without alienating the officer by unnecessarily criticizing his point of view. Remember, we all have biases. Supervisors cannot discipline officers for their beliefs. But, they do have a responsibility to try to change inappropriate attitudes. And, they must make certain that their own biases and those of their subordinates do not influence the delivery of services to all on an equal basis.

Give Subordinates the Information They Need To Function Effectively

A certain percentage of management decisions always have and always will cause worker resentment. And, those management decisions which are most apt to create worker resentment are those which involve change. "Resisting change simply because it's new and different seems to be a natural human response. We become complacent all too easily, and thus change requires a conscious effort."[4] Supervisors can minimize such resentment by supplying necessary information. For this reason it is vital that supervisors make a special effort to explain management decisions. The supervisor is responsible to portray management's position in a positive manner, even if the supervisor involved does not personally agree with that position. Criticizing management decisions to win the favor of subordinates is a serious breach of trust that must always be avoided.

Another aspect of a supervisor's role involves supplying feedback. Feedback, as the term implies, occurs when information is passed from one person to another concerning a matter that is still ongoing or one that has been recently concluded. Giving feedback is recommended whenever non-confidential information about a relevant matter is known to a supervisor but not known to his subordinates.

When Appropriate, Act as a Spokesperson for Your Subordinates

Just as management expects supervisors to defend management's position to workers, so do the workers expect

174

supervisors to relay their position to management. This emphasizes what we said elsewhere about the ambivalent role of supervisors. Operational level supervisors should be viewed as the fulcrum between the mandates of management and the feelings of workers. There is, however, a significant distinction to be made concerning this ambivalent role. As mentioned above, supervisors must support the decisions of management even if they do not personally agree with them. Equally, supervisors should support the actions of their subordinates when they agree that the actions were justified. There is, however, a presumption that the decisions of management are appropriate, but there is no such presumption concerning the actions of subordinates. There are certain qualifications that must be made so that this guideline is understood:

a. If a supervisor feels that a proposed policy, rule or procedure is unfair or otherwise inappropriate, this feeling should be communicated through the chain of command to the manager responsible for instituting it. If it is instituted despite that supervisor's objections, the supervisor is then bound, despite his personal feelings, to defend and support it.

b. If a supervisor feels that an existing policy, rule, or procedure is unfair or otherwise inappropriate, this feeling should be similarly communicated through the chain of command to the manager who has the authority to change it. But, unless and until a change is made, the supervisor must comply with it personally and insist that his subordinates also comply.

c. Supervisors must sometimes support the actions of their subordinates and back them up even if those actions were inappropriate. This responsibility is created in situations where the subordinates' inappropriate actions were in response to the instructions of the supervisor.

Maintain Objectivity

Maintaining objectivity at all times is nearly impossible. Everyone is inherently subjective. Personal biases become a problem only when they result in on-the-job subjectivity. If a supervisor makes objective decisions based on factual work-related criteria, he will be laying the cornerstone for positive and productive human relations within his work group. If he makes subjective decisions based on such considerations as gender, race, religion, or sexual orientation, he will severely undermine the development of sound human relations.

Eliminating all personal biases is not a practical expectation. However, since many biases are the result of misunderstanding, promoting understanding through education is a reasonable goal toward building a cohesive work force. Structured rap sessions designed to combat stereotypical beliefs are an extremely effective way to achieve this goal. But a trained moderator should conduct these meetings.

Respect Confidences

Supervisors must understand the human relations value of respecting confidences. Betraying a confidence is a human relations error that is impossible to reverse. Supervisors must be very careful not to promise confidentiality unless they are certain it can be maintained. Remember, however, that when some subordinates request confidentiality, they are really requesting conditional confidentiality. For example: they understand that the information they are conveying must be passed on to an appropriate unit or person in management, but they do not want the information to become available to their peers. The most common example of this occurs when a worker seeks assistance for a personal problem. Another example of conditional confidentiality is the worker who does not want to be identified as the source of the information. Typically, this occurs when a worker wants to expose corrupt or inappropriate conduct in the work unit. Therefore, when a worker requests confidentiality as a prerequisite for communicating facts, the supervisor should immediately clarify the degree of confidentiality being sought by the worker. If the worker seeks complete confidence, the supervisor must be certain he is not violating his responsibility to management before he promises it.

A supervisor must maintain confidentiality when management requests it. This means that there may be times when a supervisor is asked a question by a subordinate which he must not answer even though he has the information. If the supervisor feels there is a good reason to break such a confidence, he must first receive managerial clearance.

Maintain an "Open Door" Policy

A supervisor maintains an "Open Door" policy when it is common knowledge among his subordinates that he is both available and eager to discuss their problems. Supervisors who announce such a policy only to find that subordinates do not take advantage of it must conclude that they, the supervisors, have not established sound human relations within their work unit. If a supervisor has developed a good working relationship with his subordinates, they will come to him to express their opinions and grievances. It is a mistake for a supervisor to conclude that all is well just because he is not receiving any complaints from his subordinates. In such a situation, it is far more likely that he is viewed as unapproachable.

There is a warning about an "open door" policy. This policy has become so popular that many higher level managers employ it inappropriately and thereby violate the chain of command. Unless there is a legitimate reason to short circuit the chain of command, a supervisor's open door policy should extend only to his immediate subordinates. Without an exigency present, a manager who counsels other than his immediate subordinates is undermining the authority of the manager who is the immediate supervisor of the person seeking the counsel. However, as explained below, this rule does not pertain to the giving of routine technical skills counseling.

Emphasize Consistency When Enforcing Rules and Regulations

At no time is the human relations skills of a supervisor tested more than when he is fulfilling his responsibility to enforce the various rules and regulations that must be enforced if a law enforcement agency is to function effectively. Remember, despite the importance of maintaining good human relations, workers must comply with the mandates of the organization. The cardinal rule for supervisors to follow when enforcing rules and regulations is to maintain consistency of enforcement. It is a destructive practice for a supervisor to ignore a rule one day and enforce it the next day. Even worse is for a supervisor to ignore a rule when violated by one worker and enforce the same rule when violated by another. Worst of all is for a supervisor to enforce a rule that he ignores himself. This does not mean that the supervisor's approach to the enforcement of agency rules should be the same for all subordinates. Different people respond differently to different behavior modification and discipline. Consistency of enforcement also requires that a supervisor be aware of all pertinent rules and regulations as well as the reason for their importance.

Insofar as Possible, Involve Subordinates in the Making of Decisions Which Affect Them

Workers strive harder to achieve goals if they are involved in formulating the goals. Ownership is a vital component of planning and executing the plan. "The more that people are permitted to participate in a new project, the more they'll support it. Conversely, the more they are excluded, the more they will resist it."[5] While asking a subordinate for his opinion has great human relations value, it is also a good technique because workers often know the best way to do their job. But, the nature of law enforcement is such that it is not always feasible to consult with subordinates prior to making a decision. As a general rule, however, it is strongly recommended that supervisors seek worker input prior to the making of decisions which will affect those workers.

Emphasize Reconciliation When Settling Worker Disputes

Personnel conflicts are by far the most common problem a supervisor has to deal with. Conflict among fellow workers is inevitable. Supervisory involvement in personnel conflicts can be counter-productive. However, when people problems impact performance and service, supervisors must intervene. This intervention should begin with a fact-finding effort to determine the cause of the problem. The supervisor's emphasis must not be on who is to blame. "If at all possible, depersonalize the issue: Try to concentrate on what is right, not who is right."[6] Emphasize reconciliation and suggest ways to avoid the same problem in the future. It is absolutely imperative that disputes be resolved objectively on the particulars of each case. Supervisors must be mindful that while only two of his subordinates may be involved, everyone in the unit will weigh the fairness of the supervisory intervention.

Recognize that Human Relations Must Be Maintained

Building sound human relations with subordinates is a waste of time and effort if supervisors are not committed to maintaining those relations on a day-to-day basis. Interpersonal relationships are not static; they are dynamic. What worked well yesterday may not work well today. Times change, situations change, and people change. Supervisors must give persistent attention to maintaining human relationships, or they will deteriorate.

SUPERVISOR AS COUNSELOR

To develop and maintain effective human relations, supervisors must play many roles, from trainers to evaluators, from disciplinarians to counselors. The counseling role of a supervisor encompasses a variety of functions from instruction to personal advice. It extends from work-related details to intervention during a personal crisis. The remainder of this chapter will examine a supervisor's diverse responsibilities as a counselor.

COUNSELING SUBORDINATES WHO ARE EXPERIENCING PROBLEMS

Should a supervisor intervene when his subordinates are experiencing certain personal problems? The answer is a resounding "yes! " Officers are more than a means to carry out the agency's ends. They are people who at times develop problems due to the strenuous nature of their job. An agency's number one resource is its people. But if they are "to protect and serve", there are times they may need the same for themselves. Immediate supervisors are in the best position to be the first person to officially recognize an employee's problem. The question is which problems call for supervisory intervention?"

The Nature of Problems Which Require Intervention

Should a supervisor involve himself in all of the problems of each one of his subordinates? It doesn't take a management expert to understand that such involvement is not feasible. All-intrusive involvement would brand a supervisor as a meddler and fuel resentment among subordinates. The problems of subordinates fall into two major categories: work-related problems and personal problems. The basic rule of thumb is:

a. A supervisor's intervention is always appropriate and necessary when the problems are work-related. Most work-related problems call for instructions, clarifications, suggestions, or advice. When the work-related problem is inter-relational then the supervisor's role expands.

b. A supervisor's intervention is not always appropriate when the problems are personal or involve a person's private life. However, intervention is appropriate and necessary when:

1. a subordinate with a personal problem requests help;
2. a subordinate's personal problem results in some form of third-party complaint against the subordinate; or
3. a subordinate's personal problem affects his job performance. The extent and form of intervention is discussed below.

Which Supervisor Has the Primary Intervention Responsibility?

Once it is clear there is a need for a supervisor to become involved with an employee's problem, then it needs to be determined which supervisor has the primary intervention responsibility. The primary intervention rule designates the immediate supervisor as responsible. "Since immediate supervisors interact with their subordinates frequently, they are usually in the best position to observe changes in their subordinates' behavior and to assist in identifying and resolving their problems."[7] Of all supervisors, immediate supervisors are in the best position to see early evidence of problems and should have the best rapport to approach the individual. Through effective counseling supervisors enhance their esteem and credibility and improve the well-being of the collective work force.

What should happen when a subordinate with a problem approaches a supervisor, other than his immediate supervisor, and asks for help to deal with the problem? The approached supervisor should involve the immediate supervisor (unless an emergency exists). There are two exceptions: (1) if the problem is job-related, technical, or procedural and does not require the immediate supervisor's help, and (2) if the immediate supervisor is allegedly the cause of the problem.

When Should Intervention Take Place?

Intervention should occur without unnecessary delay. Delay almost always makes resolution more difficult. Swift intervention can be of great value to everyone concerned: the subordinate, the supervisor, the agency, and even the public being served. But this value is never realized if the supervisors are not aware either of their intervention responsibility or if they are not familiar with the symptoms which should alert them that an employee is experiencing a problem.

Examples of Intervention Responsibility

In order for a supervisor to be an effective counselor, he will need to have sensitivity to human nature and, in particular, the uniqueness of officers' problems.

Example 1:
A veteran officer approaches a watch commander in his unit who is a lieutenant but who is not the officer's immediate supervisor. The officer explains to the lieutenant that he is having a difficult time getting along with another veteran officer who was recently transferred into the unit. The problem between the two officers is a long standing one dating back to a time when they worked together in a plain-clothes assignment. The officer then asks the lieutenant for advice as to how to deal with this problem.

In this situation, the lieutenant should refer the officer to his immediate supervisor. This is an example of the primary intervention rule. Remember that there is no exigency involved in this example. If there was such an exigency, then the lieutenant would have a responsibility to counsel the officer. There is, however, nothing wrong with the lieutenant offering interim advice, such as to avoid any direct confrontation with the other officer until his immediate supervisor helps to resolve the matter.

Example 2:

An officer approaches a patrol sergeant in his unit who is not the officer's immediate supervisor. The officer informs the sergeant that he is experiencing a family problem and that, as a result of the problem, he has been contemplating suicide. The officer further explains that his immediate supervisor is on vacation and won't be back at work for another two weeks.

In this example, the sergeant should violate the primary intervention rule and counsel the subordinate even though he is not that subordinate's immediate supervisor. Remember, when exigent circumstances exist, concern for the welfare of the individual with the problem outweighs the benefits of following the chain of command and adhering to the primary intervention rule. The sergeant has a definite responsibility to get involved since the subordinate is asking for help. The unfortunate truth is that supervisory failure at critical times plays a role in the unusually high suicide rate among police officers.

Example 3:

A veteran officer approaches a watch commander who is a lieutenant but is not the officer's immediate supervisor. The officer explains he is unsure of the contents of a recently published department order concerning the procedure when requesting a leave of absence. Since the officer is in need of a leave of absence, he wants to follow the correct procedure to avoid any possible problems.

In this example, there is no reason why the lieutenant should not give the officer the information he is requesting. And, there is no need to involve the officer's immediate supervisor. This is an example of the one of the two exceptions to the general intervention rule stated above. It would be crippling to the operations of a police agency if only immediate supervisors were authorized to give simple technical skills counsel to officers.

Example 4:

Sergeant Rems, who is a patrol supervisor, was recently involved in a family dispute which required a patrol unit to resolve. The dispute involved Detective Ginty, an off-duty officer from the same department. Immediately after settling the dispute, Sergeant Rems notified Detective Ginty's immediate supervisor. Sergeant Rems informed the detective supervisor that although Ginty was not guilty of any criminal conduct, nor the cause of the family dispute, he was under the influence of alcohol and he might have a drinking problem. Shortly after receiving this notification, the detective sergeant began to notice a pattern of poor performance on the part of Detective Ginty. Included in this pattern were unexcused latenesses, poor personal appearance, and faulty report writing. At a meeting between the two to discuss this poor performance, the sergeant specifically asked the detective if he would like to discuss his family problems and/or his drinking problem.

This is an example of appropriate supervisory intervention in the personal problem of a subordinate, when it appears that the personal problem is affecting the subordinate's on-the-job performance. The mere notification from the patrol sergeant in and of itself does not justify specific intervention into the problem. But a work-related pattern of poor performance made it clear that the problems began right after the notification from the patrol sergeant. Therefore, it was proper for the detective sergeant to initiate discussion about the problem. Remember, the other two times when it is appropriate for a supervisor to involve himself in a personal problem of a subordinate are when the subordinate asks for help or when a third party complaint is made against the subordinate.

THE EXTENT AND FORM OF SUPERVISORY INVOLVEMENT

Counseling is not a periodic task of a supervisor. It should not be ignored until a problem occurs. Effective counseling demands that the counseling supervisor know his subordinates in depth. Therefore, supervisors should meet informally on a regular basis with each of their immediate subordinates. Supervisors should use these informal meetings to get to know each subordinate as an individual. Such meetings should be one-on-one, should take place at least once a month, and should last for at least twenty minutes. These meetings are extremely valuable since, if properly conducted, they are a strong indication of a supervisor's care and concern for each of his subordinates. This is very important since such indications of care and concern lead to intense loyalty upon the part of subordinates towards their supervisors. Most workers resent supervisors whom they only hear from when there is an actual problem. This resentment then becomes a barrier to effective communication.

These periodic meetings also allow supervisors to spot developing personal and work-related problems before they become too severe. Early intervention in problem situations almost always leads to easier resolution. The best way to spot these developing problems is the direct approach. The supervisor should simply ask the subordinate if he has any problems he would like to discuss. In most cases, if the subordinate believes the supervisor is trustworthy and sincere, he will confide in that supervisor if he does indeed have a problem.

EARLY WARNING INDICATORS

Some workers will not readily admit to having problems to even the most sincere of supervisors. This is why it is important for supervisors to be familiar with the early warning indicators — factors which often are indicative of personal problems. A comprehensive listing of such indicators is presented below. The most reliable of these early warning indicators is a sudden drop in performance. When a good worker becomes a poor performer almost overnight, it is a virtual certainty that he is experiencing a serious personal problem. A worker's attendance record can

184

also give insight into the existence of problems. Chronic lateness also many times stems from some type of personal problem. Supervisors should be especially aware of the early indicators associated with: depression, alcoholism, drug abuse, and suicide. While treatment of these four disorders must be left to professionals, supervisors can often detect their presence more quickly if they have a basic understanding of them, as follows.

DEPRESSION

Everyone gets depressed on occasion. Such short lived minor depression should be of no special concern to supervisors. But, when a worker seems to be depressed for an extended period of time—usually more than two weeks—the immediate supervisor of that worker should strongly consider the possibility that the worker is suffering from what is known as major depression.

Minor depression is characterized by low spirits, gloominess, dejection and sadness. Major depression has all of these same characteristics but they are much more intense. Many experts describe them as being overwhelming. The following are other characteristics commonly exhibited by those suffering from major depression:

    a. Lack of interest in everything, including those things which usually are of great interest.
    b. Spontaneous crying.
    c. Excessive tiredness.
    d. Diminished appetite.
    e. Trouble sleeping.
    f. Feelings of uselessness.
    g. Guilt feelings.
    h. Suicidal thoughts.

Many of the characteristics of depression are caused or heightened by stress. Unfortunately there is no single, specific cause of stress. For example, while major stress can be brought on by a single "triggering" event, such as a sudden death, it is believed that such stress is also caused by biological factors. These observations apply to the general population.

Law enforcement officers, however, work in an occupation that survey after survey proves to be one of the most stressful.

Most experts agree that the stressful nature of the law enforcement officer's job can quite often be traced to the following factors:

a. Unusual working schedules. Police work is a twenty-four hour a day activity. Police officers have to work irregular hours, rotating shifts, and on holidays when friends and family are at home.

b. Frustrations created by involvement in the Criminal Justice System. For example, in today's society, especially in larger cities, there is a degree of "turnstile" justice brought about by the large numbers of court cases unseen in previous times. In many jurisdictions, probation is the sentence used to dispose of over half of the felony convictions obtained. While there are many valid reasons why this is so, when police officers risk their lives to get criminals off of the street only to see them return relatively unscathed, it causes great job stress.

c. The roller coaster syndrome. This is a term we use to describe the stressful feature of a law enforcement officer's job created by the fact that the job can go from being dull and uneventful to being exciting and life threatening in the blink of an eye.

d. The nature of the clientele. It is often said that police officers frequently deal with either the worst of us or the best of us at the worst times.

e. Unfair supervisory practices. Surprisingly, unfair supervisory practices often rate as the number one cause of job stress in the law enforcement field. This is yet another argument for intensive leadership training for first line supervisors. To promote workers to supervisory positions without such training is akin to in-house creation of stressful working conditions. Such leadership training for first line supervisors is also quite beneficial as part of an agency's corruption control effort.

One final note: Top level administrators must realize that early recognition of depressed workers at the operating levels loses its value if the immediate supervisors involved do not have, or are not aware of, adequate referral sources. Supervisors must realize that attempting to be an unqualified, amateur psychologist can only be categorized as being reckless. On the other hand, a supervisor who is a sympathetic listener and who displays honest concern for a depressed worker can be the catalyst which leads to the return to normalcy for that worker.

SUICIDE

It is an unfortunate truth that an inordinate number of law enforcement officers commit suicide. The reasons why this is so are extremely complex and far beyond the scope of this book. To say that conscientious and well-trained supervisors can prevent the incidence of all suicides in any given law enforcement agency is wishful thinking that is not supported by experience or the literature in the field. But, to say that a concerned supervisor cannot prevent any suicides is also in error. A supervisor's ability to prevent suicides is increased by a greater understanding of some facts about suicide, as well as some common misconceptions about it. The following comments reveal the misunderstandings surrounding suicide.

a. It is not true that people who talk about suicide very rarely attempt suicide. In fact, there is growing evidence that just the opposite is true. People who frequently mention the possibility of suicide, quite often mean what they say.

b. As mentioned above, when a person is suffering from major depression, that person quite often has serious suicidal thoughts. This makes it even more important for supervisors to understand the early indicators of depression and to intervene when necessary to prevent the possibility of their depressed subordinates taking their own lives. It is a misconception, however, to believe that everyone who commits suicide is suffering from depression.

c. People who engage in a failed suicide attempt very often will repeat that attempt. This is a true statement. It is a misconception that there is so much shame associated with a failed suicide attempt that subsequent attempts will not follow. In fact, a great majority of people who successfully commit suicide had made earlier unsuccessful attempts.

d. Some people erroneously believe that it is a mistake to talk openly about suicide in the presence of someone who is suicidal. The truth is that talking about suicide might be beneficial to the person who is contemplating suicide.

e. It is wrong to believe that people are always openly sullen immediately before they commit suicide. The truth is that when a depressed person decides to commit suicide, that person often exhibits a cheerful disposition, brought on by the belief that his/her problems are finally going to be solved.

DRUG AND ALCOHOL ABUSE

Substance abusers, specifically those people whose work lives are impacted negatively by dependency on alcohol or other drugs, are a major concern for supervisors. Aside from the obvious fact that people who are guilty of substance abuse are dangerous to themselves and others, they are also incapable of achieving a high level of performance on a consistent basis. Substance abusers represent a high financial risk to management. They frequently steal and commit other corrupt acts, and they make mistakes which often lead to civil liability judgments against their agencies. In addition, they:

.have more than double the amount of on-the-job accidents,
.accumulate significantly higher personal medical expenses,
.have much higher rates of absenteeism, and
.file triple the amount of worker's compensation claims.

Supervisory Handling of Substance Abusers and Workers with Other Personal Problems

The question is always asked, "How should a supervisor handle a worker with a drinking or drug problem, or with some other personal problem, such as a marriage-related problem or one that has to do with children?" Our answer is always the same. Except when the law or agency policy dictates otherwise, employees with personal problems should be handled in much the same manner regardless of the nature of the personal problem. Specific treatment of emotional problems must be administered by qualified professionals. Supervisors should engage in what we call generic treatment. Generic treatment starts with recognition that the problem exists.

The most common indicators that an employee is having personal probles are as follows:

a. Noticeable change of personality.
b. Excessively nervous.
c. Accident prone.
d. Poor performance appraisals, especially sudden poor performance.
e. Frequent sick leave.
f. Frequent "last minute" requests for days off.
g. Disheveled personal appearance.
h. Confrontation prone.
i. Frequent recipient of citizen complaints.
j. Chronic lateness.

When a supervisor observes one or more of the above indicators in a subordinate, he should proceed in accordance with the intervention rules as described above. This is when formal counseling should take place. The specifics of this formal counseling effort are addressed below.

FORMAL COUNSELING SESSIONS

Once a supervisor becomes aware of the need for intervention, structured steps are needed, which should begin with a formal counseling session after the supervisor has independently gathered all of the available facts. It is important to note that this structured approach is only required for problems that go beyond the lack of technical skills. This is not to be confused with the informal periodic meetings with all subordinates mentioned above. The formal counseling session has but one purpose and that is to deal with an identified problem.

The Importance of Preparation

As mentioned above, the supervisor must familiarize himself with all the pertinent facts available concerning the employee prior to the formal counseling session. The primary reason why counseling sessions fail to achieve the desired results is lack of preparation by the supervisor. "Some people are turned-off by the idea of planning interactions with people. However, we all plan our part of relationships much of the time. We wonder whether a coat and tie are expected at a party we are attending or whether a sport shirt will do. Every now and then we talk to ourselves, rehearsing a difficult conversation we'll have during the day."[8]

As part of his preparation effort, the counseling supervisor should review the employee's personnel file, including such things as performance evaluations, disciplinary history, and attendance records. "Acquaint yourself with your employee's background, work history, and relations with others in the organization. Much of this information is available in personnel files and previous evaluations. Sometimes it is helpful to record observations about the person's behavior over a given period, such as the year between formal evaluations. You must have a clear understanding of the problem you are trying to resolve."[9]

The preparation must also involve specific review concerning the problem to be discussed. The supervisor must be prepared for the denial of any problem(s).The best way to overcome denials is to have factual information on-hand to document the existence of a problem. If, however, this factual information is negative and reflects poorly on the employee as it often will, it could very easily create immediate resentment on the part of the subject being counseled. The best way to avoid this resentment is to communicate the desire to assist in the resolving of the underlying problem.

Proper preparation also involves the formulation of questions designed to move the conversation towards relevant matters. And, it is strongly recommended that a series of questions be framed that will encourage the subject to take an active part in the appraisal of the problem and the development of solution. But supervisors should avoid the over use of accusatory questions and should never use questions that would cause fear or anger.

Logistics of the Counseling Session

It is essential that sufficient time be set aside to adequately discuss the matter in private. Depending on the nature and seriousness of the problem, more than one session might be needed. In fact, when the problem is a personal one, such as a drinking problem, several shorter sessions are preferable to fewer lengthy ones. Too much may be said at longer counseling sessions and that makes it difficult for the employee to review and digest the essence of the interview.

COUNSELING SESSION GUIDELINES

While the circumstances involved in each counseling session will dictate the supervisor's approach to that particular session, there are a number of well-established principles or guidelines that apply to all sessions.

Engage in an Ice Breaking Period

Effective counseling cannot take place if the employee being counseled is uncomfortable. The interviewer must always attempt to establish a positive rapport with the subject at the start of the interview. This can be done by bringing up a topic which is of interest to that subject. This is known as breaking the ice since it almost always results in the easing of tensions, and it is a highly recommended interview technique.

Get the Subject Involved in the Discussion

Get the subject actively involved in the appraisal of the problem and in the development of a course of action to deal with the problem. People are more committed to a course of action when they have played a hand in the developing of that course of action.

Engage in Active Listening

The most serious fault of inexperienced counselors is to do more talking than listening. Remember, the supervisor's goal is not to tell the subject what to do but to assist him in the development of his own plan of action. "As contrasted to passive listening, which requires little thought on the part of the listener, active listening can be hard work. It requires the listener to pay attention to two levels of communication. An active listener is trying to understand the issues that are being described as well as the feelings that the person to whom he is listening has about those issues."[10]

Maintain Agency Priorities

While the purpose of solving the worker's problem is at the heart of the counseling session, it is not a matter of doing so at all costs. The worker needs to understand that the supervisor and the agency are both concerned with his welfare and interested in helping to resolve his problem. But the interests of the agency cannot suffer. Supervisors must help resolve worker problems while at the same time absolutely insisting on adherence to rules and regulations and on acceptable standards of performance.

Stay Within the Limits of Your Expertise

Supervisors need to be aware of their limits and qualifications. If a supervisor has the authority and/or expertise to solve problems or to recommend ways to do so, then he should. If job-related problems have to be resolved at a higher level, the supervisor should see that they are properly referred, and should follow up. With respect to personal problems, many times a supervisor performs a great service to a worker simply by being available to listen to the worker's story. And, quite often in talking out the problem, the worker comes to his own conclusion as to its solution.

Be Familiar With and Recommend Available Problem Solving Resources

Supervisors are responsible for being familiar with the various professional resources available to their subordinates who are in need of professional counseling, such as those with a drinking problem or those under extreme stress. These resources may be located somewhere in his own agency, within the larger governmental structure, or within the private community. The manner in which the referral is made is critical. "Needless to say, the act of referring an employee for professional assistance requires the exercise of considerable skill and tact."[11] When making these referrals, a supervisor must be guided by the following points:

1. It serves no purpose to criticize an employee who is in need of professional counseling. Quite the opposite is true. A major obstacle is the prevalent belief among law enforcement people that needing professional counseling is a sign of weakness. The situation is compounded when professional treatment involves temporary removal of firearms. When this occurs, the officer often gets branded as a "rubber gun" cop. This causes many officers to refrain from seeking help because of a fear of being stigmatized by peers. The supervisor should attempt to convince the worker of the many benefits of counseling and should be very empathetic and supportive.

2. Supervisors are often required by agency policy to make referrals of workers who need help but who refuse to seek it voluntarily. While this initially may cause resentment, the alternative—the tragedies that often occur when needed treatment is not obtained—is unacceptable. However, the initial resentment of the worker almost always turns to sincere appreciation after he learns how to deal with his problem.

3. Many law enforcement officers are wary of the stigma attached to those who need professional help to deal with the many stresses of life. Therefore, supervisors should stress the confidential nature of counseling while attempting to convince subordinates to voluntarily seek professional counseling. Supervisors must be certain that any promises of confidentiality must be consistent with existing agency policy, and they should be aware of the agency procedures in place which truly provide for this much needed confidentiality.

Check for Mutual Understanding

The supervisor must make sure that there is mutual understanding with respect to what has been agreed upon during the counseling session. Unless this is done it is possible for both parties to leave the meeting with completely different ideas of exactly what took place. The best way to ensure mutual understanding is for the supervisor to summarize all essential points at the end of the meeting and then to have the subject re-state these points in his own words. Also, if the course of action agreed upon involves any sort of timetable or due dates, the time frames involved must be specific and not general. Such loose time frames as "in the very near future" or "at your earliest opportunity" are unacceptable. Rather, time frames should be stated by naming an actual due date, such as "let's get that done by May 31st."

Always Engage in Follow-Up Evaluations

It is a mistake for a supervisor to believe his responsibility is over when a counseling session is concluded, even if the result of the session was a referral to an appropriate professional counselor. Instead the supervisor has a responsibility to keep in touch on a regular basis with the worker involved until it is clear that the problem has indeed been resolved. "The manager and employee meet regularly to assess progress. If the alternative selected is not working, it may be that the problem was not properly identified. Or, if the alternative solution is not working, the manager and employee may need to select another alternative."[12]   And, when a worker has agreed to seek voluntary counseling, the supervisor must make an independent verification that the worker kept that agreement.

TEST YOUR UNDERSTANDING

1. Is the job of a supervisor strictly limited to directing the work-related activities of his subordinates? Discuss.

2. Does a supervisor have to balance the needs of the agency with the needs of his subordinates? Discuss.

3. Identify and discuss ten guidelines for a supervisor to follow when attempting to build sound humans relations with his subordinates.

4. What are "early warning indicators," and why are they important?

5. Is it necessary for a supervisor to prepare for a counseling session with a subordinate? Discuss.

6. Identify and discuss the recommended guidelines for a supervisor to follow when engaged in formal counseling of a worker who is experiencing a personal problem.

7. Is follow-up required after a supervisor has formally counseled a worker concerning a personal problem? Discuss.

FOOTNOTES

1. Robert Bolton and Dorothy Grover Bolton, *Social Style/Management Style*. (New York: American Management Association, 1984), p. vii.

2. Edwin J. Singer and John Ramsden, *Human Resources - Obtaining Results from People at Work*. (New York: McGraw-Hill Book Company, 1972), p. 32.

3. Thomas Rendero, editor, *Communicating with Subordinates*. (New York: AMACOM, 1974), p. 172. From an article by Philip Anthony and William P. Anthony, Ph.D., "Now Hear This: Some Techniques of Listening."

4. Mary Kay Ash, *Mary Kay on People Management*. (New York: Warner Books, Inc., 1984), p. 76.

5. Ibid., p. 77.

6. Donald Sanzotta, *The Manager's Guide to Interpersonal Relations*. (New York: AMACOM, 1979), p. 124.

7. Herbert J. Chruden and Arthur W. Sherman,Jr., *Personnel Management,* 5th ed. (Cincinnati, OH: South-Western Publishing Co., 1976), p. 321.

8. Bolton and Bolton, p. 84.

9. Zig Ziglar, *Top Performance*. (Old Tappan, NJ: Fleming H. Revell Company, 1986), p. 145.

10. John W. Loughary and Theresa M. Ripley, *Helping Others Help Themselves - A Guide to Counseling Skills*. (New York: McGraw-Hill Book Co., 1979), p. 16.

11. Chruden and Sherman, p. 322.

12. Ziglar, p. 143.

SUGGESTED READINGS

Blake, Robert and Jane Mouton.
The New Grid for Supervisory Effectiveness.
Austin, TX: Grid Publishing, 1979.

Bolton, Robert.
People Skills: How to Assert Yourself, Listen to Others and Resolve Conflicts.
Englewood Cliffs, NJ: Prentice-Hall, 1979.

Bradford, David and Allan R. Cohen.
Managing for Excellence.
New York: John Wiley and Sons, Inc., 1984.

Hunsaker, Phillip and Anthony Alessandra.
The Act of Managing People.
Englewood Cliffs, NJ: Prentice-Hall, 1980.

Kirkpatrick, Donald I.
How to Improve Performance Through Appraisal and Coaching.
New York: AMACOM, 1982.

Luft, Joseph.
Of Human Interaction.
Palo Alto, CA: Mayfield Publishing, 1969.

Peters, Thomas J. and Robert H. Waterman, Jr.
In Search of Excellence.
New York: Harper and Row, Publishers, 1982.

CHAPTER 9
THE SUPERVISOR AS A TRAINER

Of the abilities of a supervisor, the one which seems to go hand-in-hand with being a competent supervisor in the eyes of those being supervised is the ability to be an effective trainer. Surely there are many skills required of a competent supervisor: planning, directing subordinates, and delegating the work. Yet, his ability to train comes up again and again as the real indication of his competency.

TRAINING DEFINED

Consider the following:

During a training session conducted by Sergeant Rems with fifteen subordinate officers, the following dialogue took place:

Sergeant Rems: What exactly is training?

Officer Bailes: It's a way to help workers improve the way they presently do their job.

Sergeant Rems: Just the job they have now?

Officer Gomez: No, it could be also a way to help them learn a new job, a future job.

Sergeant Rems: That's right and when Bailes and Gomez say "a way to help" that should tell us that training involves a process or a series of defined steps. Let me ask you this: How does this process help workers with this present or future job?

Officer Jones: It teaches them to see things in a certain light. Like when we took sensitivity training because of the rise in civilian complaints.

Officer Tanker: Wait a minute. What about when it helps us do something more accurately or faster? Like when we practiced making out accident reports?

Officer Marina: Don't forget the times when training gives you more information to do a job better. You know, like when the new laws for the year come out? We all get a session in the major changes in law.

Sergeant Rems: Well, you're all right. I think you got it. Let me see if I can put it all together for us.

Rems writes on the blackboard:

Training is a process conducted by an agency to help its members to do better in their present or future jobs by influencing their attitudes, skills or knowledge.

Let's look at the components of this definition.

Process

Training is a process; a method or a course of actions which progresses forward. Process indicates that training is not a one-time event, it is ongoing. "Training by the foreman is a never-ending job. It is clear that the foreman should consider each employee as being in some stage of training."[1]

To Help its Members

Training is not unaided self-improvement, the agency is responsible for training its employees.

To Do Better in Their Present or Future Jobs

"Unless what is learned in the training situation is applicable to what is required on the job, the training effort has been of little value."[2] It must have relevancy to the work of the agency. "Relevancy must be established by explaining thoroughly why the training is being given, how it will benefit the employee, and why it is important to the work group's productivity. Don't assume relevancy; establish it firmly through a discussion with the employees."[3] It must be related to either his present or future job.

Attitudes

Training is intended to shape attitudes. A legitimate purpose of training is to give workers a different view of a situation which enables them to perform their job in a manner which results in a better product or service.

Skills

An employee can be trained to do his present job more efficiently through the development of his present skills. In addition, an employee may be prepared to do a new or future job through the development of new skills.

Knowledge

Training imparts knowledge which is required in the trainee's present or future work.

The trainee must play an active part if any real training is to take place. It is his attitudes which will be reshaped, his skills that will be developed and his knowledge which will be increased.

WHY IS TRAINING NEEDED?

One new supervisor received this good advice from an "old-time, seasoned" sergeant: "If you want to have good people in the agency, you gotta pick 'em right and train 'em right. Since we don't really have a whole lot to say about who comes on the job, training 'em right becomes our only real shot to having good people. And I'm not talking about training just for the rookies, I mean the whole job, old-time cops and bosses as well." Simple, but to the point.

Lower Turnover of Personnel

Unnecessary turnover of personnel multiplies the expenses of recruitment, examination, appointment and initial training. Law enforcement officers do not have total control over the process of hiring. However, they can heavily involve themselves in the training of their people. When this training is challenging and meaningful, an agency can expect highly skilled, competent employees with a higher level of job satisfaction.

Fewer Grievances

A highly-trained workforce results in fewer grievances. The lines of authority are clear, and employees are generally better informed concerning agency policies and procedures. Better informed employees are aware of their benefits and entitlements and understand the agency's reasons for policies and procedures.

Improved Work Product

The quantity and quality of work improves as training improves. When new skills are identified as being required, on-going training will quickly bring employees up to speed. Current trends and efficiency methods can be made available to employees through training. Also, the appropriate approach or attitude of employees in connection with the work they do will be continually strengthened.

Morale

Employees tend to be better informed about the present and less confused about the future when continuous training exists. Morale appears to be higher among well-trained workers. They accept challenges more readily and esprit de corps is evident. They feel the agency cares enough about them to spend its time and resources to help them improve, this helps them feel better about themselves.

Safety

There is a direct relationship between training and safety in the workplace. Avoiding sloppy and unsafe work habits will decrease accidents and agency loss. The agency's concern for safety increases employee safety-consciousness as the individual employee identifies the agency's concern over safety in the workplace as a personal concern for him. In addition, when an agency keeps its personnel well-trained, punitive damages from civil actions are usually lowered.

Better Supervision

When subordinates are well-trained, there is less need for constant supervision. The boss, in turn, is able to focus on his people rather than on the details of their tasks. He is freer to do the kinds of things which can pay higher benefits to the agency, such as planning, organizing and following-up.

Training is not an option, nor is it something extra to do to fill up time. It is a duty of the agency and one of the main duties of supervisors. Training is the agency's way of ensuring that each member does his job correctly, efficiently and safely.

SUBORDINATE BENEFITS FROM RECEIVING TRAINING

There are several ways employees benefit from the training:

Increased Security

Training helps an employee feel that he is important to his organization and secure in his position. He reasons that if the agency is spending time and money in training him in the most current developments in his field, then the agency must feel good about the job he is doing.

Becoming More Productive

Training increases worker efficiency and productivity. When trained adequately, the unnecessary waste of time, effort and materials is significantly reduced.

Being Identified as Upwardly Mobile

Training improves the chances of advancement, promotion and recognition. As an employee increases his value to the agency and proves he can handle additional duties and responsibilities, he gains the respect and confidence of his superiors and is identified as someone who can be given additional and more prestigious duties.

Experiencing Self-Motivation

Training increases an employee's confidence which fuels his self-motivation. When people are equipped and motivated to go beyond the routine expectations of their job they can accomplish more because they want to, not simply because they are told to. The status quo and mediocre everyday standards of most jobs can only be broken by individuals with self-motivation.

Improvement in Morale

With increased self-motivation and the opportunity for recognition, agency-wide morale naturally increases. Workers like to be involved and part of the big picture; they want to be part of something successful. Morale improves when people feel their goals and the agency's goals are the same and their contributions and opinions are valued and their skills merit further training.

SUPERVISOR BENEFITS FROM CONDUCTING TRAINING

A supervisor should not look at training as just something which might increase productivity. Training helps his people, the agency and the supervisor himself. He should see himself as having many opportunities to affect the lives of his people and to reap personal rewards as a result.

Better Knowledge of Subordinates

A supervisor who trains his subordinates takes a giant step towards knowing them. Identifying their strengths and weaknesses quickly leads to awareness of their desires, needs and potentials. Training settings provide a supervisor with a context to be involved with his people which in turn facilitates delegation, coordination, and control.

Creation of "Extra" Time

When a supervisor trains his subordinates well, he will find that time ordinarily dedicated to leading subordinates by the hand is not required. The subordinates are more confident and able to handle by themselves many problems that previously were brought to the supervisor. The boss now has "extra" time. Countless hours previously spent correcting deficiencies of subordinates are now available to the boss for other supervisory tasks such as planning.

A Safer Workplace

The productivity of the supervisor's unit increases as fewer injuries mean less time away from the job. A supervisor's concern for safety demonstrates care for his people's well-being. Recognition of this caring leads to a more tightly-knit group.

An Increased Potential for Career Advancement.

As a unit performs better, the supervisor's good reputation grows. Realizing that a supervisor is only as good as the performance of those he supervises, there is no better way for him to be recognized as doing a good job than to have his subordinates perform exceptionally. The superior performance of a supervisor's unit is sure to be noticed by the supervisor's bosses and to contribute to the career advancement of the supervisor.

Keeping Abreast of Latest Developments

If a supervisor is to train his subordinates in a certain subject and its latest innovations, he himself must first learn the subject matter. Keeping current and well-informed is a primary responsibility of the supervisor. Having to prepare to teach gives him the opportunity to keep abreast of the latest developments and innovations in the areas with which his unit is involved.

TYPES OF TRAINING

Training in a law enforcement agency is generally comprised of several types of training, each with its own purpose and trainees. Since a supervisor may be called upon to conduct any of these various types of training sessions, he should be familiar with them all.

Entry-Level Training

Law enforcement entry-level training is somewhat unique in that the trainee is compensated as he learns his profession. The law enforcement rookie is hired and put on the payroll and then usually enters a training academy. Sometimes called recruit training, entry-level training requires no prior knowledge of law enforcement on the part of its trainees.

Entry-level training provides officers with a broad-based, foundational instruction in police work. It usually runs from two to nine months and is conducted at an agency facility or at a central location, such as a state or county facility or a college, which provides training for several local jurisdictions. Ideally the instructors in such courses are a mix of trained and experienced law enforcement personnel, experts in the subject matter being taught, and academicians. Such training is expensive since, not only are there the costs of providing the training along with instructor salary costs, but also the salaries and benefit packages of the paid trainees.

The biggest criticism of entry-level training is that it does not adequately prepare recruits to deal with the real world. Critics have stated, "There is the academy way to do things, and then there is the real way that is done in the street." The skillful field supervisor will discover if such situations exist and bring any discrepancies between training and the real world to the attention of the appropriate authorities.

Field Training of the Newly Hired

Field training is on-the-job training. The trainees are shown first-hand by supervisors or other officers and peers the duties of their job. The advantage of this training is that it provides on-line realism to the performance of a task. It is done in the field, where and when it is needed, rather than in the classroom environment. It overcomes the criticism that the training provided for the newly hired personnel is nothing like what is required in the field. Great responsibility, opportunity and reward are available to the field trainer of new recruits. The quality of the training will reflect on the trainer, trainee and agency. The field trainer is directly contributing to the career of future law enforcement officials. The quality of the new recruit will also bear results in the community served by those officers. To be selected as a field trainer for new recruits should be considered an honor since a great deal is expected of a field trainer. He must not only know the job, but also the needs of the trainee. If the field trainer fails in his job, then the costs of training are compounded since the trainee will have to be re-trained.

In-Service Training

Some in-service training, such as firearms training, is required for all officers, while other types of training, such as fingerprint identification, are only required for officers who are assigned to certain units. The number of officers in attendance can be anywhere between ten in smaller agencies and as many as one hundred in the largest agencies. The length of such training can range from an hour to several weeks. It is usually conducted away from the workplace, at an academy or other central location servicing the agency.

Continuous planning addresses the need for in-service training to ensure that it takes place as needed. There must be a direct relationship between what is taught and what will be done in the field. The supervisor must be vigilant in discovering real needs for in-service training. Conversely, he must be equally vigilant and vocal in indicating when an in-service training program is no longer required. Fiscal responsibility becomes an important consideration when planning for in-service training because of the high cost of such training when one factors in the salaries of those being trained and the loss of productivity due to time away from work assignments.

Shift Training

Also known as roll-call training, shift training traditionally takes place before the shift begins. Often conducted by the supervisor of the shift, this training includes topics intended to assist the shift as it begins its duties. It could include anything from recent changes in the law to information concerning a rash of related criminal incidents occurring in the area. Shift training can also be used by a supervisor to reinforce existing procedures. This type of training is not that expensive in that it is limited to five to thirty minutes. During the shift training, the supervisor would do well to individually question subordinates about the topics covered at shift training to ensure understanding and attention during future Shift Training Sessions.

Outside Specialized Training

Agencies cannot financially justify providing all of their training in-house. Sometimes employees will be sent to a specialized training course conducted by an outside agency or college. "Most organizations utilize outside resources to supplement and complement their internal programs and activities. Outside resources become necessary when highly specialized subjects or methods are needed, or when special capabilities for instruction or for organizing materials are beyond the scope of organizational resources."[4] Specialized training includes a wide-range of subjects like accounting, budgeting, and hostage negotiation tactics. It is often more economical to contract for such training than to provide it in-house by the creation of a specialized training course.

Command Courses

Since managers and supervisors run the agency, they, too, need additional continuing education to prepare them for the increasing job demands and for future needs. "Far too many men and women find themselves members of the hourly paid work force on a Friday evening and members of the management team on a Monday morning. Somehow over the weekend it is assumed that they have acquired not only the basic skills of supervision but also, of greater significance, that attitude of mind essential to good management."[5] It can no longer be assumed that because an employee has passed a series of examinations, he will now perform adequately in the position into which he has just been promoted; training must extend to all levels.

QUALIFICATIONS OF A TRAINER

Trainers can come in all shapes and sizes, a variety of styles and approaches. But there are certain qualifications which all trainers must possess if they hope to be a successful.

Knowledge

A trainer must be familiar with what he is teaching and training. A trainer's knowledge will produce credibility.

Status

If a trainer is to be worthy of attention, then he must have status in the eyes of the trainees. Formal education or practical experience enhances the status as one qualified to train. A combination of both formal education and practical experience is the best qualification for a trainer.

Training Ability

The trainer should be aware of the fundamental principles of learning as well as the various methods of training. Some people may be very knowledgeable, but if they can't communicate, then people will not learn. It is important for a trainer to know the strengths and weaknesses of each training method so that he can use the method which is most suited for his different training needs.

Willing To Train

The most important qualification for a trainer is his willingness to train. A trainer must have the necessary patience and proper attitude required to deal with the mistakes of trainees. He must be able to offer assistance when needed without getting in the way of the trainee's progress. If there is not a willingness to do the things required of a trainer, he then cannot be successful. This is especially true of a supervisor since training subordinates is one of his primary tasks.

BASIC TENETS OF LEARNING

For a supervisor to understand the concept of learning, it is necessary for him to understand what learning is and the basic tenets or rules of learning. Learning requires change. But people often resist change, this resistance can be a block to a person's learning. A mark of maturity is to approach life as if you are always a student, ready to learn, grow, mature, and change.

State of Receptiveness

Much like soil which must be prepared for planting, a trainee must be prepared to learn. A trainer must create an attitude conducive to learning by providing motivation for the trainee to learn.

When someone sees a personal benefit in learning, he learns more willingly and readily. If a trainer can show the trainee why he should learn what is about to be taught by showing him how it will benefit him, an interest in learning will be generated by the trainee. "There must be perceivable payback to the employee. The employee faces the training with one big question: ' What's in it for me?' He must see a direct and personal benefit from the training or he will have no reason or inclination to absorb it."[6] There are several ways to accomplish this, such as pointing out how the trainee's status or salary may increase or by illustrating how the trainee's job will somehow be made easier. In our personal experience in conducting training courses, without a doubt the most highly motivated group of trainees are those preparing for a promotion examination. Realizing that their learning could lead to both increased status and salary, these candidates are extremely ready to learn.

Pleasant and Pleasurable

Can learning be pleasant and pleasurable? Once the trainer has people's attention can he continue to have learning occur? Here the skill and sensitivity to the attitude of the trainee by the trainer play a large role. With some creativity and experience, learning can be interesting, challenging and, yes, even pleasant.

Consider the following:

Sergeant Rems is training Officer Ginty in using a computer when preparing reports. Officer Ginty is not happy with this since he has no experience with computers.

Sergeant Rems convinces Ginty how much easier it will be for him to use a computer to write reports. Ginty is now in a state of receptiveness. Sergeant Rems begins by showing Ginty some basic operations on the computer. Ginty quickly masters them and after being shown a few more basic operations, masters them also. Ginty then says, "This computer stuff is O.K. I can't wait to get to the point where I can bang out a whole report on my own. What's next, Sarge?"

By realizing that nothing succeeds like success, our trainer, Sergeant Rems, made the learning experience pleasurable and pleasant by allowing our trainee to succeed early on in the learning process. If a trainee is not able to succeed in his early learning then the experience is not pleasurable, the trainee wants out, and learning grinds to a halt. It is the trainer's job to divide the learning into segments which the trainee can master and build upon success.

The Cycle of Repetition

Repeat, repeat and repeat. Having a trainee repeat an operation or procedure will obviously strengthen his mastery of the operation or procedure so that he can perform it even under the most stressful conditions. Later on, the trainee should be called upon to practice the operation or procedure so that he will not forget it. The adage, "If you don't use it, you'll lose it," is true. The trainer's challenge is to motivate trainees and enable them to see the need for repetition.

In addition, a trainer should be aware that when training workers in an operation or procedure, it is a good training method to begin by demonstrating what is the correct method. Things that are learned initially tend to stay with people. Therefore beginning a session by illustrating an incorrect method to follow and then later contrasting it with the correct method is not a sound approach for a trainer. Also, it is a good idea to connect abstract material such as legal concepts to everyday street situations. It is one thing to list on a blackboard the factors which are required before a search of a vehicle can be conducted, but it is much more lasting to illustrate by using an actual street situation and indicating how the legal concepts were correctly applied to the situation. Finally, trainers should recognize that reviews and sum-ups are important. People tend to remember that which is reinforced. Information identified as a final summary, will fix in the trainee's memory the most important part of the information imparted.

THE LEARNING PROCESS

Our treatment of how people learn as presented below is meant not as an examination of the psychological concepts which determine the way people learn, but rather as a guide to assist the supervisor in understanding his subordinates and the basic ways they learn.

Gaining Attention

We have already stated that learning requires change and that before any learning or change can occur the trainer must catch and hold the attention of the trainee. Organizational rank can demand a respectful show of attention. But a reluctant show of attention will not last for long. Once again, the best means of getting and maintaining attention is to appeal to the trainee's best interests.

Trainer Input

Cognitive information is imparted by a recognized training authority, who has a degree of credibility by virtue of his own experience and/or education. We cannot always insure that information which is imparted is adequately processed by the trainees, but we can insure that the content, delivery, and packaging are superior thereby increasing the overall quality of the instructional process. A trainer must know the material and be able to deliver it at the level of the audience.

Admitted by Senses

The information received undergoes a selection process by the trainee; all of the senses are involved in the selection process. This process simply means that one or more senses become engaged in the receiving of information, the more senses involved, the more engaging and effective the learning process.

For example, if a trainer during a weapons safety lecture shows a red-barrelled Smith and Wesson Chief .38 revolver and specifies that the revolver is red-barrelled because it has been rendered inoperable for demonstration purposes, the senses of the trainees could focus on several pieces of this information. They can focus on the caliber of the weapon, its manufacturer,

212

its type, or the fact that it is red-barrelled. However, rarely do people engaged in learning focus on several parts of the information being delivered. They tend to focus on that which is most important to them. Here because it is a safety lecture, most likely their focus would be on the fact that the weapon is red-barrelled indicating that it has been rendered safe and inoperable. After the senses choose the information to be accepted, the rest of the information is not readily retained. The information which is accepted by the senses and passed on is that which has been chosen by the senses selection process. Learning is enhanced if the trainee can involve multiple senses: if he can see the gun, hold it, and feel its weight.

Short Memory Storehouse

Information received and processed goes into a person's short memory storehouse. Here it will be held, as the name of the storehouse suggests only for a short period of time. The biggest factor in determining if it will be held for a short or long period of time is its relevance to other information in the person's long memory storehouse.

Long Memory Storehouse

The long memory storehouse is where information is kept for extended periods of time. If, for instance, the trainee has achieved considerable expertise in the field of accident investigations, additional current information dealing with accidents investigation will find its way into his long memory storehouse and be stored with relevant information. The long memory storehouse can keep information for a lifetime, whereas, the short memory storehouse turns over information regularly.

Individual Learning Speeds

Each individual learns at different rates or speeds based upon mental ability, personality, background information, and education. Remember also, that the speed at which someone learns is not necessarily an indicator of how well they retain information. Some people may not catch on fast, but once they have it, they keep it.

It is helpful to understand that people have different learning strengths and orientations. For instance, not everyone is strong in learning by reading, some people are auditory learners who learn better by hearing and interacting. Others are visually-oriented and learn best when they see something done and/or demonstrated. Still others are very kinetic, they, as most, do best with hands-on experience.

On an often over-looked point, we should not discount the impact that the physical environment has on learning. Is it too warm, too cold, too dark or too bright? If the physical environment is not conducive to learning, the learning process will be handicapped.

Understanding the factors involved in learning can help a trainer empathize and be patient with those who are being trained.

DEVISING AND CONDUCTING A TRAINING PROGRAM

What goes into planning, assembling and delivering a training program? Here are five steps:

1. Discovering Needs.
2. Setting the Goals.
3. Developing the Training Curriculum.
4. Conducting the Program.
5. Evaluating the Program.

1. Discovering Needs

The first step in devising a training program is discovering the training needs. To do this the requirements of the specific job being considered should be examined to insure that they are in keeping with agency goals. The differences between the requirements of the specific job and the present employee competence level will identify the training needs. Assessing employee competence can be done either formally through performance evaluations or informally through first-hand knowledge of supervisors.

Training is not an isolated action; it is continuous because training needs are constantly surfacing. Each time a new employee, a new procedure, or new equipment is employed, some type of training will be necessary. Supervisors need to be sensitive and responsive to the developing needs of their people.

Consider the following:

Lieutenant Rems is a shift commander. Recently he has received numerous complaints from citizens who are not satisfied with the assistance they receive when they call the precinct and speak with the person who answers the phone. In addition, more and more he has had to personally take phone calls which normally should have been handled by the precinct desk phone operator. After looking into the matter, Rems determines that the complaints are not against any one specific member of the shift but rather they seem to be against anyone who is handling the job of precinct desk phone operator. The result of this has been that Rems has had to spend time away from his other duties to more closely supervise members assigned as the precinct desk phone operator.

Rems correctly decides to assess if there is a training need. First, he reviews the department's goals in answering the precinct phone. He broadly identifies it as a way to help protect and serve the public. Then he isolates the individual job requirements of a precinct desk phone operator. For instance part of the requirements should include, providing necessary police assistance to those in need. Rems determines that to accomplish this an operator needs knowledge about services provided by the department along with conversational and interpersonal skills. The lieutenant, through his first-hand knowledge of personnel assigned to the shift, assesses how well they know the services available to the public through the department and the level of their conversational and interpersonal skills. His training need is indicated by the difference between the job requirements of a precinct desk phone operator and competence level of those currently operating the phone.

2. Setting the Goals

The goals of a training program should be as specific as possible and include answers to these questions:

a. What performance is expected of the trainee?
b. Under what conditions is the job expected to be performed?
c. What standards constitute a satisfactory job-rating?

a. What Performance Is Expected of the Trainee?

Using our above example of a precinct desk phone operator, the performance component of the goal of the training program might be stated as: Can identify the services offered by the department to the public. This is more specific than - Is aware of department services available to the public. There is no way to measure what a trainee might be aware of, but evaluating if a trainee can identify something is measurable. "Training objectives should be specifically defined and measurable, indicating the exact job skills required and expected level of performance. General statements such as, 'Develop the ability to perform the job,' provide little guidance. This statement does not specify the steps required to perform the job, the skills needed, or the expected performance level. A more appropriate training objective would use the following format: 'Produce 30 units per hour, meeting quality standards, using the following steps.' The objective statement would go on to describe the skills necessary at each step of the job."[7]   Specificity aids in measuring performance expectations.

b. Under What Conditions is the Job Expected To Be Performed?

The conditions of the training objective might appear as— within five rings answers a multi-line phone without direct supervision. The job conditions include such statements as what, if any, are the time restraints (i.e. within five rings), and what resources and equipment can be used (i.e. the phone) and which are not available (i.e. without direct supervision).

c. What Constitutes a Satisfactory Job-Rating?

If a job deals with quantifiable amounts, then establishing satisfactory job standards is a lot easier when determining training objectives. For example, a training objective for the position of crime prevention officer could include - Performs five crime prevention surveys each week.

Though some job standards are more qualitative and harder to measure, specifics can be determined with some creative thought. The key to training objectives is to be as specific as possible. Training is much like planning. They both require a goal. If you don't know where you're going, you can't hope to get there.

3. Developing the Training Curriculum

The third step can be assisted by answering the following questions:

What? —What kind of training will be given? What will be the subject of the training? What information and curriculum will be presented?

When? —What will be the duration of the training? How long will each training session take? How many sessions? Should the training be done during the regular shift, on overtime, should the shifts be changed? (e.g., If the trainee normally works midnight to 8 A.M., should the training take place during the 8 A.M. to 4 P.M. shift?) If the training is to take place during the normal shift and is only to last a few hours, then when should it be scheduled for?

Where?—At what location shall the training take place? At the precinct? At some central facility of the agency? At a local college?

Who?—Who will do the training, and who needs to attend the sessions?

How?—What method will be used to give the training? Will it be one-on-one training, a lecture, or a conference? Will video tapes or audio tapes be used?

4. Conducting the Program

Supervisors who conduct the training are advised to take the following actions in the order given:

a. Getting The Trainees Ready.
b. Showing The Trainees How.
c. Letting The Trainees Try It .
d. Finding Out If The Trainees Have Learned.

a. Getting the Trainees Ready

Put the trainee(s) at ease and begin by explaining what can be expected to occur during the training session. "Prepare the worker for training. First you need to put the worker at ease. Workers frequently are rather anxious and nervous when they are being trained. This nervousness can hinder learning. Help them understand that the training is not threatening but is designed to help them learn."[8] The trainer should explain the goals of the training so it is clear to all.

Getting the trainee ready is facilitated by these four training principles:

Motivation.

The trainee needs to know that the training will personally benefit him, and he is capable of mastering the training (refer to the earlier discussion on the benefits from receiving training).

Confidence of the Agency.

Make the trainees feel important and remind them that the agency has confidence in them and has budgeted training expenses for its personnel.

Get the Trainee Involved.

The trainer should get the trainees involved in the session as quickly as possible. This might take the form of a self introduction on the part of the trainee or his answer to a general question posed by the trainer, such as, "What do you think you will personally get out of today's training?"

Association.

Association is a training principle which calls for presenting material so that it may be related to or connected with other things familiar to the trainee. In this way the trainee is not totally overwhelmed. He is prepared by being made to feel that he already has some mastery of things which have some relation to what is about to be taught. He is not totally traveling in uncharted waters.

In getting a trainee ready to learn, the trainer should aim to get the trainee's attention, to hold it, and to spark his or her interest and desire to learn. "Learning rarely can begin until trainees are properly prepared to learn."[9]

b. Showing the Trainees How

When showing the trainees how, the most common mistake made by supervisors is assuming that the trainees know more than they actually do. As an aid in accomplishing this task, the trainer should be guided by the following training principles:

Use Examples.

A trainer should buttress information with practical examples from the everyday work setting with which the trainee can identify. Examples bring information to life and allow people to relate to the subject, the instructor, and others in the class. The most valuable resource an instructor has is his own experiences. Practical experiences which convey an important point will be remembered longer than a list of information.

Deliver Information in Manageable Segments.

The trainer should divide material into manageable segments instead of covering too much information all at once. "Trainees can absorb only a little at a time, and this information ideally should be arranged in a sequence which advances the learning from the familiar to the unfamiliar, from the easy to the difficult, from the simple to the complex."[10] Too much information at once tends to overwhelm the trainee and turns training into an unpleasant experience. By delivering information in manageable segments the trainer can make frequent checks for understanding, and if he finds there is confusion, corrective action can take place before too much misunderstanding on the part of the trainee occurs.

Travel at the Right Pace.

If the training is one-on-one, it is not too difficult for the trainer to find the correct pace to proceed. The rate of learning of the individual trainee will pretty much dictate the pace in one-on-one training. But what about a group session such as a lecture? The trainer must move the training along fast enough to keep the interest of the fast learners but not so fast that he loses the slow learners. Find the best pace and seek to maintain it so that the training session will flow smoothly.

Give Frequent Summaries.

After making key points the trainer should summarize. This helps a trainee identify what is important and check his understanding regularly. In making key points and summaries, the trainer should explain (where appropriate) the "why" of a policy or procedure.

c. *Letting the Trainees Try It*

"People learn best by doing. Skills are developed slowly and a person must practice to develop the skill. When training workers, you need to give them plenty of opportunities to practice."[11] The trainer can provide the trainee the opportunity to do the task which has been taught. This opportunity can take many shapes ranging from role playing to problem solving. Whatever shape the opportunity takes there are certain training principles which the trainer should employ:

Obtain Feedback.

By having the trainee apply what he has learned the trainer is able to get instant feedback on how well the trainee has learned. It tells the trainer what the trainee knows and in what areas the trainee requires more help and/or practice. This also gives the trainee the opportunity to ask questions and clarify details. The trainee should be allowed to deliver all the pertinent information to the trainer uninterrupted. When he can do this

220

successfully, it indicates that he can tie the pieces together and has mastered the subject matter. The trainer should not satisfy himself with yes or no answers. This will offer little accurate feedback since many people will answer yes when asked if they understand something, even though they actually do not understand. They may be too embarrassed to say no and not wish to be seen in an unfavorable light.

Correct Errors.

Errors should be corrected as they occur so that bad habits are not adopted by the trainee. However, error correction should be accomplished as tactfully as possible. It should not be overdone and thereby inhibit the trainee. It should be done, in so far as possible, in private and should not embarrass the trainee. The best type of error correction is self correction. When a trainee sees his mistake and can take the necessary steps to correct it, learning at the highest level has taken place. Not only is the trainee able to detect the error, but he also identifies a way to correct it. This requires a good grasp of the material which has been covered in the session.

Compliment Appropriately.

Before criticizing, if possible, the trainee should be complimented. This encourages the trainee and does not make it seem as if the entire experience was created to find fault. Compliments should be staggered by the trainer to provide encouragement and impetus to the trainee to help him get over plateaus in the training process when he does not see himself making any progress. Most trainers realize the need for criticism but do not see praise as being equally important. And while some trainers realize that good application of what has been learned should be complimented, few trainers realize the importance of complimenting those who have made the biggest improvement. "Positive feedback...serves as positive reinforcement. It is a reward that increases the probability that the worker will perform the task correctly. Also...look for every opportunity to provide positive reinforcement. Tell them when they did the job right or let them know when they are improving."[12]

Let Them Try It Again.

If a trainee does not master what has been taught, the trainer should re-instruct him and have him try it again in its entirety. The trainer should not consider the material mastered until the trainee can perform in its entirety what has been taught. Care must be taken that the problem may not be the performance of the trainee. The problem might lie with the training effort of the trainer. This is an often neglected part of the process. The trainer may think he has properly presented the material but in reality he has miscommunicated and is responsible for the errors in the trial performance.

d. Finding Out if the Trainees Have Learned

Is the trainee ready to do the job? If the training involved performing a new procedure, has the trainee learned it sufficiently to be able to do it under the conditions he will be called upon to operate under? Will the quality of the trainee's performance meet the standards of the agency? Is the output sufficient? The answers to these questions can be obtained through a variety or combination of individual methods. They include pencil and paper quizzes and tests, practical performance examinations where the trainee is required to perform certain physical actions, and field observations of the trainee by the trainer.

When trainees are examined to see what they have learned, they should receive immediate feedback from the trainer. In this way they can immediately set about to correct what they have not mastered. This way incorrect actions do not develop into bad habits. However, wherever possible a trainer discovering errors on the part of a trainee should, through pointed questions, attempt to lead the trainee to discovering his own mistakes and then to engage in self-correction. This builds confidence in the trainee that he can handle his own problems concerning the subject matter. Also it has a strong impact on the trainee causing him to remember the mistake he uncovered and avoid it in the future.

The testing phase can take place anytime the trainer feels the need to reinforce what has been taught or feels that the trainees are not fully grasping what is being taught. Testing identifies areas requiring re-instruction.

Finally, a supervisor should let the trainee know that he will be available to assist after the training has been completed. In this way the trainee does not see the training as the end of the assistance that is available to him. Help is available if he really needs it. It is one thing to be told by someone else that you have been trained and are now ready to do a job, but it is another thing to believe it yourself.

5. Evaluating the Program

When devising a training program, a plan for evaluating the program itself should be determined at the outset. "Evaluation is one of the great unsolved problems in the world of organizations."[13] The goal of training is the improvement of performance but accurate and objective measurements of this performance can be difficult to determine. Consequently, it can also be difficult to objectively justify the costs of an individual training program. Thus funding for training is often an uphill battle with those controlling the purse strings suspiciously examining any newly requested training courses. As a result, many agencies have court-mandated training programs funded only due to lawsuits.

Assessing the Impact of Training Programs

Has a training program had significant impact upon the trainees once they are back in the workplace? Measuring performance, in general, is difficult; it is especially difficult in law enforcement agencies where so much of what is done does not lend itself to quantifiable measurements. If the evaluation is about measuring performance, there are a variety of factors beyond the quality of the training which are outside the trainee's control, but which do influence performance, such as the level and type of supervision in the workplace. Nonetheless, adequate evaluations must be a continual process.

In assessing the impact of training, we should go beyond simply filling out evaluation forms which become an opinion poll where the participant trainees are asked to complete a questionnaire designed to indicate their feelings about the training they have just received. What should be looked at is if the supervisors of the trainees believe that the knowledge, skills and attitudes of the trainees have been impacted as evidenced by the trainees' present performance. "Just because...X attended a particular training course does not insure that...X actually benefited from the course in terms of the company objectives. His job performance, after training, should be observed and comparisons made with his performance before training on whatever measurable characteristics are considered pertinent."[14]

The clients of a public law enforcement agency (e.g., the community) are a useful barometer in determining whether the knowledge, skills and attitudes of law enforcement trainees have been impacted. Statistical analysis, when available and applicable, can assist in evaluating a training program. For instance, have personal accidents been reduced after conducting a safety training program? Does a job which was the subject of a recent training program and which used to take two hours now take only one hour? Have backlogs been reduced as a result of training in a certain function? Has the need for overtime been reduced? Surely some of these examples may have limited application in conducting evaluations of various training programs. Possibly what they really do is simply underscore the difficulty in evaluating such programs. However, a supervisor must acknowledge that training is essential, and no training effort would be complete without some attempt to ensure that the goals of the training program are being met.

COMMON TRAINING PROBLEMS

There are training problems which occur in an organization. A supervisor should be aware of such problems, because if he cannot recognize them, he cannot take steps to deal with them.

Trainer Rigidity

Too often a trainer conducting a training course refuses to deviate from what he has in front of him. Training requires a certain degree of balance and thinking on your feet. If what has worked in the past is not working in this instance, the trainer should not be afraid to make necessary adjustments to achieve the training objectives. Every trainee is an individual and as such is capable of presenting an individual training challenge. A trainer may need to make necessary alterations to fit the needs of the trainee in accomplishing the objectives of the training program.

False Assumptions

Assumptions may have their place, but in the main, it is not a wise choice faced with the alternative of facts versus assumptions. For example, consider the situation where all members of a watch have been given a copy of a recent change in the law. Now a training session has been scheduled to discuss the changes brought about by the new law. It would be a mistake for the trainer to assume that all attendees have read the new law or for that matter are well briefed on the old law. The most common mistake made when demonstrating an operation is to assume that the trainees know more than they actually do.

Overexpertise of the Trainer

A trainer can have so much expertise in his field and in his presentations that he is intimidating and considered unapproachable. Such an expert may be a plus for the agency, but if he can't reach his audience, he will not be an effective trainer. Trainers must continually find their target of delivery based on the material to be covered and the audience's level of familiarity with the material.

Trainer Paranoia

More common than admitted is trainer paranoia. This term describes a trainer who fears that if he does too good a job, the trainee will someday pass him up and become a challenge to his authority and position. So he tells the trainee just enough to get by but discourages any trainee enthusiasm or self-motivation. This is especially damaging when the trainer is also the trainee's supervisor whose job is supposed to be to assist the growth of subordinates. Supervisors should recognize that the development of subordinates, in reality, reflects well on their supervisory ability and may reduce their workload through the work efforts of a developing subordinate.

Checking for Understanding Inappropriately

While a trainer must continually check the trainee's understanding, it must be done appropriately. It serves little purpose to simply ask a trainee, "Do you understand?" More often than not the trainee will answer yes, even though there may be confusion in his mind. Specific questions elicit specific response. Questions prefaced with what, when, where, who, how and why, will generate more feedback. For example: What unit should be notified? When is the response of two units required? Who is in charge of those situations?

Not My Job

Of the common training problems experienced by law enforcement agencies, the most serious occurs when a supervisor expresses the sentiment that training is not part of his job. Often, he mistakenly reasons that there are specialists in the agency who are experts and do nothing but training. Therefore he maintains that training is not his job, and he has no time for it. Nothing could be more off-target. "The function of a company training department varies from organization to organization. But almost all training directors agree that unless supervisors are sold on training as their responsibility, the efforts of the training department won't be very effective."[15]   Training is part of a supervisor's job, and when he fails to do it, he makes his own job more difficult. Insufficiently trained subordinates will make more demands on his time since they will of necessity demand more and closer supervision. The question is not how can he afford the time to engage in the training of his subordinates, but rather how can he afford not to train them?

TEST YOUR UNDERSTANDING

1. Which ability in the eyes of those who are being supervised seems to go hand in hand with being a competent supervisor?

2. Define training and explain its components.

3. Explain why training is needed in an agency.

4. How does a subordinate gain from training?

5. How does a supervisor gain from conducting training?

6. Identify the different types of training and explain each one.

7. What are the qualifications which a trainer should possess?

8. Name and discuss the basic tenets of learning.

9. Describe how people learn.

10. What are the five steps in devising a training program?

11. Name and explain the steps in conducting a training program.

12. Explain why evaluation of a training program is difficult.

13. List some common training problems, and recommend how to deal with each one.

FOOTNOTES

1. Carl Heyes, P.E. and H.W. Nance, editors. *The Foreman/Supervisor's Handbook,* 5th ed. (New York: VanNostrand Reinhold Company Limited, 1984), p. 204.

2. Herbert J. Chruden and Arthur W. Sherman, Jr., *Personnel Management,* 5th ed. (Cincinnati, OH: South Western Publishing Company, 1979), p. 192.

3. James F. Evered, *Shirt-Sleeves Management.* (New York: AMACOM, 1981), p. 85.

4. Dalton E. McFarland, *Management: Principles and Practices,* 4th ed. (New York: MacMillan Publishing Company, Inc., 1974), p. 476.

5. Edwin J. Singer and John Ramsden, *Human Resources-Obtaining Results From People At Work.* (London: McGraw-Hill Book Company Limited, 1972), p. 78.

6. Evered, p. 85.

7. Christina Christenson, Thomas W. Johnson and John E. Stinson, *Supervising.* (Reading, MA: Addison-Wesley Publishing Company, 1982), p. 338.

8. Ibid., p. 341.

9. Lester R. Bittel, *What Every Supervisor Should Know - The Basics of Supervisory Management,* 5th ed. (New York: McGraw-Hill Book Company, 1985), p. 260.

10. Ibid., p. 260.

11. Christenson, Johnson and Stinson, p. 334.

12. Ibid., p. 334.

13. McFarlan, p. 480.

14. Chruden and Sherman, p. 194.

15. Bittel, p. 259.

SUGGESTED READINGS

Bergevin, Paul, Dwight Morris and Robert M. Smith.
Adult Education Procedures - A Handbook of Tested Patterns for Effective Participation.
Greenwich, CT: The Seabury Press, 1963.

Bienvenu, B.J.
New Priorities In Training.
New York: AMACOM, 1969.

Gagne, R.M. and L.J. Briggs.
Principles of Instructional Design.
New York: Holt, Rinehart and Winston, 1979.

Hansen, David A. and Thomas R. Culley.
The Police Training Officer.
Springfield, IL: Charles C. Thomas, 1973.

Harris, R.N.
The Police Academy.
New York: Wiley, 1973.

Lynton, Rolf .
Training For Development.
Homewood, IL: Richard D. Irwin, Inc., 1967.

Nilson, Carolyn.
Training For Non-Trainers.
New York: AMACOM, 1990.

Nilson, Carolyn.
Training Program Workbook and Kit.
Englewood Cliffs, NJ: Prentice Hall, 1989.

Staton, Thomas F.
How To Instruct Successfully-Modern Teaching Methods in Adult Education.
New York: McGraw-Hill Book Co., Inc., 1960.

CHAPTER 10
THE SUPERVISOR AS A DISCIPLINARIAN

CATEGORIES OF DISCIPLINE

Of all the management concepts that a supervisor has to grasp in order to function effectively, those involving discipline are the most difficult to understand. This difficulty exists, in part, because in management theory the term discipline is used to refer to three distinct types of discipline: (1) positive discipline, (2) negative discipline, and (3) overall discipline.

Positive Discipline

Positive discipline refers to the training and counseling of subordinates that results in willing and voluntary compliance with the rules and regulations of an organization. When a supervisor disciplines a subordinate in this manner through attitudinal or technical skills training or counseling, there are no negative connotations involved. Punishment of the subordinate plays no part in the administration of this form of discipline.

Since positive discipline seeks to promote desirable behavior, it is essential all workers are knowledgeable of what is expected of them. "Every person must know, when hired and henceforth, just what management and the immediate supervisor expect. Supervisors must communicate the kind of positive behavior expected of employees rather than dwell upon an exhaustive list of detailed prohibitions."[1] . Training, therefore, is the backbone of positive discipline. "The objectives of disciplinary action are positive. They are educational and corrective. The goal is to improve the future rather than punish for the past."[2] If a supervisor neglects his training responsibility, orderliness will suffer and the need to punish workers will abound.

Self-Discipline

An important component of positive discipline is self-discipline. Supervisors who follow the adage, "Don't do as I do, do as I say," will not be effective, in the long run, in disciplining subordinates. If a supervisor wants to effectively control subordinates and have them adhere to organizational rules, it is essential that he scrupulously follow the organizational rules.

When a supervisor, by virtue of his rank, holds himself above those rules, he will inevitably lose the respect of his subordinates. This loss of respect also accrues to supervisors who do not follow the mandates of their bosses. Supervisors who are not respected are ineffective disciplinarians.

Negative Discipline

Negative discipline refers to the meting out of forms of punishment for wrong or inappropriate job-related conduct. While both positive and negative discipline are necessary to achieve the overall objectives of disciplinary action, it is an absolute rule that, when dealing with minor violations, a supervisor should first rely upon positive discipline. Only when positive discipline fails should negative discipline follow.

Negative discipline ranges from simple reprimands to severe disciplinary measures. It is important to note that the successful administration of negative discipline does not depend on severe punishment. In some cases the mildest form of negative discipline—the verbal warning—will be all that is necessary to achieve results. When this fails, other forms of negative discipline include oral or written reprimands, fines, suspensions, demotions and separations.

It is extremely important for supervisors to document in writing the details of the need for the use of negative discipline. This documentation must be consistent with agency policy, but it does not necessarily have to become part of the disciplined employee's permanent personnel file. In less serious cases, an entry in the supervisor's daily log can suffice. Such documentation could prove invaluable in the future should it be necessary to prove a pattern of wrongdoing or verify a poor evaluation.

Overall Discipline

Overall discipline refers to the combined results of the administration of positive and negative discipline. The overall discipline of an organization is measured by the degree of orderliness present. A well-disciplined work force, therefore, does not mean one that is sufficiently punished for its job-related mistakes. Rather, it means that the work force is in voluntary compliance with the rules and regulations of the organization and works efficiently to attain the goals of that organization.

PUNISHMENT

Although punishment, at times, can be potentially counter-productive and does not guarantee improved behavior, it still must be used, if only because there is no other way to deal with a problem employee. Since punishment for minor infractions should be used only when other more positive attempts at changing inappropriate behavior have failed, punishment should be seen as a prelude to employee removal proceedings. What should also be understood and communicated to all workers is that once an employee has reached the stage where he must be punished for his job-related infractions, any repeated infractions by that employee will be dealt with by progressively severe penalties. If the cycle continues, separation would occur. This is not to say that all employees who are punished for wrongdoing will one day be terminated, since that is far from the truth. For, if administered in a fair and impartial manner and in accordance with the guidelines listed below, the use of punishment can, in most cases, bring about the desired change in the behavior of the recipient of the punishment.

Important Facts About Punishment

Regardless of whether the use of punishment has the desired effect on the recipient, such use serves notice to others that, if necessary, they will be dealt with in a similar fashion. When administering punishment, supervisors should be aware of the following:

a. Certainty of Punishment

The threat of punishment will not serve as a deterrent unless there is a feeling of certainty among employees that wrongdoing will be uncovered and that those responsible will be appropriately disciplined. And, if the discipline requires the use of punishment, then there must be a certainty that it will be dispensed. While this amounts to the use of fear to achieve the goals of management, unfortunately, fear is the only way to control some subordinates. "It is too bad that some employees obey rules only for fear of penalties. But if it is to their benefit to have jobs, and if fear keeps them on the straight and narrow, the use of reasonable penalties is of benefit to the employees themselves."[3]   Therefore, as unfortunate as it may be, fear must be a part of management's arsenal when dealing with certain employees.

b. Speed of Punishment

When punishment is required, it must be swiftly administered. Unreasonable delays are counter-productive. "When the discipline quickly follows an infraction, there is a connection between the two events in the employee's mind and hence less probability for a future infraction."[4] Delays cause great stress, not only on employees who are awaiting resolution of their cases, but also on supervisors who must continue to maintain working relationships with those employees. Law enforcement personnel should understand this concept better than most since they very often see how delay in the prosecution and punishment of criminals works to undermine the criminal justice system. Remember, however, that the need to administer punishment quickly should not interfere with the necessary professional investigation to fully document the need for punishment. "Discipline should be administered as soon as possible after the infraction has taken place or has been noticed, and after the supervisor has obtained all the facts related to the incident."[5] In those cases where such an investigation creates an unreasonable delay, the supervisor involved should keep the accused worker informed of the status of the investigation.

c. Severity of Punishment

While deterrence of misbehavior is dependent upon both the certainty and swiftness of punishment, it is not always dependent upon severity of punishment. In most cases, the severity of punishment should be predicated on the severity of the offense.

Remember, repeated minor infractions by the same worker must be met by increasingly severe punishments. The primary purpose of both positive and negative discipline is to foster improved performance. If a repeated infraction follows on the heels of the administration of positive discipline, then the use of negative discipline must be considered. And, if a repeated infraction occurs shortly after the administration of a certain punishment, then a more severe punishment must be considered.

d. Objectiveness in Administering Punishment

Fair and impartial treatment of subordinates is a fundamental supervisory doctrine that should never be violated. Therefore, supervisors must, at all costs, prevent subjectivity from clouding their judgment when deciding on appropriate punishment. Punishment which is not meted out in a fair and impartial manner will always come back to haunt supervisors. Remember, one of the benefits of administering punishment is deterrence. When co-workers of the punished employee see what has taken place, they resolve not to put themselves in a similar position. But this is not what takes place if the co-workers have good reason to believe that the punished employee was treated unfairly. Instead, a groundswell of support rises up for the disciplined employee which is accompanied by widespread resentment of the supervisor and the system. To prevent this, supervisors should never allow their emotions to dictate their actions. Theoretically, supervisors should never let anger over the wrongdoing of employees get the better of them. Nonetheless, such wrongdoing often does anger supervisors, and there is no way we know of preventing this. What we do know is a way to minimize its negative impact. The anger itself is not the problem, it is the way the anger is demonstrated that can be appropriate or inappropriate. Supervisors should never administer punishment when anger prevents them from being objective. This is one time when a delay in the administration of punishment is acceptable.

e. Consistency of Punishment

Should law enforcement agencies have uniform penalties for offenses which are automatically applied in all situations? One could argue that such a system for deciding punishments would certainly protect the agencies from the evils of supervisory subjectivity. Despite this argument, however, it is imperative that punishment fit the individual as well as the offense. There is a difference between uniform punishment and consistency of punishment. Uniform punishments fail to consider all of the circumstances surrounding misbehavior. For example, an individual's prior performance record must also always be considered when meting out punishments. Consistency of punishment means the application of like punishment for similar violations committed under similar circumstances. It is this kind of consistency that must be present if administering of punishment is to have its desired effect.

ROLE OF IMMEDIATE LINE SUPERVISORS IN MAINTAINING DISCIPLINE

The greatest challenge facing supervisors is maintaining a high-level of overall discipline in the work group. The ability to maintain a high-level of overall discipline is by far the most welcomed trait of a good leader in the eyes of his superiors.

The major responsibility for administering both positive and negative discipline belongs to immediate line supervisors. This is so for a number of reasons. The most important of these reasons is that immediate supervisors are the people who know the most about each subordinate. "The supervisor is key in the discipline process. He or she works with employees on a day-to-day basis, and thus is in the best position to observe unsatisfactory performance or behavior that violates organizational rules."[6]   This is important since, in the absence of agency guidelines to the contrary, there is no one way to deal with employee wrongdoing. Instead, the optimal way to deal with such wrongdoing is predicated on the totality of the circumstances surrounding each delinquent act.

When the wrongdoing is serious, such as corruption, or the unnecessary use of force, formal disciplinary action should be mandated. In these cases, the procedure to follow is, or should be, firmly structured by agency policy. But the course to follow when correcting minor violations should be discretionary and

236

determined on a case-by-case basis. The reason for this is that the ideal corrective action needed is predicated on complete knowledge of the delinquent employee, such as work record, disciplinary record, attendance record and a host of other facts usually known best by the immediate supervisor. The specifics of how to proceed when investigating allegations of employee misconduct is addressed in another chapter.

Acting on Wrongdoing Is Not Discretionary

So far we have established that, in most cases, it is the immediate line supervisor who must discipline wrongdoers. But an important distinction should be made if a high-level of overall discipline is to be maintained in the agency. While the form of discipline may be discretionary, the responsibility to take action is not.

All supervisors have a responsibility to take action whenever they observe or become aware of a violation of agency rules or procedures. To do otherwise inevitably leads to an erosion of overall discipline. Employees must feel certain that all un-covered wrongdoing will result in some form of supervisory intervention which will be followed by some form of discipline. Without consistency of enforcement, employees lose respect for those rules which are only sporadically upheld. If such a situation continues over a long period of time, the loss of respect extends to all rules and regulations. This snowball or domino effect builds until scandal is imminent.

Intervention by Other than Immediate Supervisors

If the supervisor who observes a minor violation is the immediate supervisor, then he will also, in most cases, administer the discipline. But, if the supervisor who observes a violation is not the immediate supervisor, then he must: (1) act to terminate the inappropriate conduct, and (2) notify the immediate supervisor and supply him with all pertinent details. This notification should be made through the chain of command. In these cases, the immediate supervisor should consider the input of the reporting supervisor when deciding on the type of discipline needed.

© 1995 by J. & B. Gould
Printed in the U.S.A.   Ms

Outdated Regulations Should Be Rescinded

Sometimes people are not following rules because the rules have outlived their usefulness. Agencies should periodically review their policies with the intent of purging them. Outdated rules and regulations are the greatest burden a supervisor can face in his efforts to maintain a high-level of overall discipline. When there are too many irrelevant or seemingly arbitrary regulations a supervisor often has to pick and choose which regulations are important and which need not be enforced. This leads to agency inconsistency since not all supervisors think alike. Inconsistent enforcement is an evil that should be avoided at all costs. Remember, inconsistent enforcement leads the worker who was penalized for a commonplace action to believe he was treated unfairly. And, the maintenance of a high-level of overall discipline absolutely requires that supervisors and workers alike view the disciplinary system as both fair and equitable.

THE ELEMENTS OF A FAIR AND EQUITABLE DISCIPLINARY SYSTEM

The goals of any disciplinary system are to promote the success of the work group by sustaining the highest possible level of performance and to maintain a work environment that is as safe as possible for all concerned. To accomplish these goals, there are certain basic elements that must be present in all disciplinary systems. These elements are:

a. Clear and Reasonable Rules and Regulations.
b. Systematic Instruction Concerning Rules, Regulations and Expected Performance Standards.
c. A Well-Informed Work Group.
d. Facts before Acts.
e. Consistent Supervisory Behavior.
f. Performance Feedback.
g. An Appeals Procedure .
h. Periodic Purging of Records.

a. *Clear and Reasonable Rules and Regulations*

It only complicates the system when rules and regulations lack clarity and reasonableness. Unreasonable rules undermine a supervisor's authority who is obliged to uphold them and frustrate the good intentions of subordinates who are required to abide by them. In turn, morale suffers and discipline begins to seem arbitrary. Rules and regulations need to be clear and reasonable so that they can be clearly and reasonably followed.

b. *Systematic Instruction Concerning Rules, Regulations and Expected Performance Standards*

As a general rule, workers do not resent penalties they know they deserve. But they absolutely resent being penalized for conduct they did not know was wrong. Therefore, the mere existence of clear and reasonable rules and regulations is worthless unless there is systematic instruction of workers to make sure they are understood. The same is true for performance standards. Workers should be well versed concerning management expectations regarding performance standards.

Immediate supervisors play a vital role in both of these matters. Since the instruction involved must be systematic and continuous, no one else in the agency is in a better position to give such instruction. And, since rules, regulations and performance standards are dynamic and not static, a big task facing a supervisor is keeping his workers properly instructed and up-to-date. To assist supervisors in meeting this challenge, copies of all changes in rules, regulations and performance standards should be given to all workers, and the workers should be made to receipt for them. In turn, supervisors should retain these receipts in the event workers claim in the future that they were not informed of such changes.

Management should be open to the suggestions by workers to changes in rules and regulations. "It is useful for management to seek employee advice on periodic revision of rules. The objective is to reduce the number of rules to the minimum and enforce those that are important. Customs and conditions change. Rules, like laws, need regular updating to achieve the respect and acceptance necessary for order in the workplace."[7]

Management open-mindedness goes a long way towards gaining acceptance of needed changes.

c. A Well-informed Work Group

It is not enough that there is understanding about acceptable conduct. Another important element of a progressive disciplinary system is giving advance warnings concerning the consequences of unacceptable conduct. These warnings must make it clear that there is a distinct difference between carelessness or unintentional wrongdoing and intentional misconduct. The former can, in most instances, be dealt with quite easily through the administering of positive discipline. The latter is much more serious, and almost always requires some negative discipline. Advance warnings should also indicate that the severity of discipline will increase with repeated infractions.

d. Facts Before Acts

"Facts before acts" is a rule that has many applications. It should be observed by all supervisors if a disciplinary system is to be judged as fair and impartial by workers. Instant career assassinations are taboo. Therefore, prior to taking disciplinary action when the merits of an allegation of work-related misconduct are uncertain, a systematic and objective investigation must be made to make certain that an accused worker is, in fact, guilty of such misconduct. (A much more detailed discussion of the making of personnel investigations appears in another chapter.) This investigation must be made before disciplinary action is initiated in cases where the guilt of a worker is in doubt.

The principle of "facts before acts" also requires that in all cases, an accused worker be interviewed and given a chance to tell his side of the story. This interview is investigative in nature. While it is important in most cases to hold this interview as soon as possible after learning of the alleged misconduct, if the incident in question is one which angered the supervisor involved, the interview should be delayed for a "cooling off period" to prevent that anger from clouding the supervisor's judgment.

This required fact finding effort must also include consideration of all of the circumstances surrounding an infraction. Only after all of the available facts have been considered should a decision be made as to the need for disciplinary action.

e. Consistent Supervisory Behavior

The hallmark of a fair and equitable disciplinary system is consistency. Fair and equitable treatment has long been recognized by management experts as one of the major job-security needs of employees. Nothing erodes the feeling of fairness more quickly than inconsistent supervisory behavior. There is simply no acceptable justification for dual standards. All employees should be treated in the same manner regardless of their race, color, creed, gender, or sexual preference. Interestingly enough, the most common reason why supervisors engage in favoritism is to reward good workers for doing a good job. While it is a recommended supervisory practice to reward good performance, such rewards must be made within the framework of agency policy. Being a good worker does not entitle a person to special treatment. Supervisors who ignore this rule seriously undermine their ability to maintain a high-level of overall discipline.

f. Performance Feedback

A fair and impartial disciplinary system must include job performance evaluations. Appraisal of subordinates is a continuous activity which should occur whenever supervisors have an opportunity to see the product of the work efforts of their subordinates. Any critical incidents observed - instances of above or below average performance - should be recorded for use when preparing formal appraisals. If merited, immediate praise should be given. Conversely, any needed constructive criticism should also be dispensed. But remember, the cardinal rule in this regard as always is to praise in public and criticize in private. Supervisors must understand that if, for any reason, they tolerate poor performance by a certain individual, they cannot in all fairness discipline any worker whose performance is equal to or better than that of the individual whose poor performance is being tolerated.

g. An Appeals Procedure

Employees who are the subject of formal disciplinary action should have the right to an appeal. "[T]he accused employee should always have the right to appeal to higher authority. Even if the person is truly guilty as charged, it may be best to hold a full hearing before higher authorities to satisfy all parties to the case that the employee has been justly treated."[8]

h. Periodic Purging of Records

A fair and impartial disciplinary system recognizes the fact that it usually serves no purpose to retain negative job-related information about an employee for more than a reasonable period of time. Purging of negative information, however, should not be automatic. Rather, such purging should be contingent upon continued good performance. For example, an employee who has been found guilty of misconduct should have that fact recorded in his personnel files. But if that employee avoids any additional instances of misconduct for a reasonable period of time then purging should take place. The period of time involved should depend upon the seriousness of the violation, so that more serious violations will remain on a person's record longer than less serious ones. However, breaking charges which are charges that could, in and of themselves, result in dismissal should not be subject to purging. When used in this manner, purging can promote good behavior and give recognition that the rehabilitation of problem employees can take place.

THE DISCIPLINARY PROCESS

The specifics of the internal disciplinary process vary from agency to agency and depend upon such factors as size of the agency, local laws, and the provisions of labor contracts. Nonetheless, in all law enforcement agencies, it is the responsibility of high-level management to establish policy governing the resolution of job-related disciplinary matters which require negative discipline. This policy should identify those serious job-related violations which could result in severe punishment, such as extended suspension or termination, which must be resolved by a formal administrative hearing presided over by a qualified person other than the supervisor who preferred the charges. The purpose of the formal administrative hearing is to decide on the guilt or innocence of the employee, and to set the penalty where guilt was ascertained.

For less serious job-related violations, the administration of negative discipline should be the primary responsibility of the immediate supervisor of the charged employee subject to the review of that supervisor's commanding officer. Regardless of specifics of the process, however, the accused employee should always have a right to appeal the finding, the penalty, or both.

Responsibilities of Immediate Supervisors Regarding Administrative Hearings

Immediate supervisors are not relieved of further responsibility just because a subordinate either is required to or elects to have an allegation adjudicated via a formal administrative hearing. Remember, in matters of internal discipline, the burden of proof is on the agency, and the agency expects the immediate supervisor to shoulder this burden if the charge is one which he initiated.

The supervisor involved should prepare for testifying at such a hearing in the same manner as any law enforcement officer would prepare for giving testimony. Immediately prior to the hearing date, the supervisor should review all of the information available to him. This should be a relatively easy task if the supervisor made detailed notes of the events surrounding the violation. In addition, the supervisor should review the accused employee's work history and prior disciplinary record and should be prepared to make a recommendation as to a fair and equitable punishment should a finding of guilt be reached.

The supervisor's responsibilities in the matter do not end when the hearing is concluded. Unless it is contrary to agency policy, the immediate supervisor should be the one who notifies the subordinate of the findings of the tribunal as well as the nature of any penalty that has been imposed. It is vitally important that this task be performed promptly and in a highly objective manner. Regardless of how the subordinate or the supervisor view the penalty, the supervisor is obligated to support it. If the subordinate perceives it as being too harsh, the supervisor must avoid the temptation to place the blame on the "higher-ups." Likewise, if it is seen by the subordinate as being lenient, the supervisor must refrain from any suggestion that such leniency stems from behind the scene action inappropriately taken by the supervisor on behalf of his subordinate. However, if the supervisor in fact played a key role in the assessment of the penalty, as is often the case, then the supervisor must assume some responsibility for it. In this instance, it is important for the supervisor to make it clear to the subordinate that his input was not designed to either sink the subordinate or to get him off the hook, but to arrive at a penalty that had the best chance to achieve its intended goal.

Administering Positive Discipline

When positive discipline is called for, it is usually best to handle the matter informally. Formal disciplinary charges are not needed since there will be no penalties imposed. It is the responsibility of the immediate supervisor to administer positive discipline or to arrange for it. This discipline almost always involves some combination of communication, training and counseling. Many times the discipline can be applied at the time the misconduct is observed. Follow-up is always required, however, to make sure that the situation has been corrected.

In some cases, such as when professional counseling or specialized training is required, the supervisor involved does not conduct the training/counseling, but still plays an important role. This role involves such things as motivation and follow-up to insure that a transfer of attitudes, skills, and knowledge to the actual work setting has occurred and that the matter has been resolved.

Administering Negative Discipline

Deciding upon appropriate punishment is the single most complex decision in the entire disciplinary process. In cases

244

where an immediate supervisor is responsible for the decision, that supervisor must do the following:

a. Review the subordinate's work history, prior disciplinary record, and the nature and cause of the specific violation.

b. Make certain of the exact limits of his authority as specified by department policy, especially with respect to restrictions on penalties imposed. The ramifications of a supervisor exceeding his authority in these cases are severe even when an honest mistake is made. If the supervisor has any doubt concerning the extent of his authority, he should check with his own boss.

c. Research how similar matters have been handled in the recent past. This is important to insure the consistency that is so vital if the disciplinary system is to be fair and equitable to all employees.

d. Review and consider all of the circumstances which were involved in the incident in question.

The Disciplinary Action Interview

A disciplinary action interview is conducted by an immediate supervisor to inform a subordinate of the results of an investigation made by that supervisor into the subordinate's alleged job-related misconduct. During this interview the employee is also informed of the nature of any punishment to be imposed as a result of confirmed misconduct. This interview should be held as quickly as possible after the supervisor's fact-finding effort discussed above is completed. If an inordinate delay is unavoidable, the accused subordinate should be informed of that fact and of the cause of the delay. The following guidelines for conducting this interview should be adhered to by the supervisor:

a. Hold the interview at a time and in a place that ensures privacy and allows freedom from interruption.

b. Have all of the essential facts available during the interview and review those facts just prior to the interview.

c. Be sure to respect confidential sources of information. If the disciplinary matter being resolved was initiated by a tip from one of the subordinate's peers or from a member of the community, there is no justification for revealing the identity of that person. There is, however, significant justification for protecting that person's identity even if the person did not specifically request such protection. In these cases, it is essential that the provider of information be shielded from any and all forms of retribution. Of course, any information supplied by such a person must be corroborated by the supervisor before it can be used against an employee.

d. Be serious, but do not treat the subordinate like an adversary. On the contrary, try to convince the subordinate that helping him is a high priority.

e. Use facts to make your case and not conjecture. Try to get agreement on key points.

f. Listen carefully for new information. "Let the employee speak—be a good listener; don't rush the meeting. Allow the employee to give his or her side of the story. A good rule is to show that you are listening by asking questions that indicate you are receiving the message being delivered."[9]

g. Communicate that the behavior that occurred is in question, not the subordinate himself. "To elicit a positive response, the supervisor must be sincere, criticize performance rather than attack an employee's character, and try to project a positive attitude."[10]

h. Attempt to convince the subordinate of the need for improvement, if such a need exists, and try to get a commitment from the subordinate to do his best in the future.

i. Practice empathy.

j. Ask if the subordinate has a personal problem, and offer assistance if such a problem exists. But, make it a point that the existence of a personal problem does not excuse misconduct.

k. Set specific time frames for any agreed upon course of action.

l. Check for understanding by having the subordinate summarize key points in his own words.

m. End the interview on a positive note.

The Importance of Follow-Up

In all cases where work-related misconduct was confirmed, it is essential that supervisors follow up shortly after a disciplinary

246

action interview. "The ultimate purpose of disciplinary action is, of course, to assure good productivity by developing good discipline. Its aim is to reduce repetition of disobedience. It cannot repair the damage done. Hence, disciplinary action must be evaluated in terms of its effectiveness after it has been applied. That means more careful supervision of those who were disciplined."[11]

OBSTACLES TO THE EFFECTIVE ADMINISTRATION OF DISCIPLINE

Maintaining an acceptable level of overall discipline is an essential task of all supervisors. There are obstacles to overcome, mistakes that can be made, and pitfalls to be avoided. These are some of the more common obstacles:

a. Being Overly Reliant on the Fear of Negative Discipline

It is a serious mistake for supervisors to immediately resort to the threat of negative discipline when things go wrong. These supervisors erroneously believe that threats are their greatest asset and they overuse them. Some of them make this mistake because they know that relying on negative discipline requires less effort than engaging in positive discipline. What makes matters confusing is that this negative approach can often be successful in the short run. After a period of time, however, threats lose their motivating force, and the supervisor finds himself backed into a corner. These supervisors usually do not learn until it is too late that the system won't tolerate a boss who institutes an inordinate number of formal disciplinary actions.

b. Being Overly Lenient

Some supervisors, especially newly promoted ones, erroneously believe that being lenient will make them popular with the troops and that popularity is the key to their success. In the real world, supervisors who are too lenient make their jobs more difficult in the long run. Many workers will not hesitate to take advantage of a boss who looks the other way when a violation takes place. Instead of gaining popularity, the supervisor loses respect. The situation is aggravated by the fact that it is difficult, if not impossible, for a lenient boss to reverse his approach. Conversely, new supervisors who start out being extremely firm can gradually ease up as they gain confidence, experience, knowledge, and understanding of the personality of each worker under their supervision. "It is always easier to begin with a firm approach, with the emphasis on the letter of the law. As you gain self-confidence and knowledge of your duties, you can shift your emphasis to the spirit of the law and temper your judgments within the framework of the company policies."[12]

c. Acting with Incomplete Information

Things aren't always as they seem. It is wrong to assume the worst when things go wrong. Before accusations of wrongdoing are leveled, a supervisor must make certain he has enough information to sustain such accusations. Internal resolution of a disciplinary matter is administrative in nature and does not require that an employee be proven guilty beyond a reasonable doubt. In the absence of some contractual or local rule to the contrary, the standard of proof that should be established is a "preponderance of the evidence." This, of course, means that more than half of the evidence available must point to an employee's guilt before a judgment of guilt is rendered.

d. Inadequate Case Preparation

The consequences of a finding of "not guilty" in a formal administrative tribunal (whether it be the initial formal disciplinary hearing or an appeals proceeding) is extremely damaging to the supervisor and to the agency. The acquitted employee seldom forgives the agency and usually remains, at best, a marginal employee who criticizes the agency at every opportunity. In most cases, fellow workers side with their colleague. In short, the morale of all concerned suffers. For these reasons, once a supervisor is convinced of the need for negative discipline in a particular matter, it is imperative that he be adequately prepared to establish guilt. He must act on the premise that he will be vigorously cross-examined in every case which involves a formal administrative hearing, in the same manner that law enforcement officers are cross-examined during a criminal trial in which they are the arresting officers. The backbone of the supervisor's case must be verifiable facts, and he should not rely in any way on speculation. It is vital that detailed notes are made and kept for future reference. It is not uncommon for long periods of time to pass between the administering of negative discipline and an appeal from that action. Unless they are written down, it is a strong possibility that many relevant details in such cases will be forgotten.

e. Public Disciplining

Criticism should, with one exception, be a private matter. There is no justification for unnecessarily damaging a worker's reputation and/or self esteem by ridicule or embarrassment. The one exception to this rule occurs when, in order to terminate inappropriate ongoing conduct, it becomes necessary for a supervisor to do or say something in the presence of others that is easily interpreted as being critical of a subordinate. For example, a supervisor must immediately intervene in a situation where a subordinate is being verbally abusive of a citizen even if a number of other officers are present. Such public display of criticism should be limited to whatever is necessary to terminate the inappropriate conduct. Any further discussion in the matter must be held in a private setting.

f. Being Vengeful

It is unethical for a supervisor to allow his personal biases to affect the way he treats his subordinates. Consistent enforcement of rules is the cornerstone of maintaining orderliness in the work group. Even so, some supervisors often yield to the temptation to single out and personally attack certain workers only because they dislike them. These supervisors fail to realize that it is impossible to mask unfair treatment over a long period of time. And, quite often, the unmasking occurs during formal disciplinary hearings which in turn results in decisions unfavorable to the supervisor. This, in turn, could and should result in the supervisor facing disciplinary action. Personality conflicts are bound to occur. But the only time an employee's personality should be the subject of disciplining action is when his or her personality interferes with job performance or has been problematic in relationships in the department and community.

g. Ignoring Anonymous Information

There is often much value in anonymous information. Unfortunately, some supervisors discount such information in the belief that the supplier of the information is seeking to create a problem for one or more officers for some vindictive purpose. While this is may be true in some instances, if the information is factual and does result in the discovery of wrongdoing, then the motives of the supplier of the information are irrelevant. In many cases the individuals who supply anonymous information are well-intentioned people who are aware of the possible negative ramifications of going public with their information. In any case one thing is certain: a supervisor who does not follow up on anonymous information is ignoring his responsibility to help maintain a high-level of overall discipline.

h. Inappropriate Transfer of Personnel

Supervisors must understand that assignments should be based on ability and not inability. In the management of personnel, transfer of personnel is an entirely legitimate and necessary management tool. Some of the proper uses of personnel transfer are: to increase the versatility of workers via different exposure, to meet fluctuations in workloads, and to allow for equitable distribution of opportunities for promotion and desirable working conditions. But, as a general rule, it is a poor management practice for a supervisor to use transfer to pass a problem subordinate to another supervisor. Instead, supervisors should rely on consistent application of discipline to deal with problem employees. Transfers should only be considered after all other disciplinary alternatives have proven unsuccessful. There are times when a change in environment will solve a problem. But, such a transfer should never be made without adequate notification to the new supervisor of the reasons for the transfer.

TEST YOUR UNDERSTANDING

1. Discuss the differences between positive discipline and negative discipline.

2. Does punishment always have to be certain to accomplish its purpose? Discuss.

3. Does punishment always have to be swift to accomplish its purpose? Discuss.

4. Does punishment always have to be severe to accomplish its purpose? Discuss.

5. Who has the primary responsibility to administer both positive and negative discipline? Discuss.

6. Should a supervisor act every time he observes a violation of agency rules and regulations? Discuss.

7. Why is it important for an agency to rescind outdated rules and regulations?

8. Discuss the elements of a fair and equitable disciplinary system.

9. Is deciding upon an appropriate punishment an easy or difficult task? Discuss.

10. Discuss the guidelines for the holding of a disciplinary action interview.

11. Discuss the obstacles to the effective administration of discipline.

FOOTNOTES

1. Dale S. Beach, *Personnel - The Management of People at Work,* 5th ed. (New York: MacMillan Publishing Company, 1985), p. 373.

2. Keith Davis, Ph.D. and John W. Newstrom, Ph.D., *Human Behavior at Work - Organizational Behavior,* 8th ed. (New York: McGraw-Hill Publishing Co., 1989), p. 424.

3. Michael J. Jucius, Ph.D., *Personnel Management,* 9th ed. (Homewood, IL: Richard D. Irwin, Inc., 1979), p. 475.

4. Davis and Newstrom, p. 425.

5. Jack Halloran, *Supervision - The Act of Management.* (Englewood Cliffs, NJ: Prentice-Hall, Inc., 1981), p. 196.

6. Donald P. Crane, *Personnel: The Management of Human Resources,* 2nd ed. (Belmont, CA: Wadsworth Publishing Co., 1979), p. 201.

7. John M. Ivancevich and William F. Glueck, *Foundations of Personnel/Human Resource Management.* (Plano, TX: Business Productions Inc., 1986), p. 571.

8. Beach, p. 378.

9. Ivancevich and Glueck, p. 586.

10. Crane, p. 205.

11. Jucius, p. 475.

12. Halloran, p. 202.

SUGGESTED READINGS

Baer, Walter E.
Discipline and Discharge Under the Labor Agreement.
New York: American Management Associations, 1972.

Benton, Lewis R.
Supervision and Management.
New York: McGraw-Hill Book Co., 1972.

Bradford, Boyd.
Management - Minded Supervision.
New York: McGraw-Hill Book Co., 1976.

Byars, Lloyd L. and Leslie W. Rue.
Personnel Management: Concepts and Applications.
Philadelphia, PA: W.B. Saunders Company, 1972.

Harrison, Edward L.
"Legal Restrictions on the Employer's Authority to Discipline."
Personnel Journal, Vol. 61, No. 2 (Feb. 1982)

Higgins, James M.
Human Relations - Behavior at Work, 2nd ed.
New York: Random House, 1987.

Luthans, Fred and Mark Martinko.
The Practice of Supervision and Management.
New York: McGraw-Hill Book Co., 1979.

Pigors, Paul and Charles Myers.
Personnel Administration.
New York: McGraw-Hill Book Co., 1977.

Van Dersah, William R.
The Successful Supervisor in Government and Business, 4th ed.
New York: Harper and Row Publishers, 1985.

CHAPTER 11
THE SUPERVISOR AND COMPLAINTS FROM SUBORDINATES

DEFINING COMPLAINTS FROM SUBORDINATES

There are many types of complaints, as the definition bears out: a complaint is an expression of grief, regret, discomfort, dissatisfaction, pain, censure, or resentment. Supervisors should not get involved in all of the complaints of their subordinates. Such a "mother hen" supervisory style is entirely inappropriate. On the other hand, supervisors who do not get involved in certain employee complaints, by their lack of action, seriously endanger both employee morale and productivity. It is important, therefore, for supervisors to know which employee complaints merit supervisory intervention and which do not.

For purposes of supervisory intervention, a complaint is any action or statement by a subordinate which comes to the attention of a manager and which clearly indicates displeasure concerning an on-the-job relationship or a condition of employment. These are the complaints which require some form of supervisory intervention. For purposes of this discussion, complaints which require supervisory intervention will be referred to as "work-related complaints." If work-related complaints are ignored or improperly handled in their early stages, they can grow and fester into serious problems. Little problems become big problems if they are not addressed quickly and effectively. "To avoid having to file a formal grievance, the strategy for the supervisor is to take care of small complaints quickly as they develop—this step will avoid larger ones later on."[1] Of all managers, the key ones to address employee complaints in a timely and effective manner are the immediate supervisors.

Key Points Concerning Work-Related Complaints

The following are key points about the definition of work-related complaints which supervisors must understand:

1. Work-related complaints do not have to be fully verbalized to merit supervisory intervention. As indicated above, any action or statement which clearly indicates displeasure sufficiently

warrants intervention. This doesn't mean that a supervisor must hold a private meeting with a subordinate every time he hears a complaint. But it is a supervisor's responsibility to watch for situations which have the potential to evolve into major complaints from subordinates, and to intervene as soon as possible. To meet this responsibility, supervisors should familiarize themselves with the most common symptoms of employee dissatisfaction such as a sudden deterioration in performance, excessive lateness, and a pattern of absenteeism on the first scheduled work day after regularly scheduled weekly leave.

2. Supervisors must intervene as described above in any work related employee complaint regardless of the merits of the complaint. Sometimes complaints are based upon a person's perception rather than on the reality of a situation. Therefore, some complaints have a subjective base, while others have an objective base. "Even if you know there is no basis for the complaint, the employee thinks there is. Therefore, if it is important enough for the employee to bring it to your attention, it should be treated as an important complaint by you."[2] For the person with a complaint, perception can be reality. If a supervisor is not sensitive to a complaint just because it is based on the employee's misunderstanding, lack of knowledge, faulty perceptions and the like, the employee with the complaint will grow hostile and resentment will set in. Quite often, this hostility and resentment spreads. "[B]eing heard can lessen that sense of being 'dismissed' and powerlessness that will trigger an even greater outpouring of complaints."[3]

The Scope of Employee Complaints

Employee complaints which require supervisory intervention fall into two broad categories.

1. Complaints that are sensory in nature. These are complaints which can be evaluated by means of the human senses. Such complaints can involve tangible objects that can be felt and touched, such as department-issued portable radios that do not work well or patrol cars with faulty brakes. They could also involve non-tangible matters, such as insufficient ventilation, or excessive noise.

2. Complaints that are non-sensory in nature, such as low pay, outdated work rules, or harassment.

Complaints that fall into the first category are easier to verify since they are more objective. They are more objective because they are easily validated. For example, either a portable radio works or it doesn't. Once confirmed, they are also the easiest ones to resolve unless such resolution requires a significant expenditure of funds.

Complaints that fall into the second category are much more difficult to deal with since they are more subjective and are not easily verified. For example, what exactly is considered a low pay scale? Then, even if such complaints are verifiable, their resolution is often extremely difficult, if not impossible. If a pay scale is established as being too low, what can a supervisor do about raising it? For such complaints, it is the attitude and manner with which a supervisor deals with them that is vitally important. If the supervisor does everything within his power to resolve an employee complaint and fails to do so, the supervisor's stock in the mind of the employee could nevertheless go way up because the "boss" tried.

Characteristics of an Effective Employee Complaint System

An effective employee complaint system is one which provides for the acceptance and investigation of all work-related complaints. An agency that has such a system safeguards itself against charges of apathy or lack of concern for its employees. In addition, faulty agency policies and procedures are often uncovered as a result of employee complaints. For this reason, an effective employee complaint system is viewed by some management experts as a form of quality control.

While the operation of an effective employee complaint system is somewhat expensive, the return that is realized in the form of increased morale and productivity more than offsets this expense. While the specifics of any agency's employee complaint system vary from agency to agency, to be effective, such systems must contain the following characteristics:

Effective Complaint Systems Should Have More than One Entrance Point, and Anonymous Complaints Should Be Accepted

It is not a good management practice to insist that workers identify themselves in order to lodge a formal work-related complaint. A worker who wants to make such a complaint, but doesn't want to be associated with making it, should have a way to make that complaint. Remember, it has been established time and time again that anonymous information often proves to be valuable. Therefore, at a minimum, every agency should have and publicize to their employees at least two ways for employee complaints to be lodged. One way should always involve the complaining worker making his complaint directly to his immediate supervisor. Another method could be either a suggestion box system or a telephone hotline setup for employees to use anonymously. In any case, an employee who desires anonymity should always be accommodated. Likewise, an employee who is willing to identify himself to the investigator of a complaint but prefers to otherwise remain anonymous should also be accommodated.

Effective Complaint Systems Should Protect Those Who Complain

Fear of reprisal is the single biggest reason why management does not become aware of work-related employee complaints soon enough to prevent widespread problems. "Some workers fear supervisory retaliation if they present a grievance, especially if they win it. It is important for supervisors to convince workers that they want to hear grievances and to settle them. Supervisors should approach grievances in a problem-solving frame of mind, rather than with the idea: 'This is a fight—it's either them or me.'"[5] Every agency should have a well-publicized policy which forbids reprisals against those workers who make work-related complaints. In the event that such a policy is violated, punitive action must be taken against those responsible. If workers believe that reprisals will be made against those who complain, then hostility can develop and productivity and morale will certainly suffer. Supervisors should, therefore, encourage the registering of complaints and demonstrate that reprisals won't occur. This will allow the employee to feel safe. It also helps for supervisors to adopt the attitude that complaints are inevitable and they offer supervisors an opportunity to enhance relationships with subordinates.

Effective Employee Complaint Systems Should Provide for Equitable and Objective Investigations Into All Complaints

Employee complaint systems are worthless unless they assure complaining parties of an equitable and objective investigation by a neutral party, preferably the immediate supervisor of the complaining member, unless that supervisor is in some way involved in the complaint. The investigator must have the authority to either take corrective action or recommend that corrective action be taken to resolve valid complaints. "When complaints do arise, every reasonable effort must be made to settle the majority of complaints at the level where the complaint originated."[4] When it is not possible for the immediate supervisor to be neutral, as when the immediate supervisor is directly involved, some other manager must be given this investigative responsibility. Who this other manager is depends on agency policy and the circumstances of the complaint.

It is imperative that each and every anonymous complaint be investigated. Anonymous complaints which do not require corrective action should be closed only after it has been satisfactorily established that the complaint has no merit. The problem with the investigation of anonymous complaints is well known to law enforcement people. Quite often, without additional information from the maker of the complaint about the specifics of the complaint, the investigation fails. Because of this, complainants in sensitive cases should identify themselves only to the investigator of the complaint. Note, however, that while such a provision makes for more successful complaint investigations, it also increases the chances of anonymous complainants being identified and thereby undermining the credibility of the entire complaint system.

Effective Complaint Systems Should Provide Feedback on the Disposition of Complaints

The most common weakness of employee complaint systems is a failure to provide feedback on the dispositions of lodged complaints. Bear in mind that many complaints are based on a worker's assumption that an inequity exists. But often it is determined that the inequity was the result of the worker's misunderstanding of the facts. In such cases, no corrective action is required and none is taken. Yet, in many such cases, no effort is made to inform the complainant of the findings of the investigation. And, in a great majority of such cases, no effort is ever made to inform the general worker population of such findings. This, despite the fact that the supplying of feedback about the results of complaint investigations has the potential to strengthen confidence in the complaint system. It also serves to reduce the multiple lodging of the same complaint. For these reasons it is strongly recommended that all agencies keep their employees informed about employee complaints made and the disposition of such complaints.

Effective Complaint Systems Should Have an Appeals Process

An employee complaint system will not be fully accepted by workers unless there is an appeals process built into it. Furthermore, supervisors should not view an employee's decision to appeal as a personal affront. Those authorized to hear appeals must always support sensible and logical decisions rendered by supervisors. In cases where such a decision made in good faith is reversed, the supervisor must be given a way to save face. If, for example, an otherwise sensible decision was improper because of information not known to the supervisor, then the entire matter should be referred back to that supervisor to reconsider in the light of the additional information.

PREVENTING COMPLAINTS

Supervisors should have a preventive approach toward complaints which seeks to uncover and eliminate those conditions and practices which are fertile ground for complaints. The following is a listing of the most common causes of work-related employee complaints along with recommendations designed to minimize the impact of these causes.

Inappropriate Supervisory Practices

Workers want to be respected by their supervisors. Very few, if any, complaints are generated simply because a supervisor finds it necessary to instruct or criticize a subordinate. However, many complaints emerge because of the manner in which a supervisor instructs or criticizes. This further supports our position that a supervisor's interpersonal skills are his most important asset. There is never sufficient justification to belittle or ridicule a worker. Conversely, supervisors should always show concern for the feelings of their subordinates. Supervisors will prevent many complaints if they apply the principles in this text. Most especially they should:

1. Refrain from the use of vulgar or intemperate language.
2. Refrain from playing favorites.
3. Give public recognition for good performance.
4. Criticize in private whenever possible.
5. Enforce rules and regulations in a consistent manner.
6. Rely primarily on positive discipline to deal with minor violations.

Violations of the Provisions of Collective Bargaining Agreements

In those agencies which have collective bargaining agreements, violations of these agreements generate a significant number of complaints. Many of these violations occur simply because supervisors are not sufficiently aware of the terms of the collective bargaining agreement. Of all the common causes of work-related employee complaints, violations of contractual provisions are the easiest ones to avoid.

Such avoidance can be achieved by:

1. Publication by agency administrators of those provisions of the collective bargaining agreement that regulate the making of personnel decisions.

2. Publication by agency administrators of the specifics of those cases in which employee complaints concerning contractual violations were upheld.

3. Inclusion by agency administrators of a review of pertinent contractual provisions in the supervisory training curriculum.

4. Direct liaison at the local level among supervisors and employee representatives of the recognized employee collective bargaining unit, who are often referred to as delegates. Far too often, supervisors create relationships with these delegates which can only be described as adversarial. Supervisors often overlook the fact that the primary function of delegates is to insure that workers are treated in accordance with the terms of the contract. Since such treatment is—or should be—also a major concern of supervisors, a liaison between a supervisor and the delegate representing that supervisor's subordinates is the best way to avoid inadvertent contractual violations.

Physical Plant and Equipment Problems

Dissatisfaction with the working environment creates a large portion of employee complaints. Such complaints range from dissatisfaction with outdated facilities to complaints about shoddy maintenance. Since these complaints are easily verified but not easily resolved, if the resolution requires a significant expenditure of funds, they present a significant challenge to supervisors. This challenge can best be met by bringing these complaints to the attention of higher authorities (through the chain of command) and by taking vigorous action to correct those deficiencies which do not require significant capital outlay. Maintaining the cleanliness of the physical plant, for example, should be a top priority. One final note: supervisors must be relentless in their efforts to bring about repair or replacement of any deficiency in the physical plant or with operating equipment which impacts on safety, regardless of any economic

262

considerations. It is one thing to put up with outdated restroom facilities and quite another to tolerate faulty two-way radios. Should such safety problems continue after calling them to the attention of higher authorities, supervisors are obligated to lodge their own complaints.

Outdated Agency Rules and Regulations

Outdated rules and regulations generate many employee complaints which, in turn, present a significant dilemma for supervisors attempting to enforce them. The dilemma is that supervisors often cannot present any logical reason for their enforcement. Their only recourse is to quote the rules and insist on compliance.

Prime examples are regulations which are viewed by employees as infringements of their individual rights, especially when such regulations impact on their off-duty conduct, such as rules which control where they live and what they say, e.g., their criticism of the agency. Another example involves personal appearance. Rules governing facial hair and jewelry create significant employee dissatisfaction, some which is justifiable in view of the changing norms of society.

When rules generally viewed by employees as unnecessary are reviewed and determined appropriate, the supporting rationale should be circulated throughout the agency. This is an extremely important responsibility of management since workers tend to accept rules more readily when they understand the necessity for the rules.

Uncovering Employee Complaints

The supervisor who sits back and waits for specific complaints to come to him is making a mistake. The pro-active supervisor has his ear to the ground, hears problems coming and deals with them before they generate complaints. Employees take their complaints to supervisors who they have learned to trust. As a general rule, a newly appointed supervisor hears complaints only through the grapevine. Once a supervisor earns a reputation as being truly interested in resolving complaints, more and more of his subordinates will bring such complaints directly to him.

RECEIVING COMPLAINTS

In most cases, it is the immediate supervisor who should accept, investigate, and resolve the majority of work-related employee complaints. All such complaints, even those which have no basis in fact, must be treated seriously. "Even with chronic complainers, it's good to keep in mind that this time around, the grievance may be justified. Just because you've heard it before—'that jerk in statistical services really fouls us up'—doesn't mean it isn't true this time. Or perhaps this particular person is the only one with the courage to tell you....Listening, coupled with solution-oriented questions about the problem, makes sure that you don't make false assumptions about the validity, or lack of validity, of complaints."[6]

It is often quite traumatic for an employee to bring himself to make a complaint. Much damage to the subordinate-supervisor relationship can occur if the supervisor receiving an imagined complaint treats the complaint too lightly or, worse yet, ridicules or belittles a subordinate for his erroneous perceptions. An "open door" policy—being available and anxious to assist subordinates—is the best way to develop the trust necessary for subordinates to risk making complaints. "The kind of boss someone can talk to is a boss who will always listen carefully, take even seemingly small complaints seriously, be available, and show care and concern."[7]

Too many supervisors view the fact that they receive very few complaints as meaning that all is well. A scarcity of employee complaints is probably indicative of a supervisor who, for some reason, has not yet won the trust of his subordinates. This probability becomes a certainty if it can be established that the subordinates of such a supervisor are lodging of complaints via the system's alternative entrance point. A supervisor who finds himself in this position must understand that the situation can be reversed through hard work. He should re-evaluate his supervisory approach and make a concerted effort to establish sound human relations with his subordinates.

HANDLING COMPLAINTS

Handling employee complaints is a severe test of a supervisor's technical skills, his interpersonal skills, and his analytical skills. More than any other task, resolving employee complaints requires all of a supervisor's skills. Without question, however, the most difficult task of investigating a complaint occurs when it is determined that the employee is being unfairly treated by a higher internal or external authority. In such a case, the ambivalent role of the supervisor demands that the supervisor support the employee's complaint. "In handling an employee's complaint, follow all of the appropriate guidelines. Be willing to take the employee's complaint to a higher level if you believe that he is right. If you disagree with him, tell him the reasons for your disagreeing."[8] When supporting a complaint in this manner there are two extremely important guidelines that must be followed. First, the supervisor should avoid any attempt to fix blame for the unfairness. Who is to blame is not the important issue, resolving the complaint is. Second, supporting arguments must be in the form of communicable facts and not suspicions or hunches.

The supervisor who follows these two guidelines will grow in the eyes of both his superiors and his subordinates.

Steps in Dealing with Complaints

The following steps outline the process of handling work-related employee complaints:

Receive the Complaint Properly

Complaints should not be taken on the run. It is vital for a supervisor to give the complaining employee an attentive and complete hearing without interference. The amount of time needed to be set aside depends on the complexity of the complaint. A supervisor who does not have sufficient time available to discuss the complaint fully should schedule an appointment to receive the complaint as soon as possible. If, however, the nature of the complaint clearly indicates the need for immediate action, the supervisor should clear his schedule and commence an investigation as soon as possible.

The guidelines when receiving the complaint are:

1. Remain calm. Understand ahead of time that employees with complaints are prone to become upset and agitated. Supervisors are expected to remain calm and in control of the situation even in the face of emotion and agitation. Effective problem solving cannot take place in the absence of self control on the part of the investigator.

2. Do not begin the inquiry by using a series of pointed questions to get the facts involved in the complaint. Instead, begin by having the worker tell the story in his own words. As the employee's account unfolds, try to get him to discuss his feelings and motives as well as his perception of the facts.

3. Take notes as the employee relates his story. In addition to the value of recording what is being said, note taking serves to indicate to the worker that you are taking his complaint seriously.

4. Refrain from passing judgment, offering opinions, or otherwise interrupting as the employee's story unfolds. Concentrate on the perceptions of the employee. The time to give your opinions and/or to ask clarifying questions comes later in the interview.

5. While listening, try to determine the real cause of the complaint. Quite often, the complaint as originally stated changes form as the discussion continues, and the actual pressing issue emerges. Only when the true problem is isolated can the employee's complaint be resolved.

6. Don't interrupt just because the employee is engaged in a certain amount of repetition. Talking about one's problems with an empathetic listener is therapeutic. "Putting problems into words provides a release for frustration, fear, anger over assumed slights—any of the myriad feelings that can underlie something that's gone wrong."[9] Having to clarify one's thoughts so as to accurately communicate them to another often makes a person come to sensible conclusions on his own.

7. After hearing the complaint without interruption, the supervisor should ask questions designed to clear up details that are not clear to him. Then the supervisor should repeat the essentials of the story back to the employee to make sure that there is mutual agreement about what is being said. Unless the

supervisor makes certain at this point that accurate communication has taken place, everything that follows could very well be a waste of time.

Determine the Status of the Complaint

After allowing the employee to talk in detail about the complaint, and after confirming that accurate communication has taken place, the next step for the supervisor to take is to determine the status of the complaint. The supervisor does this by analyzing the facts and fitting the complaint into one of the three following categories:

1. No valid complaint exists.
2. A valid complaint exists which has an immediate remedy.
3. A valid complaint exists which has no immediate remedy.

Take Action or Defer Action Depending on the Status of the Case

The steps toward resolving the complaint depend on the status of the complaint:

1. No Valid Complaint Exists.

In many instances, the employee comes to the conclusion that his complaint is not valid as result of going over the details with a supervisor. However, if after relating his story the employee still believes he has a legitimate complaint, the supervisor must convince him otherwise by using facts. It is a big mistake at this point for the supervisor to simply tell the employee that his complaint is not a legitimate one. The supervisor's position must be buttressed by facts.

If the supervisor is unsure of the facts or needs more information, he should state that to the employee. At that time a follow-up interview should be scheduled. The course of action to be taken at the follow-up meeting depends on the specifics of the facts discovered.

2. *A Valid Complaint Exists Which Has an Immediate Remedy.*

If the complaint is one which the supervisor is authorized to attempt to resolve, either by agency policy or the provisions of an existing collective bargaining agreement, and if no more facts have to be gathered or verified, the supervisor should act immediately to resolve the complaint. To do this, the supervisor should ask the subordinate for his recommended solution. If the employee suggests an appropriate solution, then the supervisor should accept it. Or, at the very least, the supervisor should attempt to use the employee's suggested solution as the basis for a compromise solution. Remember, when a complaint can be solved in a number of ways, the best way to solve it is the way the employee thinks it should be solved, as long as the employee's solution is appropriate. The reasoning behind this is simple: people work harder to make solutions work if they have direct input into the solution.

In those cases where the course of action decided upon is not one suggested by the employee, it is imperative that the supervisor explain the reasons for his decision. If agency rules or regulations are involved, quote them and explain their applicability to the situation.

3. *A Valid Complaint Exists Which Has No Immediate Remedy.*

If the complaint is such that, because of agency policy or provisions of an existing collective bargaining agreement, it must be resolved by a higher authority, then resolution must be deferred. Here it is imperative that the complaining employee be given a specific time frame within which an answer can be expected. In these cases the supervisor is responsible for making sure the employee is presented with the decision as soon as it is available. The reasons for any decisions subsequently reached must be carefully explained to the complaining employee.

Explain the Appeals Process

Workers presented with decisions regarding complaints they have made must always be told of the steps they can take to appeal those decisions. A supervisor should encourage a dissatisfied worker to appeal. Such a response is often what is needed to convince the employee that the decision rendered is appropriate. If the supervisor does his job as outlined above, he has nothing to fear from an appeal. Even if it is determined upon appeal that the supervisor made an honest mistake, if the system is designed the way it should be, then the supervisor will be given a way to save face. For example, if a supervisor's decision was predicated on a misinterpretation of a certain policy, the supervisor should be given the correct interpretation and be told to reconsider his decision. In that way the supervisor can avoid the impression that he was forced by higher authority to reverse himself.

Keep Superiors Informed

A supervisor who takes corrective action to resolve a valid work-related employee complaint, should put all the facts in a written memorandum and forward it to his boss. Supervisors have an obligation to keep management informed of negative as well as positive developments. A copy of this memo should be retained by the supervisor in the event that any decisions have to be defended before an appeals board.

Engage in Follow-up

In all cases, good supervisory practices mandate that supervisors touch base with employees who have lodged complaints within a reasonable period of time after a resolution to that problem was implemented. This follow-up is important for two reasons: (1) to make certain that the problem has been solved, and (2) to reassure the employee that his lodging of the complaint will not be held against him. The follow-up should include a sincere invitation from the supervisor to bring any additional complaints directly to him.

COMPLAINTS INVOLVING A COLLECTIVE BARGAINING AGREEMENT

Some management experts refer to all work-related complaints as grievances and then make a distinction between contractual grievances and non-contractual grievances. Others, including your authors, feel that the difference between contractual and non-contractual complaints is so important that it is best to use two different terms. The term we recommend when referring to a complaint which alleges a violation of an existing collective bargaining agreement (commonly known as the "contract") is a "grievance." "A grievance—whether by a single worker or by the entire union—is a complaint that management is violating some provision of the union contract."[10] For our purposes, a grievance is a special kind of work-related complaint.

The Handling of Grievances Must Be As Stated in the Contract

The cardinal rule for dealing with grievances is that they must be handled in accordance with the terms of the contract. Supervisors must understand that there is never sufficient justification for violating the contract. Furthermore, unless otherwise stated in the contract, employees cannot voluntarily exempt themselves from the provisions of the contract. In actual practice, grievances are usually handled in the same manner as all other work related complaints. This is because most collective bargaining agreements allow for resolution of grievances at the local level. The first procedural step in the formal grievance agreement between Teamsters Union Local 695 and the County of Waukesha, Wisconsin Sheriff's Department, is: "1. The employee and/or his Union representative shall attempt to settle the issue with the immediate supervisor."[11] Because of the value of resolving complaints expediently at the local level, in agencies where this is not the case managers should make it a priority to amend the contract, if possible, to make it that way.

The Primary Difference Between Handling Employee Complaints in General and Handling Grievances

The primary difference between handling complaints in general and handling grievances is in the procedures to follow if resolution cannot be achieved at the local level by immediate supervisors. In both instances supervisors forward a written summary to a higher authority for resolution. When the complaint is other than a grievance, the higher authority considers the complaint itself and the mandates of department policy. In

270

these cases, the decision of the higher authority is final. Unless the complaining employee takes the matter to court, it is never subject to external review.

When the unresolved complaint is a grievance, the procedure is much more structured, as it is in all instances controlled by the wording of the contract. This structure usually includes definitive time frames which must be followed. In addition, the typical contract provides for some type of external arbitration should internal attempts at resolution fail.

The Contractual Grievance Procedure and Other Guidelines for Handling Grievances

To avoid improper handling of grievances as well as confrontations with the authorized employee bargaining unit, supervisors should be well-versed with the grievance procedure as it is contained in the collective bargaining agreement (which should be reproduced and available to all employees as part of the agency's written procedures). In addition, supervisors should be aware of the following guidelines concerning grievances:

a. A supervisor should begin his investigation of every alleged grievance with the assumption that it has merit.

b. A supervisor investigating a grievance must have at his disposal the specific wording of that portion of the contract that was allegedly violated.

c. Grievances should never be settled outside of the terms of the contract, even if the employee agrees to such a settlement.

d. Supervisors must never negotiate an agreement to settle one grievance in exchange for the withdrawal of a different grievance. While this type of trading is appropriate at a higher managerial level when such negotiation is being conducted with the employee's collective bargaining representatives, it is never appropriate at the local level.

e. Supervisors should never deviate from the precise wording of the contract when attempting to resolve grievances.

DOCUMENTING COMPLAINTS

All work-related complaints, including grievances, should be documented in writing by the supervisor who took the complaint. However, the extent of this required documentation varies depending on the circumstances. For example, written reports concerning relatively minor complaints which are resolved at the local level can be informal and brief. Conversely, when a written report concerning an employee's complaint is going to be used by a higher authority to resolve a complaint which cannot be resolved at the local level, the written report involved must be quite comprehensive and specific. Such a comprehensive written report is also required in cases where a higher authority is considering an employee's appeal or when higher authorities are ruling on an employee's grievance.

Contents of a Comprehensive and Specific Employee Complaint/Grievance Report

A comprehensive written report of a complaint, including a grievance, should include the following information if available. (Note: when any of this information is not available, the reasons why must be addressed in the report. Also note: when there are conflicting opinions, each opinion must be included.):

a. The identity of the complaining member.

b. The identity of the supervisor who received the complaint.

c. The identity of all other employees and/or supervisors involved.

d. An explanation of the substance of the complaint. What is it all about?

e. If the complaint is a grievance, the specific section of the contract should be accurately stated.

f. The time frames involved in the complaint. If available, the exact time of occurrence should be included. If the complaint is about something which continued over a period of time, the exact time periods involved, if available, must be included.

g. The locations involved in the complaint. Note that when the exact location is a critical consideration, a diagram must be included with exact measurements.

h. A statement explaining why the incident being complained of happened.

i. A statement outlining the remedial action being sought by the complaining member.

j. The recommendations of the investigating supervisor.

272

TEST YOUR UNDERSTANDING

1. Should supervisors intervene and try to resolve all of the complaints of their employees? Discuss.

2. Does a work-related employee complaint have to be supported by facts before it merits supervisory intervention? Discuss.

3. Name and discuss five characteristics of an effective employee complaint system.

4. Discuss four conditions or practices which commonly generate employee complaints.

5. Should a supervisor automatically conclude that all is well with his subordinates simply because no one is making any complaints to him? Discuss.

6. Identify and discuss the steps a supervisor should take when dealing with the work-related complaints of his subordinates.

7. What is a grievance? Are grievances handled differently than other work-related employee complaints? Discuss.

8. Discuss the documentation of work-related employee complaints.

FOOTNOTES

1. Natasha Josefowitz, Ph.D., *You're The Boss! - A Guide To Managing People With Understanding and Effectiveness.* (New York: Warner Books, Inc., 1985), p. 212.

2. Charles S. George, Jr., *Supervision In Action - The Act of Managing Others.* (Reston, VA: Reston Publishing Co., Inc., 1977), p. 158.

3. Robert M. Bramson, Ph.D., *Coping With Difficult People.* (New York: Anchor Press/Doubleday, 1981), p. 53.

4. Louis V. Imundo, *The Effective Supervisor's Handbook.* (New York: AMACOM, 1980), p. 182.

5. Keith Davis, Ph.D. and John W. Newstrom, Ph.D., *Human Behavior At Work - Organizational Behavior,* 8th ed. (New York: McGraw- Hill Book Co., 1989), p. 450.

6. Thomas L. Quick, *Person to Person Managing: An Executive's Guide to Working Effectively With People.* (New York: St. Martin's Press, 1977), pp. 63, 64.

7. Josefowitz, p. 87.

8. Imundo, p. 182.

9. Bramson, p. 53.

10. Louis E. Boone and David L. Kurtz, *Contemporary Business,* 4th ed. (Chicago, IL: The Dryden Press, 1985), p. 211.

11. Allen Z. Gammage, Ph.D. and Stanley L. Sachs, M.A., *Police Unions.* (Springfield, IL: Charles C. Thomas Publisher, 1972), p. 148.

SUGGESTED READINGS

Baer, Walter S.
Winning In Labor Arbitration.
Chicago, IL: Crain Books, 1982.

Edwards, Richard.
Rights At Work - Employment Relations
in the Post- Union Era.
New York: The Twentieth Century Fund, Inc., 1993.

Fulmer, Robert M.
Supervison: Principles of Professional Management.
Beverly Hills, CA: Glencoe Press, 1976.

Jandt, Fred E. and Paul Gillette.
Win-Win Negotiations: Turning Conflict Into Agreement.
New York: John Wiley and Sons, Inc., 1985.

McPherson, Donald S. with John Gates Conrad.
and Kevin N. Rogers.
Resolving Grievances - A Practical Approach.
Reston, VA: Reston Publishing Co., Inc., 1983.

Scott, William G.
The Management of Conflict - Appeal Systems in Organizations.
Homewood, IL: Richard D. Irwin, Inc. and
the Dorsey Press, 1965.

Trotta, Maurice S.
Handling Grievances - A Guide for Management and Labor.
Washington, D.C.: B.N.A., 1976.

CHAPTER 12
THE SUPERVISOR AND COMPLAINTS
AGAINST EMPLOYEES

DEFINING COMPLAINTS AGAINST EMPLOYEES

For our purposes, a complaint against an employee (or a personnel complaint) is an allegation of job-related wrongdoing or of criminal misconduct which is lodged against an employee of a law enforcement agency. The nature of the complaint may vary from a minor violation of organizational rules to a serious criminal violation. A personnel complaint must involve an allegation of job- related employee wrongdoing or criminal misconduct, therefore, not all complaints about the way an employee handled a situation qualify as personnel complaints.

Complaints About the Appropriateness of Established Procedures

Sometimes citizens who complain about a patrol officer's conduct are unknowingly complaining about agency policies or judicial decisions limiting the authority of the police. Quite often, citizens do not understand the reasoning and necessity for policies, rules or judicial decisions. In many instances citizens interpret an officer's unwillingness to take action as negligence or apathy, when in reality he is following the mandates of his agency. Misunderstanding then leads to complaints. For example, store owners often complain to the police about youth congregating in front of their stores. They want the police to make the youngsters move along. In most instances, however, the police do not have the authority to stop people from congregating in the streets. Consequently, when an officer fails to grant the store owner's request, he interprets the officer's non-intervention as an unwillingness to help and lodges a complaint against the officer.

When this type of complaint is made, and there is no other allegation of misconduct, it should not be classified as a personnel complaint. The onus is on the supervisor to explain the situation to the complainant. When the complaint is about an internal policy or rule, if appropriate, the supervisor should bring the matter to the attention of higher authorities.

Complaints About the Validity of Police Action

It is quite common for citizens to complain about the validity of summary police action involving the making of arrests or the issuance of citations. The most typical of these complaints is that the officer who took the summary action was mistaken and that the citizen is in fact "not guilty". Traffic incidents account for most of these complaints. Police supervisors are constantly dealing with complaints from citizens such as, "I wasn't speeding," or, "The light was green when I passed the intersection."

When such complaints do not also allege other misconduct, they should not be handled as personnel complaints. Instead, they should be referred for adjudication to the criminal court or administrative tribunal having jurisdiction. In these cases the supervisor should explain to the complainant that such matters must be resolved by someone representing the judicial branch of government, e.g., a judge or arbiter. In addition, the supervisor should supply the complainant with all the objective information he needs to have his day in court, such as the location of the court and the appointed times of the proceedings.

There are times when, after taking summary action, a police officer realizes he made a reasonable mistake. Most of these incidents involve the making of summary arrests. What typically occurs is that an officer, relying on information known to him at the time, arrests a person based on probable cause. But a continuing investigation reveals that the person arrested did not commit the crime charged or any related crime (or it is determined that no crime at all has been committed). When this occurs, unless contrary to the laws in the jurisdiction, the officer should release the arrested person as soon as he realizes that he no longer has probable cause. If possible, the officer should obtain the consent of his supervisor prior to effecting the release, but if this means continued detention of the arrested person in the absence of probable cause, then the release should be made without the supervisor's consent In all such cases, the releasing officer should inform his supervisor and submit a written report containing the circumstances of the initial arrest and the subsequent release.

278

DETERMINING THE MERITS OF ALL COMPLAINTS

The cardinal rule of handling personnel complaints is that all personnel complaints must be investigated as to their merit. "[P]olice agencies should accept all complaints, whether received in person, by telephone, by letter, or anonymously."[1] It is a mistake to dismiss such complaints out of hand. "[N]o member of any agency should have the authority to quash or 'informally handle' complaints because, for example, he or she believes that the complainant has spelled out no clear misconduct."[2]

If an initial inquiry into the merits of a personnel complaint does not reasonably support the existence of misconduct, then the case can be closed. But a decision to either close a case or pursue it further must be made based on all of the available facts. To act on a matter in the absence of all of the available facts is a basic error that supervisors must scrupulously avoid.

Accepting Anonymous Complaints

History supports the fact that some of the most serious and infamous instances of police misconduct were initiated by anonymous information. "It takes a considerable amount of courage to walk into a strange police station to complain about officers who work there, so police should be required to accept complaints, even if those who wish to lodge them choose to communicate by phone or letter, even anonymously."[3] Anonymous complaints must be investigated as to their merits.

TWO CATEGORIES OF PERSONNEL COMPLAINTS

Personnel complaints are classified into two distinct categories depending on the origin of the complaint: (1) external complaints and (2) internal complaints.

External Complaints

External personnel complaints come from someone not associated with the agency of the accused person. External complaints are further subdivided by the source of the complaint. If a complaint comes directly from someone who was victimized by the alleged misconduct, it is known as a "first person" complaint. If it comes from a representative of the victim (an attorney, a cleric, or an elected official) then it is referred to as a "spokesperson" complaint. Spokesperson complaints should never be rejected simply because they do not come directly from the victim. All personnel complaints, regardless of their source, must be investigated if only to determine the merits of the complaint.

Victimless Police Misconduct

On occasion, a personnel complaint is made by a civic-minded citizen who observes victimless police misconduct. For example, a citizen might report that he observed a police officer who appeared to be intoxicated. For our purposes this is considered to be a first-person complaint. Even though there was no victim, the complaint should be investigated in the same manner as any other first-person complaint. But, it is not necessary for the complainant to identify himself or to submit to an interview before any credence is given to his complaint. When there is no detailed information available, independent follow-up should be made in an attempt to establish the validity of the complaint.

Internal Complaints

If a personnel complaint comes from an employee and is directed at a fellow agency employee, it is referred to as an internal complaint. The most common internal complaint occurs when an immediate supervisor accuses an employee of wrongdoing after personally observing what is, or seems to be, misconduct. Other examples include observation of misconduct by other than immediate supervisors, misconduct uncovered via staff inspections, and deficiencies uncovered by agency auditors. An employee must be allowed to lodge a personnel complaint against one of his or her peers or against his superiors. For example, complaints of sexual harassment against any

280

employee must be taken and fully investigated regardless of who makes the complaint.

REGULATION OF NON-JOB-RELATED CONDUCT

In the past, it was quite common for law enforcement agencies to have a host of regulations regulating the non-job-related conduct of their sworn officers. However, many of those regulations have been determined to be violations of the individual rights of officers, especially those rights guaranteed by the First Amendment of the United States Constitution. The essence of the courts' position has been that an officer cannot be punished for non-criminal actions unless it can be established to the satisfaction of the courts that such actions were job-related, impaired the officer's job efficiency, and seriously damaged the operational effectiveness of the agency. "Therefore, there must be a connection between the prohibited conduct and the officer's fitness to perform the duties required by his position. In addition, the conduct must be of such a nature as to adversely affect the morale and efficiency of the department or have a tendency to destroy public respect for and confidence in the department."[4] Consequently, certain conduct which was once interpreted as "conduct unbecoming a law enforcement officer" can no longer be so interpreted. This includes conduct which may be viewed by some as immoral. As a result, officers now have greater freedom to do things such as: express themselves while off duty, participate in politics, and accumulate debts.

This is not to say that the off-duty conduct of officers should never be of any concern to their agency. Some conduct can be contested if it can be shown that it interferes with or affects the ability of an officer to do his job. However, contesting off-duty conduct is not an easy task. Recent court decisions have upheld the rights of officers to engage in controversial off-duty behavior.

Consequently, supervisors should not formally contest an officer's off-duty conduct unless it is a clear violation which the agency governs. Supervisors who ignore this rule are exposing themselves and their agency to considerable liability problems.

These supervisors must accept the reality that standards of conduct for officers thought to be enforceable just a few years ago are no longer subject to agency control.

Legal Advice Must Be Made Available

Because of the complex and dynamic nature of the legal issues involved, it is a mistake for agencies to rely exclusively on the ability of their supervisors to decide whether or not to pursue personnel complaints which are not clearly job-related. Whenever uncertainty exists as to the merits of a complaint, a far wiser course of action is to make legal advice readily available to supervisors.

RECORDING PERSONNEL COMPLAINTS

All external personnel complaints must be put in writing as soon as they are received, and assigned a control number. "Every police agency should develop procedures that will insure that all complaints, whether from an external or internal source, are permanently and chronologically recorded in a central record."[5] Agency policy should allow for the lodging of complaints in person, by telephone, or by mail. The policy should also allow personnel complaints to be lodged at any agency facility regardless of the assignment of the individual who is the subject of the complaint. This is a very important consideration. It is wrong to require a person to go to a particular police facility to lodge a personnel complaint. Some complainants would rather forget about their complaint than run the risk of coming face-to-face with the subject of their complaint or with any of his colleagues. And, every time a citizen forgets about a complaint, it is likely that the agency misses an opportunity to obtain information that has the potential to help it improve its operation.

External Complaints Made in Person

When a complainant comes to an agency facility to lodge a personnel complaint, he or she should be interviewed by a supervisor. The complainant should be requested to list the basic facts of the complaint in his own handwriting. Information needed to contact the complaining person, and description of the exact nature of the alleged misconduct must be included. General statements by complainants such as, "I was treated in a discourteous manner," or "I was physically attacked by the officer," are not satisfactory. The complainant should specify the exact form of the alleged misconduct. Agencies should have standard forms to record information on and the necessary personnel to assist such complainants and/or witnesses, if necessary.

External Complaints Received by Mail or Telephone

When a personnel complaint is received in the mail, the original letter can serve as the official complaint. The agency control number should be placed at the top of the first page of the complaint letter.

When a personnel complaint is received by telephone, the supervisor who receives the call should assign a qualified worker to record the complaint in his own handwriting. If a standard agency form exists, then it should be used.

MINOR INFRACTIONS

The manner in which personnel complaints should be handled depends, more than anything else, on the seriousness of the offense. "The scope of an internal investigation of misconduct should be proportionate to the severity of the infraction alleged."[6] Complaints involving minor infractions are best handled by the immediate supervisor of the offending employee. "Such problems of discipline are traditionally handled best by those who are most intimate with the subordinate. Their disposition does not need the formality that the handling of serious breaches of conduct requires."[7]

The first step in the investigation of allegations of minor infractions is to verify that an infraction indeed occurred and that the officer who committed the infraction has been identified. Of course, if the infraction was observed by the delinquent employee's immediate supervisor, such verification is not needed. In all other cases, involving allegations of minor infractions, including those which were initiated via an external complaint, this verification must be made before any other action is taken. Great harm often results when an employee is wrongly accused, regardless of the seriousness of the accusation. Once it has been established that a minor infraction occurred and that a certain officer committed it, the following procedures should be followed to dispose of the matter:

1. Discuss the Matter with the Offending Employee

Once a supervisor has verified that a minor infraction has occurred and the offending employee has been identified, a prompt, private, and relatively informal discussion of the incident should be conducted between the offending officer and his immediate supervisor. If appropriate, the supervisor should set the stage for discussing the infraction by saying something positive about the offending officer's overall performance record. The supervisor then presents the specific details.

In the case of minor infractions which were observed by an employee's immediate supervisor, this discussion can often be conducted on the spot. If, however, the offending employee has in the recent past been the recipient of positive discipline due to similar infractions, consideration must be given to handling the present infraction in the formal manner usually reserved for handling more serious infractions. This is an example of how a progressive disciplinary system should work. If positive discipline fails to achieve a desired change in behavior, then it must be followed by the application of negative discipline.

In those cases where the infraction was minor and the offending officer does not have a history of similar infractions, the most important issue for the supervisor to resolve is the reason for the commission of the infraction. If the infraction was unintentional and was the result of a lack of understanding of agency policy, then it can very simply be handled via the application of positive discipline in the form of technical skills training. If, however, it was intentional, then it becomes a more serious matter and requires, at the very least, some form of attitudinal training accompanied by a warning that future intentional misconduct will be met by progressively severe disciplinary action. Guidelines for deciding on the appropriate positive or negative disciplinary action needed in these cases is covered elsewhere in this text.

2.. Check for Understanding

It is absolutely necessary for the supervisor to check and make sure there is good understanding concerning the resolution of the infraction. The best way to do this is to have the employee state in his own words what he believes has been agreed upon. While the employee is relating his perceptions to the supervisor, it is essential that the supervisor listen attentively and make clarifications, if necessary.

3. Make a Record of the Incident

A record concerning the basic facts involved in the minor infractions and the action taken to resolve them should be made. Such records prove invaluable to supervisors if future events require them to document past misconduct of their subordinates. "For such purposes, complete records of received complaints, their investigation, and their disposition should be maintained."[8]

The complexity of the record depends on the circumstances in the case. In the great majority of cases involving minor infractions, all that is required is a brief notation which captures the essential facts. For ease of retrieval, it is recommended that supervisors make these notations on individual "conduct cards" for each of the officers they supervise.

Only when a minor infraction is committed by an employee with a recent history of similar behavior or when the matter is going to be reviewed by a higher authority is a more comprehensive reporting format required. An essential element of such a comprehensive record is a cross reference to past infractions. Naturally, if the past infractions weren't properly recorded as discussed above, it would be difficult, if not impossible, to retrieve this information.

It would be completely inappropriate to make a record concerning an observed minor infraction without discussing the incident with the offending employee. Some supervisors engage in this practice to "cover" themselves while at the same time avoiding the unpleasantness that is always present when it becomes necessary to criticize the actions of another. This practice is wrong for a number of reasons. First, supervisors are expected to deal forthrightly with all uncovered misconduct of their subordinates. Second, a supervisor who engages in this practice ignores the disciplinary principle that employees must always be given an opportunity to explain their behavior before disciplinary action is taken. Third, employees who learn that such covert record keeping has been taking place invariably become quite resentful, and justifiably so.

As mentioned above, the unpleasant nature of criticizing the actions of a worker can often be minimized if the supervisor involved prefaces his critical remarks with some form of realistic praise. For example, if an officer who is otherwise a high performer has a lateness problem, the supervisor should begin a discussion of the lateness problem with praise for the officer's overall performance record.

4. Follow-Up

As is the case with all problem solving efforts, supervisors must follow up to determine the results of actions taken to correct minor deficiencies. The nature of the follow-up depends on the circumstances of the original infraction, but it should always be structured so as to avoid embarrassing the employee. Concerning this required follow-up, while it should be discreetly conducted, it is a mistake to mask it, to conduct it in a covert manner, or, worst of all, to deny it. In fact, it should be made clear to the employee during the earlier discussion of the incident that follow-up will most certainly occur. The offending employee should also be informed during this initial discussion that continued infractions will be met with progressively severe disciplinary action.

SERIOUS COMPLAINTS

Supervisors assigned the responsibility of handling personnel complaints of a more serious nature than minor infractions should follow the strategy below:

1. Be Certain of the Exact Nature of the Alleged Misconduct

If the recording of the complaint was done properly, the exact nature of the alleged misconduct should be readily available. If

286

it is not, the investigator must obtain it before he proceeds with his investigation. It is at this point that the investigator should seek legal advice if it is unclear as to whether the alleged wrongdoing is either criminal or job related. Remember, it is wrong to interfere in the private lives of employees unless there is a proper agency interest involved, e.g., the employee is engaged in criminal conduct or in misconduct which negatively impacts on his work performance.

2. Conduct an Investigation to Determine the Facts

The strategy involved in conducting personnel complaint investigations is much the same as that which would be used in other investigations: interviews of victims and witnesses might have to be conducted, an interview or interrogation of the accused officer must be conducted, pertinent factual information must be gathered, and physical evidence may have to be collected and analyzed. "All supervisory personnel shall intensely investigate all personnel complaints initiated by them or assigned to them, gathering all available information from all known sources."[9]

3. Analyze the Available Facts and Arrive at a Disposition

Once the fact finding effort is concluded, all of the available facts must be considered, and a decision must be made concerning the guilt or innocence of the accused employee. If the evidence does not reasonably support the allegation, then the case should be closed after the employee is properly notified. Such a notification should be made as quickly as possible. If the evidence reasonably supports the allegation, then the appropriate corrective action must be decided upon. This is done by considering all of the circumstances surrounding the incident, including such things as the intent of the offending officer, his prior record, and the recommendations of his immediate supervisor. Unless agency policy dictates otherwise, the employee should be informed of the results of the investigation during a disciplinary action hearing. (Details about how to conduct such a hearing are covered in a previous chapter.)

4. Follow-Up

In those cases where corrective action was taken, the immediate supervisor of the offending officer should follow up to make certain the disciplinary action that was taken had the desired effect. If necessary, the matter must be reopened.

Personnel Complaint Investigations Are Somewhat Unique

There are two considerations that set apart personnel complaint investigations from most others. First, the manner in which these investigations are conducted can, more than any other type of investigation, impact upon the productivity and morale of the agency. For this reason, supervisors conducting these investigations must be fully acquainted with, and carefully comply with, both the judicially created and contractually guaranteed "due process" protections which apply to employees who are the subject of personnel complaint investigations. "[W]here an officer's reputation, honor or integrity are at stake because of government-imposed discipline, due process must be extended to the officer."[10] ("Due process" will be discussed later in this chapter.)

The second consideration that sets all personnel complaint investigations apart from most other investigations is that the investigator must often concern himself with more than simply determining whether job-related wrongdoing or criminal conduct in fact took place. In other words, "guilty" or "not guilty" is not the only issue. Once the investigation confirms that wrongdoing took place, then it must focus on the degree of culpability of the offending officer. Was the violation an intentional act, an act of carelessness, or due to a lack of understanding? The answers to these questions are needed so that the appropriate positive or negative discipline can be applied to correct the behavior of the offending officer, or to bring about his separation from the agency, if necessary.

INTERVIEWING VICTIMS AND WITNESSES

Personnel complaint investigations require the investigator to interview those who were victimized by the alleged misconduct and any available witnesses. The seriousness of the charge, the complexity of the case, and the nature and amount of information possessed by the subject of the interview are all factors that will determine the amount of time needed for the interview.

In most cases the person reporting the incident and the victim of the alleged misconduct are one and the same. This, however, is not always the case. With "spokesperson complaints," the complainant is a representative of the victim, such as an attorney, clergy person, or elected official. In these instances, it is critical that the investigator insist upon interviewing the victim personally to get a first-hand account of the incident.

The Importance of the Skill of the Interviewer

It is wrong to assume that a person with information needed to further an investigation will voluntarily disclose it simply because an investigator needs the information. In many cases, it is the interviewing skills of the investigator which determine the degree of disclosure.

The Time, Place and Setting of an Interview in a Personnel Complaint Investigation

Interviews of any alleged victims and witnesses should be conducted as soon as possible after a personnel complaint is lodged. But there are some factors which have priority over the timeliness of an interview. Privacy and freedom from interruption and possible inconvenience are other important considerations. Therefore, immediacy may have to be sacrificed in some instances in deference to a lack of privacy or in order to prevent significant inconvenience or interruption. Any condition which significantly detracts from the subject's ability to concentrate on the interview should be avoided. It is best to avoid holding detailed interviews at a station house or other agency facility. Unless the subject objects, the best place for a detailed interview is at the subject's home or place of business.

Other Interview Guidelines

Listed below are other important guidelines for supervisors when interviewing victims and/or witnesses in personnel complaint cases:

1. Do not in any way show animosity towards the complainant. The complainant should be treated with the utmost courtesy. "Courteous receipt and proper processing of complaints should be absolutely required of [all officers] who learn that a civilian wishes to complain about officers."[11] After the complaint has been taken, the supervisor should make it a point to thank the complainant for the information he supplied.

2. Do not, under any circumstances, show a lack of belief in the subject's story as it is being told. "Refrain from being judgmental regarding individuals who complain. To dismiss a complaint cavalierly, simply because of a judgment that the complainant is a 'screwball' or a 'pain in the ass,' is to blow the whole ball game."[12] If it becomes clear that a victim's complaint is based on incomplete or inaccurate information, the supervisor should relate the facts to the victim after the complainant has finished his account. This should never be done, however, unless the supervisor is absolutely certain that the facts in the matter contradict the complainant's story.

3. Do not, under any circumstances, interview witnesses in a group. Witnesses waiting to be interviewed should be separated from other witnesses. If this is not done, there is the risk of contaminating someone's version of what happened by statements made by others.

4. If a complainant is apparently intoxicated, re-interview him when he is sober. However, under no circumstances, should taking the complaint be postponed simply because the complaint is under the influence of alcohol. Fairness to the officer being accused of misconduct, however, demands that the supervisor officially record his belief that the complainant was intoxicated and the reason for his conclusion. Copies of such a record should not be given to the complainant.

5. Be prepared prior to the interview. Acquire as much information as possible about the person to be interviewed. In cases involving more serious allegations, a records' check should be

made to determine the credibility of the subject of the interview and whether he has had any previous encounters with the police. This is not to say that a person with a police record should always be discredited. It is a fact, however, that certain individuals complain about police misconduct as a strategy for their defense against charges of criminality.

6. Be considerate of the physical, mental, and emotional state of the person to be interviewed. In some cases, it might be best to obtain some basic facts and then schedule a detailed interview for a more conducive time in the immediate future.

7. Exercise special caution when interviewing juveniles. Notify the parents/guardians and inform them about the nature of the interview and the time and place of the interview. In personnel complaint cases there is no reason why a parent/guardian should not be permitted to be present at the interview.

8. Begin the interview with a warm-up period, break the ice and establish rapport with the person being interviewed. It is essential that the interviewer avoid any appearance of being in an adversarial role.

9. After the warm-up period, ask the interviewee to relate his story in his own words. After the story has been related the interviewer should ask questions which should follow a logical sequence.

10. Be alert and sensitive to indications of a complainant's possible motives for lodging the complaint. This is not meant to suggest that employee wrongdoing can be excused because of the motives of the complainant, because it can't. Therefore, it is not uncommon for people who are seeking revenge to lodge false complaints against police officers. But motives can be important clues in determining the merits of complaints.

11. Conclude the interview on a positive note once you are satisfied that all relevant information has been obtained. The subject should be given a way to contact the interviewer should the need arise and should be told that he will be notified of the disposition of the complaint. In closing, the interviewer should always express appreciation for the subject's cooperation.

Note Taking During the Interview

Taking notes during the interview significantly increases the value of the interview. To allay any suspicions about note taking, the interviewer should always briefly explain at the start of the interview that the notes are meant to prevent subsequent re-interviews brought about by the inability of the interviewer to remember all of the pertinent facts discussed. If, however, the subject adamantly objects to the taking of notes, then the interview should be held in the absence of note taking. When this occurs, it is absolutely essential that the interviewer makes notes immediately upon the conclusion of the interview.

Note taking cannot be a substitute for careful listening. The interviewer should not get so caught up in taking notes that he fails to show interest in the immediate discussion. Therefore, taking notes should be kept to a minimum and include only vital details. For this reason, as soon as possible after the interview, the interviewer should review his notes and make them more complete and understandable.

Documenting the Interview

In the great majority of personnel complaint investigations, the handwritten notes of the interviewer can serve as sufficient documentation of the interview. However, in personnel complaint investigations involving serious charges which may ultimately be resolved in criminal court or at an administrative hearing, it is desirable to have the subject's statement put in writing and have him sign it. The necessity of obtaining such a signed statement increases dramatically in cases where there is a distinct likelihood that the subject may change his story for material reasons after speaking with an attorney, or when there is a possibility that the subject will not be available at a subsequent hearing.

INTERVIEWING THE ACCUSED EMPLOYEE

At some point during a personnel complaint investigation, the accused employee must be interviewed. When the complaint involves a minor infraction, this interview should be held very early in the investigation.

When the complaint involves a more serious matter, however, it is usually best to delay interviewing the accused officer until the investigator has interviewed the complainant and available witnesses and collected and reviewed as many relevant facts as are available. It is only when the accused employee has information that has to be obtained before the investigation can go any further that an interview with him should be conducted early in the investigation of a serious personnel complaint. The exact point at which the accused employee should be interviewed, therefore, is discretionary with the investigating officer and should be decided on a case-by case-basis.

Interviewing in Cases Involving Possible Criminal Activity

Often, a personnel complaint includes allegations of criminality. Therefore, concerning the investigation of personnel complaints, not all face-to-face fact finding efforts between an investigator and an accused officer are interviews. Depending on the circumstances, some of them are interrogations. There is a significant distinction to be made between a personnel complaint interview involving a non-criminal infraction, and a personnel complaint interrogation involving an allegation of a criminal nature. This distinction is at the heart of a dilemma that is created when a law enforcement supervisor is investigating an employee of a law enforcement agency who is suspected of committing a criminal offense. Before discussing the specifics of this dilemma, a brief review of the Miranda rule is needed.

Custodial Interrogation Requires the Administration of Miranda Warnings

Interrogation is generally defined as the asking of guilt seeking questions in a criminal investigation. Not all interrogations require the administration of Miranda warnings. But with one exception, when the interrogation involved is custodial in nature—when the subject is not free to leave—then Miranda warnings must be administered, and the subject must waive his rights before questioning, if the results of the interrogation are to be used against him at a criminal trial. But the results of a custodial interrogation held in the absence of a waiver of Miranda rights are admissible at an internal administrative hearing. The one exception to the rule which states that custodial interrogation requires the administration of Miranda warnings involves questioning in a situation involving a matter of public safety.

The Specifics of the Dilemma

As mentioned above, when a law enforcement supervisor is conducting face-to-face questioning of an agency employee who is suspected of criminal conduct, a dilemma is created for the supervisor. The ingredients of this dilemma, some of which have been discussed above, are as follows:

a. When an employee of a law enforcement agency is directed to be present while on duty at a particular location for questioning, the employee must comply or else he is subject to disciplinary action for disobeying a lawful order. Therefore, such questioning is deemed to be custodial in nature unless the employee is told he is free to leave. If, however, he is told that he is free to leave, then he must be allowed to leave without jeopardy if he decides to leave.

b. Unless there is a local statute to the contrary, employees of law enforcement agencies can be required to answer questions which are specifically directed and narrowly related to the performance of their official duties. Refusal to answer such questions can result in termination of employment.

c. Statements made during the questioning cannot be used against the employee in a criminal trial unless they are preceded by a valid waiver of Miranda rights. But if an employee refuses to waive his Miranda rights, then all questioning must cease.

d. If custodial interrogation takes place in the absence of the Miranda warnings, statements made may be used against the employee in an administrative hearing but not at a criminal trial.

Let's suppose that a supervisor is required to interview an officer as part of an investigation when there is a likelihood that criminal charges may result from the investigation. In such a custodial situation, if the supervisor asks questions in the absence of Miranda and requires the subordinate involved to respond, then the information is not admissible in criminal court, no matter how incriminating it may be. On the other hand, if the supervisor administers Miranda, then he is giving the subordinate involved an opportunity to refuse to answer any questions. This then is the dilemma. In such a situation, should the supervisor conducting the investigation give the subordinate Miranda warnings and thereby give him an opportunity to remain silent, or should he require the subordinate to respond in the absence of Miranda, knowing that the responses will not be admissible in criminal court?

This dilemma must be resolved on a case by case basis depending on the circumstances in the case. In resolving it, the supervisor must decide if it is better to get information which he will not be able to use at a criminal trial or to invite the subordinate's silence by the giving of Miranda warnings.

Miscellaneous Guidelines for Interviewing/Interrogating the Accused Officer in Personnel Complaint Cases Involving Serious Charges

Listed below are additional guidelines that should be followed when interviewing/interrogating an accused officer as part of a personnel complaint investigation involving other than minor infractions:

a. Prior to the questioning, the accused officer should be informed of the identity of all persons present and the reasons why they are present.

b. Prior to the questioning, the accused officer should be told the exact nature of the accusations.

c. One representative from the accused officer's line organization should be permitted, upon the request of the subordinate, to be present at all times during the questioning.

d. The interview/interrogation should be conducted at a reasonable time, preferably when the accused is on duty during daytime hours.

e. The interview/interrogation should be recorded either mechanically or by a stenographer.

f. "Off the Record" questions should not be used, nor should offensive language, threats, or promises of rewards for answering questions.

g. The duration of questioning periods should be reasonable with breaks allowed for meals, personal necessity, telephone calls, etc.

h. The accused officer should be provided with a transcript or a tape of the proceedings, as soon as possible, after its conclusion, but in all cases, prior to the holding of a hearing or a trial in the same matter.

REMOVAL OF FIREARMS FROM INTOXICATED OFFICERS

It is a grievous error to allow intoxicated law enforcement officers to retain their firearms. Upon observing an officer who appears unfit for duty due to intoxication, a supervisor must detain that officer pending an investigation to determine if the member is indeed unfit for duty. The form and extent of this investigation and who conducts it depends on the law, contractual agreements, and agency policy. As a general rule, however, the person conducting the investigation should use common sense standards to determine if an officer should be required to surrender his firearms. Should such a surrender be required, disciplinary action must always be initiated. In all such cases, however, the officer involved should be required to attend counseling sessions as described elsewhere in this text.

PROTECTING THE RIGHTS OF ACCUSED EMPLOYEES

The provisions of statutory and case law, contractual agreements, and past practices of an agency which protect the rights of employees who are the subject of personnel complaint investigations must be strictly followed. "Administrative directives should clearly delineate the rights and responsibilities of employees at every level in the department."[13] It is a well-established judicial doctrine that arbitrary deprivation of such rights will result in court reversal of agency imposed punishment. In such cases there is also a strong possibility that the employer may be civilly liable.

Therefore, it is recommended that all law enforcement agencies afford their employees who are the subject of personnel complaint investigations involving serious misconduct certain rights which are described below. It must be emphasized, however, that these rights represent minimum requirements. Agencies should look to their own local law, contractual provisions, or past practices in providing protection of rights to accused employees. They must do so or suffer the consequences of such things as reversal in court, reinstatement with back pay, awards for pain and suffering, and legal costs.

a. Formal Notice of the Specifics of the Charge

When an investigation into the merits of a personnel complaint reasonably supports the complaint, the accused employee must be formally notified. This notification should be in written form and must contain the specifics of the charges. The notice must be specific enough to allow the employee an opportunity to adequately defend himself. Gone are the days when it was sufficient to inform the employee that he is being charged with "conduct unbecoming a law enforcement officer." Not describing the officer's alleged misconduct in specific enough terms opens the door for court reversal of any punitive action taken against the employee.

Personal service of this kind (referred to in many agencies as "charges and specifications,") is the preferred method of service. Upon being served, the accused officer should be required to sign the charges and specifications, keep a copy, and return the signed original to the server. Service of the charges must be made sufficiently in advance of the hearing to provide the accused sufficient opportunity to prepare his defense.

When personal service of charges and specifications cannot be affected, a record of the attempts made and the reason for their failure should be kept. In these cases the charges and specifications can either be sent by certified mail to the last known address of the employee, or they can be delivered to a responsible adult at the employee's usual residence. In these cases, written documentation of the method of service employed should be kept as part of the case file.

b. Notification of the Nature of Any Evidence To Be Used Against the Employee

The purpose of instituting procedural due process requirements in personnel complaint investigations is to guarantee fair and equitable treatment. Such treatment demands that the accused be given an opportunity to adequately defend himself. Due process is violated if evidence, which is to be used against the employee, is kept hidden from the employee until the hearing or court proceedings.

c. Permit Employee to Obtain Counsel

Prior to questioning an employee who is the subject of an official investigation, the employee should be permitted to obtain counsel if a serious violation is alleged. The investigating officer should notify the employee at least two business days prior to the date of the questioning so that the employee may obtain and/or confer with counsel. While this right to counsel has the potential to delay the proceedings, the benefits far outweigh the danger of a slight delay in the process. If an investigation is professionally conducted there is little to fear from the presence of a defense attorney. Representation by counsel tends to reduce the number of court reversals.

d. Allow the Employee To Mount a Defense

Any employee charged with serious wrongdoing must be allowed to present his side of the case. This includes permission to call his own witnesses and to present evidence to counter the allegations.

e. Generally Permit the Accused To Confront and Cross-Examine Witnesses

In administrative hearings, employees facing serious allegations should be entitled to confront and cross-examine witnesses. There are times, however, when good cause exists for not allowing such confrontation and cross-examination. For example, such good cause would exist if a witness against an employee is a field associate—an employee who has agreed to act as a sentinel over employee behavior and whose identity the agency has promised to keep confidential. When the general rule of confrontation is violated, the burden is on the agency to establish the existence of the required good cause to the satisfaction of the hearing officer.

f. Maintain a Disinterested Adjudication Body

Agencies should make a special effort to maintain a neutral body to weigh the evidence in serious personnel complaint cases in order to assess the culpability of accused employees and to set punishments when charges against employees are sustained. "Although such boards are time-consuming, most police managers and agencies believe they should be an integral element of administering internal discipline. The boards provide a diversity of opinion for the final adjudication, and allow for greater participation in the process by persons involved in the complaint investigation."[14] Decisions by such a body should be put in writing and should include the rationale for actions taken.

HANDLING COMPLAINTS OF SEXUAL HARASSMENT IN THE WORKPLACE

Throughout the law enforcement community, and indeed throughout the nation, as a result of the break down of gender-based barriers in employment, there has been considerable attention given to the issue of sexual harassment in the workplace.

There are two types of sexual harassment. The first, and most commonly known type, occurs when there is unwelcome sexual behavior directed toward one employee by a supervisor or another employee that carries an implied or stated condition of continued employment, promotion, assignment or transfer based upon the employee's response. The second, and lesser known type of sexual harassment, is committed by a supervisor who tolerates a work environment where sexual harassment unreasonably interferes with an individual's work performance or creates an intimidating, hostile or offensive working situation. Both of these types of sexual harassment are prohibited by law.

Supervisors Must Maintain a Work Environment Free of Sexual Harassment

Supervisors are not immune to being named in civil liability suits just because they do not harass anyone. Supervisors can be named in a sexual harassment complaints if they have failed to take appropriate action to terminate it. In addition, supervisors must make certain there is no retaliation of any form taken against someone who lodges a complaint of sexual harassment. Supervisors should make subordinates aware that such retaliation is just as illegal as the actual act of harassment. Although women are most often the target of sexual harassment, men also can be sexually harassed.

Agencies must make it easy for employees to lodge sexual harassment complaints. It is important that agency policy specify that counselors and supervisors will treat each complaint confidentially. This means that information obtained from the complainant should not be discussed with other personnel except as necessary to investigate and resolve the complaint.

NOTIFICATION OF THE PRINCIPALS

It is a good community relations strategy to make sure that civilian complainants are notified of the disposition of their complaints as soon as possible after the case is resolved. In cases where a complaint has been sustained, the complainant should be so informed and should be told that appropriate disciplinary action has been taken against the offending employee. The specifics of the disciplinary action should not be conveyed since the complainant has no need to know of all of the circumstances considered in arriving at that decision. When a complaint is unfounded or otherwise unsubstantiated, the complainant should be told of that fact along with the general rationale for that finding.

Just as it is a good policy to promptly inform a complainant, it is also good policy to promptly inform the accused employee.

"The complainant and the officer should be notified of the decision and of the basis for it."[15] Unless contrary to agency policy, notification should be made by the immediate supervisor during a disciplinary action hearing.

MISCELLANEOUS GUIDELINES

The following guidelines apply to all personnel complaint investigations:

a. Supervisors must constantly strive to avoid any unnecessary damage to the reputation of an employee who is the subject of a personnel complaint.

b. Supervisors should never coerce an accused employee to resign or retire in exchange for dropping charges. Such coercion almost certainly will cause court reversal and reinstatement should the employee decide at a later date to sue. Whether or not an employee should be allowed to resign or retire voluntarily to avoid disciplinary action is a matter of agency policy. If consistent with policy, however, voluntary resignations and retirements are more preferable to forced ones.

c. It is a mistake to bring the complainant and the accused officer together in a face-to-face confrontation to try to determine the truth of the matter. When the problems that could arise out of such a confrontation are weighed against possible advantages, it becomes clear that it is an inadvisable strategy.

d. In cases of minor infractions where the accused officer admits he was discourteous or otherwise acted improperly, the matter should never be settled solely by the issuance of an apology to the complainant. Some other form of positive or negative discipline must be applied. To allow an apology to settle a personnel complaint does not, in any way, help prevent recurrence of the inappropriate behavior. Besides, once such a precedence is established, some workers will conclude that a simple apology will get them off the hook for their misdeeds.

e. In cases where the identity of an officer in question is uncertain, show-ups should be avoided since they are much too suggestive. Allowing the complainant to view pictures is acceptable, if the guidelines for this mode of identification, as established by the courts, are followed. Most importantly, there should be no attempt made to influence the complainant to select any particular photo. Lineups are also an approved method of establishing identity in personnel complaint cases. When the complaint does not involve a criminal matter the employee may be ordered to stand the lineup. Failure to comply is a serious breach of discipline. Remember, however, that while lineups have passed judicial muster, they are demeaning to police personnel including those officers who are used as fillers. They should, therefore, be used only when necessary and when allowed by agency policy.

f. Supervisors who uncover misconduct among their subordinates must always consider the "tip of the iceberg" possibility. In other words, if it is determined that one subordinates is ignoring a particular rule or regulation, then it is possible that other subordinates are doing the same. Such a possibility should then be explored, but such exploration must be accomplished as tactfully as possible.

TEST YOUR UNDERSTANDING

1. What is a personnel complaint?

2. Is it a good policy for a law enforcement supervisor to investigate the merits of all personnel complaints? Discuss.

3. Discuss the value of anonymous complaints.

4. Name and discuss the two categories of personnel complaints.

5. Is it a good idea for a law enforcement agency to attempt to regulate all of the off-duty conduct of its officers? Discuss.

6. Should all external personnel complaints be recorded? If so, how?

7. Discuss the procedure that should be used to handle minor infractions.

8. Discuss the strategy for handling more serious complaints.

9. Discuss the interview of the complainant in a personnel complaint investigation.

10. Discuss the interview of an accused officer.

11. What is the dilemma facing the investigator when interviewing the accused officer if the personnel complaint being investigated is a criminal offense? Discuss.

12. Name and discuss the due process protections that should be built into personnel complaint investigations.

FOOTNOTES

1. William Bopp and Paul Whisenand, *Police Personnel Administration,* 2nd ed. (Boston, MA: Allyn and Bacon, Inc., 1980), p. 249.

2. Jerome H. Skolnick and James J. Fyfe, *Above The Law - Police and the Excessive Use of Force.* (New York: The Free Press, 1993), p. 232.

3. Ibid., p. 231.

4. Charles R. Swanson, Leonard Territio, and Robert W. Taylor, *Police Administration - Structures, Processes and Behaviors,* 2nd ed. (New York: Macmillan Publishing Co., 1988), p. 343.

5. Bopp and Whisenand, p. 252.

6. Stanley Vanagunas and James F. Elliot, *Administration of Police Organizations.* (Boston, MA: Allyn and Bacon, Inc., 1980), p. 292.

7. Ibid., p. 293.

8. Ibid., p. 292.

9. Bernard L. Garmire, Editor, *Local Government Police Management,* 2nd ed. (Washington, D.C.: International City Management Association, 1982), p. 416.

10. Swanson, Territo and Taylor, p. 340.

11. Skolnick and Fyfe, p. 232.

12. Louis A. Radelet, *The Police and the Community,* 4th ed. (New York: Macmillan Publishing Co., 1986), p. 253.

13. Ibid., p. 265.

14. Bopp and Whiseneand, p. 257.

15. Ibid., p. 239.

SUGGESTED READINGS

Dudley, William, editor.
Police Brutality.
San Diego, CA: Greenhaven Press, Inc., 1991.

Earle, Howard H.
Police - Community Relations: Crisis In Our Time, 3rd ed.
Springfield, IL: Charles C. Thomas, 1980.

Fishman, Janet E.
Measuring Police Corruption.
New York: John Jay Press, 1978.

Sherman, Lawrence W.
Scandal and Reform: Controlling Police Corruption.
Berkeley, CA: University of California Press, 1978.

Simpson, Anthony E.
The Literature of Police Corruption.
New York: John Jay Press, 1979.

Tonry, Michael and Norval Morris, editors.
Modern Policing.
Chicago, IL: The University of Chicago Press, 1992.

Trojanowicz, Robert C.
The Environment of the First-Line Police Supervisor.
Englewood Cliffs, NJ: Prentice-Hall, Inc., 1980.

Weston, Paul B. and Philip K. Fraley.
Police Personnel Management.
Englewood Cliffs, NJ: Prentice-Hall, Inc., 1980.

Wilson, O.W.
Police Planning.
Springfield, IL: Charles C. Thomas Publisher, 1977.

CHAPTER 13
PROBLEM SOLVING

PROBLEM DEFINED

Our working definition of a problem is: any condition which negatively impacts on the work environment or work product of the law enforcement agency. This includes everything from inadequate supplies to a rise in burglaries in a certain area. Based on our definition, the potential exists for agencies to experience a large variety of problems. Due to the wide-reaching responsibilities of law enforcement agencies and their twenty-four-hour-a-day availability, this is, indeed, the case. However, our focus is not on the variety of problems, but rather on how supervisors can deal with problems - that is, engage in problem solving. We believe that no matter what the problem, there are basic actions which should be taken in dealing with problems. A systematic approach can be used to discover the problem and then deal with it. Such an approach is invaluable to law enforcement supervisors who are often faced with the task of seeking and ferreting out problems and bringing about solutions.

A RECOMMENDED APPROACH TO PROBLEM SOLVING

Problem solving involves both discovering a problem and then dealing with it. The process is made up of five steps which are divided into two phases. The first phase, the determination phase, consists of two steps. The second phase, the correction phase, consists of three steps.

Phase One: The Determination Phase

Step 1. Identification of the Problem.
Step 2. Analysis of the Problem.

Phase Two: The Correction Phase

Step 3. Planning the Solution.
Step 4. Implementing the Solution.
Step 5. Evaluating the Solution.

Phase One: The Determination Phase

The purpose of the determination phase is to correctly determine when and where a problem exists and then ensure that the problem has been accurately described in terms of its nature and magnitude. The two steps are: identification and analysis.

Step 1. Identification of the Problem

This is the sine qua non of problem solving. It is indispensable and is the most important step in problem solving. If a problem is not accurately identified, then even the most ingenious solutions are futile. In this step the supervisor determines what conditions have the potential to impact negatively on the work environment or work product. "Locate the problem and state it clearly. Be sure the problem as stated is the real problem and not a symptom or just part of the problem."[1] Not to identify and isolate the real problem is like going to a firearms range and shooting at the wrong target. Your perfect grip, aim, squeeze of the trigger and breathing may result in hitting a target over and over, but if it's the wrong target then all your perfect efforts were a waste of time.

Unique Role of the First-Line Supervisor

The first-line supervisor is in a unique position to act as a problem solver for the agency and to begin the problem-solving process by identifying the problem. He must be keenly aware of those conditions which demand attention and settlement. He is the member of the management team who is closest to the operating level. If anyone is in a position to uncover problems, he is, and he can do it using a variety of sources available to him:

a. Clients and community residents—Those who work or live in the area are excellent sources for identifying problems. Contact with them should be on a continuous basis and not only as a result of complaints about local conditions or services. If Mr. Smith, the dry cleaner, and Mrs. Thompson, who runs the day care center, voice the same criticism or complaint, chances are there is something that should be pursued to determine if a potential problem exists. These people are right in the middle of things and are extremely qualified to help in identifying problems.

b. Working subordinates—If Detective Green and the custodian, Mr. Barton, independently relate the same condition to the supervisor, it is a sure bet that there is something that should be investigated. Because they are actually doing the job, they are closest to the job's environment and work product. They can tell the boss what is really going on. Informal conversations have the ability to reveal things that never find their way into a formal report. The supervisor who listens carefully to his subordinates and has the confidence of his subordinates will receive information from them which has the potential to identify problem areas.

c. Personal discoveries—Past experience and job knowledge uniquely qualify a supervisor to be sensitive to and observant of problems. The dedicated supervisor who is constantly vigilant for the existence of possible problems is an asset to the organization. However, personal initiative and observation which have so much potential for problem solving are often under-used. There are at least two reasons for this. First, at times the supervisor is too close to the situation to see that something is not right. What is wrong may have been going on so long that it is not seen as a negative but rather as just part of the overall makeup of the everyday work environment. Secondly, there is a tendency to follow the old saw, "Why fix what ain't broken?" This mentality maintains that: we have gotten along this far without any great difficulty, so why should we go around and look for trouble? But that is exactly what a supervisor should do. He should look for trouble—meaning that his identification of problem areas is a big part of his job.

d. Agency records—Examining agency records should be a normal part of a supervisor's routine. Here patterns can be uncovered. Arrest reports, crime complaint reports, reports of accidents, etc., can all be used as a source to identify problems. For instance, arrests made only at the end of a shift by a certain officer thereby requiring overtime may be a symptom of illegal activity occurring earlier in the shift or a pattern of abuse of overtime. Agency records hold clues and cues to identifying problems.

e. Other public agencies—The supervisor should attempt to communicate with members of other public agencies that have responsibilities in the same geographic area. These agencies need not be law enforcement agencies. Actually, some of the most serious potential problems affecting a law enforcement agency can be uncovered by communication with non-law enforcement agencies. Social services agencies which have received complaints of child abuse have provided information about drug sales by the parents responsible for the alleged child abuse. One public agency sharing the same target clientele as another, can often provide information which may turn up a problem for the other agency.

f. Local newspapers—A supervisor should be totally aware of what is appearing in the local press. Feature articles, editorials, and op-ed articles should be scrupulously followed by a supervisor. However, to become aware of agency problems by the media is the least desirable way for a supervisor to find out about a problem. It opens the agency to criticism that the agency either does not know what is going on in its own shop or that it acts only if pressured into doing something.

The Importance of Verification

Before we jump to step two (analysis of the problem) identification must also include verification. A supervisor cannot go any further in real problem solving until he has accurately identified and adequately verified the problem. A breakdown in the process often occurs when people confuse symptoms of a problem with the root cause of a problem. When this mistake is made, well-intentioned efforts can be exhausted to no avail simply because the actual problem wasn't adequately verified.

Consider the following:

Sergeant Rems received numerous complaints from local merchants that the double parking in front of their stores prevents them from getting deliveries in a timely manner. One immediate response by Rems may be to have a sector car respond and issue traffic summonses. But the sergeant wants to make sure that this is actually a traffic problem. The first thing Rems does is discuss the issue with patrol officers who cover that street. He finds out that there is a traffic problem there, but that it is actually caused by men patronizing prostitutes in a building near the merchants' businesses. Rems decides to have action taken beyond merely issuing traffic summonses.

By attempting to verify the problem, Rems was able to accurately identify the problem. If he had not done this he would have merely been treating a symptom rather than tackling the solution. His efforts prevented the misuse of time, effort, and resources. "Too often businessmen are superficial in diagnosing their problems. They assume they know what the problem is when it is actually much deeper that it appears. Just as a medical diagnostician seeks beyond the symptoms to find the real cause of an illness, so the manager must not confuse symptoms with causes. The manager must dig deep to find the root cause of a problem. The symptom might only mask what really has caused the gap between what is happening and what was supposed to happen."[2]

Step 2. Analysis of the Problem

Law enforcement is such that it often demands quick responses to life threatening situations. These kinds of immediate responses have their place, but they tend to condition the law enforcement supervisor to come up with rapid solutions to all the problems he encounters. In the analysis step the details of the problem are exposed. It is not a knee jerk, rapid-fire operation. It takes a supervisor's time, patience, effort and investigative skills.

The question is, "What should be analyzed?" The answer is, anything that can expose details of the problem. This is a formidable task. However, by examining the general elements of a problem its details can be revealed.

Element of those involved:

This includes a review of those who are involved or associated with the problem such as persons making complaints, witnesses, and those complained of, (including criminal perpetrators where the problem involves criminal actions). Wherever possible those connected with the problem should be interviewed. Background information on them should be examined to clear-up details. If a supervisor receives a complaint that officers assigned to the shift are harassing neighborhood youths, certainly a review should be conducted to ascertain which officers are alleged to be involved. How are they alleged to be harassing the youths? What is the background of the officers involved? What is the background of those making the complaints? It is vitally important that the actions and background of those connected with the problem be examined so there can be a true analysis of the problem.

Element of the physical environment:

Does the physical environment contribute to the problem? For example, if the problem is that muggings have increased in a certain area, what does the area look like? Is there poor street lighting? What are the patrols in the area like? If the problem is pedestrian fatalities due to motor vehicle accidents, are there adequate traffic control devices? Is the street extraordinarily wide causing pedestrians to cross in a hurried manner while ignoring existing traffic signals?

Element of social clues:

If the problem is fighting between youth gangs, are there ethnic or racial differences contributing to the confrontations? If two officers do not seem to work well together, could it be because of the age difference between them? A supervisor must be constantly aware of how social conditions contribute to real problems.

Element of chain of events:

How do events and the chain of events produce or fuel conditions which caused the problem? How will changing or altering such events help deal with the problem?

Consider the following:

Recently there has been a rash of assaults on grade school children by older children who attend a nearby junior high school. The assaults occur while the grade school children are waiting at their bus stop. Investigation reveals that the nearby junior high school dismisses its students at the same time that the younger grade school children are waiting at their bus stop. There is obviously a chain of events contributing to the problem.

Aside from dealing specifically with those who are committing criminal acts, a change in the dismissal time of one of the schools would assist in dealing with the problem.

After a problem is identified, an analysis of the problem should factor in the various elements which contribute to the problem and the solution.

Phase Two: The Correction Phase

After a problem has been correctly identified and analyzed, the determination phase is completed. Now that the supervisor knows what he is up against, the correction phase can begin. The remaining three steps of problem-solving process are: planning the solution, implementing the solution, and evaluating the solution. It is at this point that all the problem identification and analysis are finally given practical solutions. But just as treating symptoms instead of real problems is inadequate, so, too, poorly planned and implemented solutions which do not adequately solve the problem are a waste of resources and pointless. It is imperative that problems receive concrete solutions. This can only be attained by detailed planning.

Step 3. Planning the Solution

The supervisor as a problem solver, should set his goals, figure out who and what is available to help him, and decide what actions will be taken by whom to accomplish the goals. Most people don't lack for ideas for solving problems, but the process often bogs down because of a lack of initiative and discipline to act upon the ideas.

Setting Goals and Objectives

Being specific is essential to setting goals. Without specificity, the solution cannot be broken down into manageable parts and tasks. Goals should be articulated in realistic terms so that implementation and evaluation are obvious. For example, it is unrealistic to state your goal as: eliminating all traffic accidents forever. This would be a great accomplishment, but one which is highly improbable. Goals should be quantified wherever possible and include time tables or due dates. As stated earlier, goals become objectives when time frames are set.

An example of an unacceptable objective in connection with incidents of burglaries would be "to reduce burglaries in the area." Stated in realistic terms an acceptable objective would be "to reduce burglaries by 10% on Post 12 within the next 60 days." Now this is attainable, manageable and something people can get a handle on because it is specific. When goals and objectives are specific enough and people go on and reach them, it gives them a great sense of accomplishment and success which is a big boost to morale.

When setting goals and objectives, if practical, the input of those individuals involved with the problem should be sought. "Problem solving and decision making are often improved by seeking help from those individuals or groups of employees who are best informed about and/or most closely involved in the problem and in implementing its solutions."[3] The supervisor should seek such assistance to ensure that the goals and objectives are realistic and attainable. Otherwise the problem-solving effort will be seen as just another creation of management without any link to the real world.

Having said all this, putting legs on the goals is the next critical step. You cannot just pin a goal up on a bulletin board and expect it to happen. Specific steps must be determined. For example, continuing with our burglaries objective, the next question should be: What can we do at various agency levels to reduce burglaries by 10%? The supervisor and whoever else is involved in the process of goal-setting will need to do some "brainstorming". Brainstorming is making an exhaustive list of ways to accomplish the goals, all the ideas on the list might not be enacted, but the list gives you specifics to choose from. For instance, our list for reducing burglaries might include: (1) increased patrols, (2) a study on the most effective ways other agencies have used to reduce burglaries, (3) community education about the value of home security systems, (4) increased neighborhood-watch programs, (5) patrol officers awareness of recently paroled felons with burglary convictions, etc. Once a supervisor makes a list of specific manageable tasks then it becomes possible to see how the problem will be tackled.

Available Help

What assistance is available to help deal with the problem? Who or what can a supervisor call on to do some of these integral tasks? It is a good idea to outline those resources (personnel and equipment) that might be able to assist. For example, the list should include the resources of the unit, the agency, other public agencies, persons in the private sector and members of the community. Examples of resources of persons in the private sector could include banks, insurance companies, and local merchants, while examples of members of the community could include members of the clergy and other community leaders. Don't hesitate to seek as much assistance as possible.

Actions To Be Taken

What should be done and who should do it? This is another place where the problem-solving process can breakdown. The supervisor cannot do it all himself, he needs to ask for specific help and delegate tasks. Each specific step in the solution will need its own action steps. For instance, if it is decided that community education is part of the solution, then who will be asked to teach the class? How many sessions will be held? Where will it be held? And how will it be advertised? Or if patrol officers will be made more aware of recently paroled felons: Do we have an adequate computer system to make this possible? If not, how and when will one be purchased? How can we increase communication with parole boards to have more information ready? What new equipment/technology do we need to help parole officers be more aware and effective?

The key is action steps: what actions will be taken by whom and when shall they be done. After determining what help is available and exactly who will do what, the problem solver should contact these resources, tell them what he would like from them and get a commitment. Later on, it will be his job to coordinate the efforts of all the resources that are assisting him and keep them informed of the progress that is being made in dealing with the problem.

Step 4. Implementing the Solution

This is where the action is. What has been planned is now put into action.

Coordination

All actors who have a role in implementing the solution must be in the right place at the right time to perform as they have agreed to perform. This task of coordination is the job of the problem solver.

Feedback

A system which provides feedback for the problem solver must be in place to retrieve information about progress towards solving the problem. "The finalization of a decision does not mean that management can sit back and expect that what has been decided upon has been carried out. It is important to build into the solution to any problem a feedback mechanism that will keep management informed of the results."[4] If there are any glitches, they should be identified and brought to the attention of the problem solver so that corrective action can be taken as soon as possible. In implementing solutions some flexibility may have to be introduced into the process, but that can only take place if the problem solver has provided for feedback mechanisms to alert him to the need for minor adjustments.

Documentation

As far as possible, meticulous documentation should be kept on what is being done. This allows the problem solver to explain in detail through records what has been done to deal with the problem. It will provide valuable notes for future problem solving. It also permits others in the agency to share in this experience when dealing with similar problems. Most importantly, it provides the ability to evaluate the solution.

Step 5. Evaluating the Solution

This is the final step of the problem-solving process. Did the solution meet the intended goals or objectives? If not, why not?

316

Does it continue to appropriately deal with the problem or has the problem reoccurred? "Managers need to monitor decision implementation to be sure that things are progressing as planned and that the problem that triggered the decision-making process has been resolved."[5] If the evaluation of the solution shows that the problem has not been solved, then the evaluation can be used to provide additional information about the problem so that another approach may be taken to solve it.

Even when apparently successful efforts are used to solve a problem, the solution, with its results, must be evaluated to ensure that it brought about the intended results.

Consider the following:

To reduce traffic accidents, Sergeant Rems increased enforcement in the area which experienced the rise in accidents. The next month the number of traffic accidents dramatically decreased. Initially, people believe that Rems's solution worked. But, a closer evaluation revealed that there were other factors at work: (1) the area contains two large universities which were closed during the month, and (2) a major highway which normally brings traffic into the area was temporarily closed for repairs, causing traffic to be detoured out of the area. Both of these factors contributed to a decrease in traffic in Sergeant Rems's target area. With less vehicles in the area, accidents naturally decreased dramatically. It may not have been due to the increased traffic enforcement as originally thought.

Evaluation and follow-up to the implementation of solutions is the most overlooked part of problem solving. Most problem solvers, once obtaining results, are content to leave the condition behind them and move on to something else. The true problem solver, however, doubles-back to make sure the specific goals or objectives have been met, that it is a result of what has been done, and also ensures that the condition is not re-occurring.

PROBLEM SOLVING: PROACTIVE OR REACTIVE?

Should problem solving be proactive or reactive? Actually it is of necessity, both. It is not uncommon for the supervisor to be approached by subordinates and hear, "Boss, I got a little problem." When a supervisor reacts to this (which is in reality a request for assistance), he is engaging in reactive problem solving. Reactive problem solving is responding to problems as they come along. Since a certain portion of problems are unpredictable, a supervisor must always be prepared for reactive problem solving, i.e., waiting for problems to come to you. But proactive problem solving is the opposite, it is taking the offensive and looking for the problem before it finds you.

Proactive Problem Solving

The supervisor must be persistent in seeking and ferreting out potentially problematic situations before they are formally brought to his attention and, ideally, before they become full-fledged problems. "As a supervisor you are often faced with many problems, more than you can possibly handle at any given time. These problems are sometimes brought to your attention forcefully. But to be really effective, you can't wait for problems to arise. You need to take the initiative and analyze your operations, looking regularly for problems and potential problems."[6]

The key to proactive problem solving lies in using available resources. Early detection of problems can be achieved through the use of resources such as agency records and information obtained from subordinates and people outside the agency. Uncovering patterns is the surest way for early detection of problems.

If a supervisor receives separate and different complaints from seemingly unrelated sources about the same officer, the supervisor should attempt to identify if any underlying problem exists concerning the officer. Putting isolated facts together and establishing patterns which may indicate the existence of a problem is at the heart of proactive problem solving.

THE PROBLEM-SOLVING MEETING

When a problem affects an entire unit, the supervisor should use a problem-solving meeting to address it. Certain issues are very conducive to group discussion format, while others are not. For example, group meetings are helpful for issues such as: decreasing accidents involving agency vehicles, reducing paperwork, improving maintenance of equipment, etc. But it would not be appropriate to use a problem-solving meeting to decide how to specifically deal with an employee's poor performance. The problem-solving meeting has its place, but it should never be used as a substitute for the supervisor making his own administrative decisions.

The problem-solving meeting employs an open dialogue format. The participants discuss a problem which affects the entire group under the direction of a chairperson. Their aim is to come up with a solution to their collective problem.

Preparing for a Problem-Solving Meeting

The preparation by the chairperson prior to the meeting is critical for the meeting's success. Prior to the meeting, the chairperson should clearly define the problem and the aim of the meeting. A meeting without purposeful leadership will prove as unwieldy as an agency without leadership. The chairperson is responsible for selecting those whom he thinks should attend the meeting. This group of people should represent a cross-section of those in the unit and should be limited to 15 (chairperson included). The reason for limiting the size of the group is that when more than 15 attend it becomes too difficult to manage the group and its discussion.

Prior to the meeting, each attendee should receive a copy of the agenda, a description of the problem and any data which might assist in formulating a position on the issues. Care must be taken by the chairperson not to influence and prejudice the thinking of those invited to attend the meeting. The thoughts they bring to a meeting must be their own if a true consensus is to result.

In addition to the chairperson preparing for the meeting, each invitee must prepare for the meeting by reviewing the agenda and clarifying anything that he does not understand. If it is expected that the invitee is to make any kind of presentation, he should gather beforehand the necessary information and data he needs.

At the Meeting

The chairperson should direct and regulate the flow of discussion so as to involve everyone present. The discussion time should be structured in three phases: the opening, the discussion of issues, and the summary.

The Opening

The chairperson should greet the attendees and ensure that each one knows who is in attendance. The meeting should begin promptly in a cordial atmosphere. The chairperson should begin by clearly reviewing the reason for the meeting and outline the procedure to be followed in conducting the meeting. To get the discussion started, the chairperson should direct a question to the group or a specific individual.

The Discussion of Issues

It is the chairperson's job to stimulate discussion and keep it flowing by involving each person in the discussion. He must guard against any one individual monopolizing the discussion or having the discussion stray from the subject agenda. From time-to-time the skilled chairperson will summarize to clarify what has been accomplished and to keep the discussion on target. The most common error made by an inexperienced chairperson is to pass immediate judgment on remarks made by an attendee. "Don't criticize ideas while generating possible solutions. Criticism during the idea-generation stage inhibits thinking. Also, because discussion tends to get bogged down in criticizing early ideas, only a few ideas are generated."[7] Instead, "the supervisor records all ideas suggested by the group, with ground rules prohibiting criticism, ridicule, and premature evaluation of the merit of any idea."[8] Criticism and judgment during this phase of the discussion of the issues stifle discussion and inhibit participants.

The Summary

The importance of the summary cannot be overstated. It is here that the group comes to a consensus on what has been decided. It is the chairperson's job to ensure that no misunderstanding exists concerning agreements and assignments. The chairperson should underscore what has been agreed to and make sure that any assignments are understood. Those who are expected to perform any tasks as a result of the meeting should clearly understand what is expected of them and by when. If any follow-up meetings are to be held, it is much more efficient to agree to their scheduling at this time while all those who will attend are present.

IN CONCLUSION

Problem solving is one of those tasks that a supervisor must deal with constantly. The problem-solving abilities of supervisors will separate the excellent supervisors from the average supervisors. Problem-solving calls for a proactive approach to identifying problems combined with the confidence and wisdom of knowing you have identified the real problem and not just its symptoms. Problem solving should move along an orderly progression of steps designed, wherever possible, to involve those concerned with the problem in coming up with the solutions to the problem. "In most cases, participation in the problem solving process increases understanding and acceptance of the final decision."[9] Lastly, the supervisor's problem-solving efforts must include an all-important evaluation to determine if the problem has been truly solved. While problem solving is no easy task, the supervisor who becomes successful at it will be recognized and respected by his subordinates.

TEST YOUR UNDERSTANDING

1. What is the definition of a problem?

2. What are the two phases of problem solving?

3. What are the two steps of the first phase of problem solving?

4. What are the three steps of the second phase?

5. Which step is known as the sine qua non of problem solving and why?

6. Why is the role of the first-line supervisor unique?

7. List some resources available to the problem solver.

8. In which step are the investigative skills of the supervisor taxed along with his patience?

9. What elements should be analyzed so that the details of a problem may be revealed?

10. When planning a solution, what actions should a supervisor, as a problem solver, take?

11. What actions are a part of implementing a solution?

12. Describe the last step in problem solving.

13. Should problem solving be a proactive or reactive action? Explain why.

14. What kinds of problems can be handled by a problem-solving meeting? Explain your answer.

15. How should a chairperson prepare for a problem-solving meeting?

16. How should a chairperson of a problem-solving meeting, conduct such a meeting?

FOOTNOTES

1. Rensis Likert and Jane Gibson Likert, *New Ways of Managing Conflict.* (New York: McGraw-Hill Book Company, 1976), p. 126.

2. Dale Carnegie and Associates, *Managing Through People.* (New York: Simon and Schuster, 1975), p. 60.

3. Lester R. Bittel, *What Every Supervisor Should Know - The Basics of Supervisory Management,* 5th ed. (New York: McGraw-Hill Book Company, 1985), p. 152.

4. Carnegie and Associates, p. 88.

5. Kathryn M. Bartol and David C. Martin, *Management.* (New York: McGraw-Hill, Inc., 1991), p. 272.

6. Christina Christenson, Thomas W. Johnson, and John E. Stinson, *Supervising.* (Reading, MA: Addison-Wesley Publishing Company, 1982), p. 220.

7. Bartol and Martin, p. 269.

8. M. Scott Myers, *Every Employee A Manager.* (New York: McGraw-Hill Book Company, 1981), p. 140.

9. Ramon J. Aldag and Arthur P. Brief, *Managing Organizational Behavior.* (St. Paul, MN: West Publishing Company, 1981), p. 266.

SUGGESTED READINGS

Bransford, John.
The Ideal Problem Solver: A Guide for Improving Thinking, Learning and Creativity.
New York: W.H. Freeman, 1984.

Delaney, William A.
The 30 Most Common Problems in Management and How To Solve Them.
New York: AMACOM, 1982.

Jackson, Keith F.
The Art of Solving Problems.
New York: St. Martin's Press, 1975.

Kempner, Charles Higgins.
The Rational Manager: A Systematic Approach to Problem Solving and Decision Making.
New York: McGraw-Hill, 1965.

Margerison, Charles J.
Managerial Problem-Solving.
New York: McGraw-Hill, 1974.

Roth, William F.
Problem Solving For Managers.
New York: Praeger, 1985.

CHAPTER 14
SUPERVISING FIELD OPERATIONS

While much can be said about the law enforcement officer in terms of attitude, insight, and empathy for citizens, the true product and measure of law enforcement service is the results an officer achieves in various field incidents. By the nature of field service, much of what an officer does is removed from the eyes of an immediate supervisor. Therefore, the need for guidance in the form of guidelines is obvious.

IMPORTANCE OF WRITTEN LOCAL GUIDELINES

Guidelines should be written and tailored to the specific requirements of the clients/citizens in individual jurisdictions. In this chapter we will deal with a variety of field incidents and the general guidelines to be followed.

Why Guidelines at All?

Most law enforcement officers, because of the nature of their job, are given a tremendous amount of discretion. This discretion is especially evident in field operations occurring at curbside, in the street. "Discretion is not only proper, but it is a necessary part of police work."[1] Law enforcement officers simply do not have the resources to enforce every statute in each instance of a violation. However, to keep such discretion from becoming capricious and arbitrary, guidelines must be established by the agency. The use of guidelines serves as a check against unbridled discretion.

Guidelines also serve as a standard for officers to aid them in ensuring that certain "must do" steps have been taken in field operations. Guidelines aid the supervisor in evaluating the performance of an officer during certain field operations. For example, "Did the officer get certain specifically required information?" Or, "Did the officer notify his immediate supervisor of the results of certain actions taken?" Guidelines allow officers to evaluate their own actions. "Did I get certain required information?" "Did I advise the client or victim of available resources?"

Training new personnel is easier with the existence of guidelines. Training an officer in handling a situation without existing guidelines leaves the result largely up to the individual expertise, ability and dedication of each instructor. Twelve different instructors, can result in twelve potentially different training results.

Why Written Guidelines?

Guidelines governing field operations should be written. This allows an officer to review in advance what actions should be taken in a particular situation. Written policies and procedures are easier to disseminate to an entire agency than the spoken word. Confusion and misinterpretation can be reduced. Written guidelines are easier to change. Written guidelines serve as a protection for both the agency and the individual officer. A failure by an individual officer to follow written guidelines is certainly more easily documented and provable than if the guidelines were only spoken. Conversely, if an officer can show that he, indeed, followed the written and recorded guidelines of his agency, then he is in a better position to rebut any criticism of his handling of a situation.

Local Guidelines

Guidelines should be local in that they should be able to deal with the peculiar needs of the agency. That does not mean that guidelines used by a state-wide law enforcement agency could not be used by a comparable county or municipal law enforcement agency. It does mean that guidelines must be able to adequately deal with the individual demands created by a particular agency when dealing with a specific field operation.

Although our guidelines can be used by a variety of agencies, restrictions may exist from agency to agency and individual requirements mandated by different geographical jurisdictions should be considered and adhered to. Remember, guidelines are not meant to deal with every incident and situation imaginable. Guidelines do not cover every eventuality.

Too often managers and supervisors believe that the thicker and bigger the book of operational guidelines, the more successful will be the operation. Nothing could be further from the truth. As a book of operational guidelines grows and grows, it becomes a mass of reactive messages. That is, every time an incident occurs, reaction takes place and a rule is created to deal with it. Soon we have a thick book but it is little more than a thickened scar tissue of unrelated and fragmented rules. The wise manager and supervisor detecting this quickly realizes that the problem is more than likely a deeper one of possibly overall lack of training or poor morale within the agency.

GENERIC RULES FOR SUPERVISORS: UNUSUAL OCCURRENCES

While it is difficult to mandate specific actions at all unusual occurrences, there are certain actions which should be taken at any such occurrences.

Definition of Unusual Occurrences

An occurrence which has any of the following traits could qualify as being unusual: seriousness, sensationalism, peculiarity, vastness, news worthiness, causing public unrest. The list could go on and on. Probably the most important factor in determining whether or not an incident should be considered an unusual occurrence is the need to know expeditiously on the part of the head of the agency.[2] Should the "Chief" know about this one and should the "Chief" know about it now? An affirmative answer to either of these questions qualifies an incident to become an unusual occurrence.

Emergency Action

The supervisor must ensure that proper emergency action is taken at the scene of an unusual occurrence. While the actual steps of the supervisor may be different from agency to agency due to size of the agency and reciprocal agreements with other agencies, his principal goal is always the same. He should seek to establish, as much as and as quickly as possible, control of the situation. He should not take the attitude that higher ranking members of the agency will probably respond, so he should delay any action until they arrive. If something needs to be done, he should do it. Steps to first safeguard life, then property, should be taken in that order. Steps geared to protect the rights of individuals over the reputation of the department should be followed.

Consider the following:

Supervisor Rems responds to an arrest of a radical community leader. The newsworthy arrest is determined not to be valid in that insufficient probable cause existed. If the arrested person is immediately released the department will appear foolish and its reputation marred. Nonetheless, the supervisor, in accord with agency guidelines, immediately orders the release of the prisoner.

The supervisor acts correctly. The rights of an individual come before the reputation of the agency.

Notifications

In unusual occurrence situations, information must be quickly transmitted from the scene, and it is the job of the supervisor on the scene to see that this is done by notifying the next higher level of command. This information can be further communicated to higher levels of command either by the same supervisor or by each succeeding level of command.

When making the notification to the next level of command, the supervisor should include requests for assistance, if this has not yet been done. If technical assistance or further life-saving assistance is required, the supervisor makes sure this is obtained. If higher ranking members of the agency are required to respond, the supervisor on the scene also requests their response to the scene.

A checklist of information for notifications would include:

a. Clear and concise description of the incident—We have had a street collapse; there has been a gas explosion.

b. Location and type of premises involved—At 207 East 158 Street, a six story multiple dwelling.

c. Whether a field command post is being established—At 3105 Park Avenue, the Ager Real Estate Company, a field command post is being established.

d. Resulting conditions—Overnight lodging is required for the evacuated occupants of the premises; traffic will be shut down in all three of the southbound lanes of the expressway.

e. Specific personnel requirements—A minimum of three members is required to safeguard property strewn about in adjacent areas due to the explosion; additional traffic control consisting of two traffic control agents is required to detour vehicular and pedestrian traffic from the area.

f. A preliminary account of the dead and injured—Six confirmed dead and fourteen injured at this time.

g. A request to check on the dispatch of the appropriate amount of ambulances and to alert emergency rooms—We'll need three ambulances and have the trauma team at the hospital stand by for an officer with a gunshot wound.

h. Specialized units and equipment—Have the Harbor Unit respond to the Hudson River at West 158 Street; have a unit with a dog noose respond.

Support units exist, as their name indicates, to support line units engaged in field operations. However, support units cannot do their job unless they receive proper notifications containing required information from the line unit at the scene, and that is the supervisor's job.

Reports

A report should be prepared by the supervisor on the scene detailing what has occurred, since he is in the best position to recognize, record and report what has taken place. There is some debate over the format of such a report. Should it be a structured form with captions to be completed or should it be an unstructured narrative report? A structured report is certainly easier to complete and provides standardization which lends itself to computer data storage. However, an unstructured narrative report is wider reaching and has the potential to capture information not obtained by a structured report. At the very least, the report of an unusual occurrence should answer the questions: when, where, who, what, how and why.

Once a report is prepared there is always a chance that persons outside the agency will see the report. However, if certain information is sensitive (e.g., the identity of the victim of a sex offense), it should not be included. Instead a statement such as "a female known to this department" should be included in place of the name of the victim.

At times there is confusion over whether the incident is unusual. If doubt exists over whether or not an incident is unusual, it is recommended that the report and notification be made. The time proven saying, "If you have any doubt, make it out," applies.

FIELD COMMAND POST

The purpose of a field command post is to coordinate police personnel and equipment at the scene of an emergency. A field command post should be established when the circumstances indicate a need for police operations over a period of time, and, in addition, telephone communication and on-site record keeping will improve the handling of the incident.

Duties of the Supervisor

The supervisor in charge of a field command post should notify his supervisor of the incident and include the following:

a. The location and nature of the incident.

b. The location and telephone number of the field command post. Generally the location selected should be:
-Easy to find.
-Safely outside any area of danger (fire/gunshots).
-Near phone lines and electrical power.
-In an area where personnel and equipment can be assembled.

A neutral site should be used. If the incident is a labor dispute, the appearance of favoritism should be avoided by not establishing the field command post on either the facilities of labor or management. Also if time and resources permit, effort should be made to find an alternate location for the field command post in the event the initial selection proves to be unsatisfactory.

c. A request for equipment to assist in setting up the field command post (e.g., command log to record assignments and events, communication equipment, distinguishable logo flag to identify the command post).

Continuing, the supervisor should then:

a. Assign a capable member to make entries in the command log and act as liaison with the press.

b. Prominently display the distinguishable logo flag so that additional personnel responding to the scene will be able to readily identify the field command post.

Duties of Member Maintaining the Field Command Log

The person responsible for the field command log should:

a. Open the log by entering his name and that of the supervisor in charge along with badge or identification numbers.

b. Enter the date, location, telephone number of the command post, and include a brief description of the incident.

c. Enter the names of other supervisors and names of representatives of other agencies.

d. Enter any notifications made as well as describing any further unusual occurrences.

When recording of the names of personnel other than supervisors who respond to the scene, it is probably better to record their names on a separate form, such as some type of detail roster, because of the potentially large number of personnel that might be required to respond. This roster should be kept with the command log for ready reference.

Closing the Field Command Post

The supervisor in charge should:

a. Make similar notifications to those made when the field command post was established indicating it has now been closed.

b. Reassign personnel that have responded to the incident and are no longer needed.

c. Make appropriate entries in the command log indicating that the field command post has been closed.

d. Ensure that equipment from the scene is properly returned. Locations for field command posts can vary from a special mobile bus which the agency uses specifically for such incidents to a private citizen's place of business or even home. When a private citizen volunteers such assistance, formal recognition should be afforded the citizen by the agency.

LABOR DISPUTES

It is the duty of law enforcement personnel policing a labor dispute to preserve the peace and protect life and property at the scene. It is not their duty to settle disputes over working conditions or salaries. Labor disputes unlike most field operations are not spontaneous. They usually occur after a period of negotiations and, then, after the parties concerned openly admit they cannot come to an agreement. This allows the agency sufficient time to plan and prepare for the culmination of a labor dispute, namely the strike.

Supervisor's Role

The field supervisor should respond to the scene upon being notified that a strike has or is about to take place. He should ensure that action has been taken to preserve the peace and prevent injury and destruction of property. The field supervisor should first separately interview a representative of management and labor and obtain background information to aid in the preparation of later reports. The information obtained should include such basic information such as the names of labor and management representatives, why the strike is taking place, and the times any remaining employees and pickets will be present.

After these separate interviews, the field supervisor should bring together the representatives and advise them jointly that:

a. Force, violence and violations of the law will not be tolerated.

b. The role of the agency is strictly neutral.

c. The use of the streets and sidewalks by persons not involved in the strike will not be interfered with.

332

d. The use of professional agitators will not be tolerated.

e. The number of pickets will be determined by the policing agency and not the representatives of labor or management.

The field supervisor will then go about requesting an appropriate assignment of personnel and equipment. In determining personnel assignments, the following factors should be considered:

a. Size of the premises involved and its location.

b. Location of loading docks, exits, and entrances used by employees as well as customers.

c. Times non-striking employees enter and leave the premises for meals or any other reason.

d. Times deliveries are made to the premises.

e. Location of bus or train stops used by non-striking employees.

f. Any other location of which the policing agency should be aware (e.g., a local check cashing place which is used by non-striking employees to cash their pay checks).

If necessary, a field command post should be established and a report on the incident prepared by the field supervisor. The most important issue for a law enforcement agency policing a labor dispute is that the agency must remain impartial. Even the appearance of partiality must be avoided. Impartiality extends to the use of amenities on the premises of management or labor. The facilities of management or labor are not to be used as a field command post.

Arrests

If arrests must be made, they should be made quickly, efficiently and as quietly as possible and the violator removed immediately from the scene. The members on the scene should keep in mind that people involved in a strike are not usually hardened criminals, and so should not allow themselves to be taunted into making arrests. It calls for a great deal of restraint on the part of those members of the agency present. It would be wise for police supervisors at the scene of a strike to give this advice to officers policing a strike, "Remember, if you weren't here in uniform policing this strike and instead were just walking along off-duty in civilian clothes, none of those picketing here would give you a second look, much less dare try to taunt you. Don't take any of this personal."

MISSING PERSONS

There has been an alarming number of persons in our country who voluntarily or involuntarily are "missing"; they seem to vanish without a trace. Law enforcement has recognized this trend and steps have been taken to increase the coordination between agencies charged with the responsibility of finding missing persons. Through the use of shared computerized data and assistance from various sectors of the media, law enforcement has realized a modicum of success in finding missing persons.

But the problem has been compounded by individual jurisdictions with different definitions of what constitutes a missing person.

Definition

To empirically define a missing person is difficult since there are different legal mandates in different jurisdictions. However in 1975, a missing person file was added to the nationwide National Crime Information Center (NCIC). This allowed local law enforcement to enter missing person data into the FBI's NCIC computer and make inquiries, and get instantaneous responses. The criteria for entry into this file included:

"Persons of any age who were missing and had a disability which subjected themselves or others to personal and immediate danger.

Persons of any age who were missing and were in the company of another under circumstances indicating their physical safety was endangered.

Persons of any age who were missing under circumstances indicating that the disappearance was involuntary.

Persons who were missing and who were unemancipated juveniles as defined by the laws of their state and did not meet the entry criteria of the other three categories."[3]

What we offer instead of an all-inclusive definition of a missing person is categories of persons who should definitely not be considered missing persons. They are:

a. Adults (e.g. 18 years old or older) who voluntarily leave home for personal reasons such as domestic or economic reasons.

b. Persons wanted for crimes.

c. Persons wanted on civil or criminal warrants.

Some confusion exists between an unidentified person and a missing person. In an unidentified person case, you have the person but don't know who he is. In a missing person case, you know who the person is, but you don't have the person; he is missing.

Time Requirements

There should be no requirement that a person be missing for a certain period of time before he can be considered missing. If someone was talking about committing suicide and was last seen walking near the river, he is no less missing now than he will be in 24 hours. However, someone who came to town to go swimming and suddenly cannot be found by those accompanying him in his party, should be searched for initially, but any formal report of a missing person should be recorded and investigated by the appropriate law enforcement agency in the jurisdiction where the missing person resides. This is done due to the belief that the best information about the alleged missing person is most likely to be found in the town where the missing lives. Also it is most likely that if the missing is to turn up on his own, he would either return to his home or communicate with someone in the locale where he resides.

Initial Actions

The supervisor should respond to the scene and make sure the responding officers have obtained a good description of the missing person from the complainant, including the clothing he was last seen wearing along with the location where he was last seen. If the missing person is an inpatient in a hospital or an institution, a search of the premises is in order before looking any where else. The supervisor should make sure overhead commands have been notified and the records of the local precinct and of the centralized missing person unit have been checked. While the policy on beginning an immediate search for the missing may vary from agency to agency, it is strongly recommended that immediate action be taken in cases where the missing are:

   a. Mentally or physically handicapped persons,
   b. Possible involuntary disappearances,
   c. Children under 16 years of age,
   d. Possible drowning victims,
   e. Senior citizens sixty-five years old or older.

When an investigation is conducted, it is extremely important to keep meticulous records of persons interviewed and the addresses of premises searched. If the investigation reveals that the missing has been the victim of a crime, the missing person case should be closed and made part of the case alleging that he is a victim of a crime.

HIGH-SPEED PURSUITS

High-speed pursuits cause a large number of injuries to law enforcement officers. The all too familiar movie scene of an officer pursuing a suspect while driving up one-way streets with lights flashing and sirens wailing has unfortunately been glamorized over and over again. This poor attempt at glamorization mixes with a feeling shared by many officers that it is a personal affront when a suspect attempts to flee the scene in a vehicle after being directed by the officer to "pull over." The result is a combination which produces a high speed pursuit that often proves deadly to the officer or innocent bystanders. Therefore, local guidelines should be established to determine the need for a vehicle pursuit, and when such a pursuit is necessary, how to conduct such a pursuit. In absence of such local guidelines, the following is offered as a reference to assist in the handling of high-speed pursuits.

Policy Question: To Chase or Not To Chase?

A pursuit by vehicle should not be initially undertaken nor continued whenever the risks to the police and/or the public outweigh the danger to the public if the perpetrator/suspect is not immediately caught. What must be remembered is that there is always tomorrow. If such immediate risks are more than the danger the perpetrator/suspect poses if he eludes the police, then the officers involved should make every effort to get sufficient information so that an apprehension can be made at a future time.

Definitions

a. "Main vehicle" is the vehicle that started the pursuit.
b. "Backup vehicle" is the first additional vehicle to assist in the pursuit.

Duties of the Main Vehicle

When an officer attempts to stop a vehicle which will not comply and instead flees the scene, the officer must determine the need to start or continue a vehicle pursuit. His decision should be based upon agency policy and weigh certain factors: "What have I got at this time? Is this solely a traffic offense, or is this an armed, dangerous, and violent escaped felon?" He should also ask, "What time of day is it? Are the roads wet and slippery because it is raining? Is this the outskirts of town or the crowded commercial business hub? And how familiar am I with this particular area?" Probably the most forgotten factor for the officer to consider is, "How good is my vehicle?" Just because you are driving an official vehicle does not mean it can successfully apprehend any other vehicle on the road. Some agencies have moved to smaller engine vehicles not only for economic reasons, but also as a way to limit potentially dangerous high-speed pursuits.

If the decision is made to engage in a pursuit, the officer assigned to the main vehicle should notify the dispatcher and inform him of the location and a description of the fleeing vehicle and its occupants. Contact with the dispatcher should be continual with changes in direction of travel indicated as they occur. In communicating with the dispatcher, two errors on the part of the officers involved often crop up. One is that officers seem to depress the transmitter of the radio key unnecessarily which plays havoc with the reception of the transmissions by other concerned units. The other error, and the one most often committed by officers involved in the pursuit, is not keeping radio transmissions brief and not speaking in a normal tone of voice. Excitement begets excitement. While realizing it is very difficult to do, it cannot be overstated that the need for evenly voiced transmissions is a must. Such transmissions assist in keeping a pursuit as it should be - that is, a professional undertaking designed to compel a non-compliant person into complying with the officers while constantly being aware of the danger to the public at large as well as to the officers.

If the pursued vehicle is lost or the pursuit is terminated, the officer should notify the radio dispatcher.

Duties of the Backup Vehicle

The officer assigned to the backup vehicle should immediately acknowledge the "backup" assignment with the dispatcher. He should maintain a safe distance from the main vehicle. It is recommended that at least five (5) car-lengths distance be maintained from the main vehicle. He should not pass the main vehicle unless requested by the main vehicle, or if some other situation exists such as an accident or mechanical trouble.

Duties of the Supervisor

The supervisor should direct and control the pursuit and any apprehension effort. By monitoring the radio, the supervisor should limit the use of the radio by units other than the main and backup vehicles. Vehicles other than the main and backup vehicles should be prevented from forming a caravan behind the pursued vehicle. The main and backup vehicles should be the only vehicles in close pursuit of the pursued vehicle. When necessary, the supervisor should terminate the pursuit despite the fact the perpetrator/suspect has not been apprehended. Although it may be an unpopular decision, it may very well be the wise decision. In cases where the perpetrator/suspect has eluded the police, the supervisor should coordinate a search of the area where the pursued vehicle was last seen. If appropriate information about the vehicle and the perpetrator/suspect has been obtained, it is often more productive to search in a specific area than continue the high speed pursuit and risk injury to innocent parties or the officers themselves.

After a pursuit has been terminated, the coordinating supervisor should prepare a report detailing the events and results of the pursuit. Such a report serves two purposes. First it reveals if agency policy was followed, and second, it allows the agency to evaluate the tactics used during pursuits in order to maintain the highest safety standards.

Tactics

Although each agency should develop local guidelines, these are some general tactics to consider:

a. There should be no driving alongside a pursued vehicle.

b. Ramming the pursued vehicle with an officer's vehicle should be prohibited.

c. The positioning of an officer's moving vehicle so that it will be struck by the pursued vehicle should be prohibited.

d. Roadblocks should be permitted only when directed by supervisory authority.

e. Vans and scooters should not be used in high speed pursuits.

f. Use of unmarked vehicles should be limited.

g. Two-wheel motorcycles may be used initially, but their use should be terminated upon arrival at the scene by a four wheel vehicle.

HOSTAGE/BARRICADED PERSONS

Law enforcement officers are presented with a unique set of problems in dealing with hostage/barricaded persons situations. A person who commits a crime and then seeks to prevent his arrest by fleeing and barricading himself in a building or other premises is considered a barricaded person. Also considered a barricaded person is someone who is discovered during the commission of a crime and barricades himself at the scene to prevent his apprehension by the police. When such a person takes a hostage, the situation becomes a hostage persons incident. In either type of situation, the need for specific policy guidelines are a must for a law enforcement agency. As always the needs of the individual agencies as well as local laws and mandates should determine policy for the individual agencies. However, certain guidelines can be based on prior experiences by law enforcement. Because of the similarity between hostage persons incidents and barricaded person incidents, the guidelines that follow have applications to both types of incidents.

Initial Actions of Responding Officers

The goal of the first officers on the scene is the same as the overall goal when dealing with such incidents, namely to handle the situation with maximum safety to all persons concerned. After determining that it is a valid incident, the officers should verify that help in the form of any available specialists and the supervisor is on the way. Pending the arrival of help, the subjects, if at all possible, should be confined and isolated. Firearms control should be maintained. Because such events often bring about large crowds, police lines should be established early on since it becomes increasingly difficult to move bystanders later. Any witnesses should be identified and asked to remain. They will prove extremely useful in developing a profile of the subjects involved, in making any arrests and in aiding in prosecutions which may result from the event.

From the outset, the initial responding officers need to realize that the response to hostage/barricaded persons situations represent somewhat of a departure from traditional police responses. If the barricaded subject is contained and poses no immediate threat, no attempt should be made to take him into custody. The arrival of the supervisor should be awaited. When there is time to negotiate, all the time that is necessary to ensure the safety of all persons involved should be used. Deadly force should be used only to protect lives of those present and then only as a last resort. It is this "buying time" through the use of specially trained negotiators that is somewhat unique.

Why Is Time Important?

No two such confrontations are exactly alike. Therefore it follows that no one response can be devised to deal with all such confrontations. However, experience has shown that time is a most important factor in such instances. The first fifteen to forty-five minutes are the most dangerous.[4] Buying time can result in the following:

a. Generally the more time a captor and the hostage spend together, the more they become acquainted and develop feelings which decreases the likelihood that the captor will harm the hostage. Curiously enough, something called the "Stockholm Syndrome" sometimes occurs. This is where the hostages also develop feelings of "everlasting gratitude"[5] for their captors.

b. It allows the police to develop intelligence which leads to specific plans that are tailored for the particular incident.

c. It allows the police to apprehend the subject if the appropriate opportunity presents itself.

d. It allows the hostages to "escape" if the right circumstances present themselves. (A word of caution here. Such actions must be taken based on an individual and accurate assessment of the situation at hand and should not be undertaken unless the hostage is absolutely certain of the success of his efforts.)

e. Being able to buy time allows authorities to buy still more time through a continuation of the negotiations.

Duties of the Supervisor

The responding supervisor should make sure that firearms control has been established and continues to be maintained. Those at the scene should not use their firearms unless their lives or the life of another at the scene is in immediate danger. The supervisor should request enough personnel support to assist in crowd control and also verify that any specially equipped personnel and available specially trained negotiators are responding.

It will be necessary to establish a field command post to coordinate activities at the scene. Because of the number of personnel responding, an area for their briefing and assembling should be selected by the supervisor. The area in the vicinity of the incident should be divided into an inner and outer perimeter. The size and location of such perimeters of course depend on the particular incident at hand. However, the inner perimeter should be an area which is frozen to all unauthorized persons, admitting only certain selected official personnel as permitted by agency policy. The field command post should not be within the inner perimeter, and if the use of gas is to be considered, the command post should be upwind from the scene. The outer perimeter should be an area from which civilians have been removed and from which official personnel not involved in the incident are excluded. Even after the incident has ended, the outer perimeter should continue to be maintained so that if members of the press are now to be admitted into the outer perimeter they can be easily identified and separated from curious citizens.

Specially Trained Negotiators

A great amount of training at the county, state and federal level is available for officials conducting negotiations in hostage/barricaded persons incidents. The degree and specificity of the training must be dictated by the needs of the agency. However, as is often the case, there are certain general traits that should be exhibited by negotiators.

a. Their appearance and bearing should be one which creates a perception on the part of the barricaded person or hostage taker that they are persons of authority.

b. While they present themselves as persons of authority, they should not portray themselves the ultimate decision maker. This allows the negotiators to defer decisions, thus buying more time.

c. They should possess a calm and evenhanded demeanor, and should not express negative attitudes which could intensify

342

the confrontation. Negotiators should remember that the hostage taker, the captor, is in a "fight or flight state."[6]

d. Negotiators should operate on the premise that practically everything is negotiable except:

1. Weapons will not be supplied. If the subject presently is in possession of a bogus or unloaded weapon, supplying weapons obviously only creates a worse danger.
2. No additional hostages are to be given or exchanged.
3. There can be no releasing of other prisoners who are presently in lawful custody.

Types of Hostage Captors or Barricaded Persons

Each hostage taker or barricaded person is an individual with an individual makeup and individual thoughts. In dealing with such persons, it has been found to be helpful to try to create various profiles which indicate common characteristics.

a. The Professional Criminal Who Has Had His Escape Blocked

This is usually the easiest type of captor for law enforcement officials to deal with after the situation has stabilized. The reason is that he is relatively rational, and usually comes to terms with the authorities after assessing the situation and balancing the odds of his actions. In most cases unnecessary violence and useless injuries are thus avoided.

b. The Emotionally Disturbed Person

He presents complex problems. Less predictable since he is not rational, such a person harbors great conflict and inner frustration. Hence, particular attention should be given to the words he uses and the demands he makes. He may enjoy being the center of all the attention, a position in which he rarely finds himself. Time is important here since such persons expend a great deal of energy due to being emotionally tense and thus can eventually wear themselves down.

c. The Terrorist

Such persons create the greatest difficulty for law enforcement. They see themselves as freedom fighters seeking justice. They claim to have a strong resolve to die for their cause. However, with the passage of time even such a resolve has been seen to deteriorate, leaving them open to committing errors which have allowed authorities to ultimately take them into custody before injuries occur.

Multiple Hostage Situations

Some terrorist organizations train their members to simultaneously engage in multiple incidents so that the response of law enforcement officials will be divided and thus diminished. A dangerous characteristic of such terrorist actions is that the terrorist subjects at each location compete with each other, thereby toughening their determination not to give in as long as their colleagues at other locations continue to hold out. It is difficult to conduct negotiations in such circumstances since the actions of one hostage group tend to reinforce the other. As difficult as it is to deal with such a situation, certain actions are recommended:

a. If multiple situations develop simultaneously, they should be deemed to be related until concrete evidence indicates otherwise.

b. If not related, then proceed as in any other hostage/barricaded person incident. But if related, then as soon as possible, any communication between the terrorists should be severed.

c. Also, if related, each field command post at the scene of each incident should stay in constant contact with a separate central coordinating unit so that information between the authorities at each incident can be centrally analyzed and quickly shared.

d. Decisions regarding negotiation efforts should be coordinated by one separate central coordinating unit, if the incidents are found to be related.

344

Direct Action

Each decision that is made must be made with the understanding that the lives of the hostages, the public at large, and the officials involved are sacred. If a captor kills one of the hostages, then a decision must be made whether to take direct assaultive action or continue dialogue. While it is true that if a barricaded person kills one hostage, he may kill more, it is not always the case. However, as soon as one hostage is killed, all available intelligence must be updated with an eye toward determining if this is totally due to the depravity of the barricaded person or if the conduct of the hostage precipitated the fatal action. An evaluation must be made to determine if direct action intended to rescue the hostage would endanger the hostage more than the anticipated actions of the barricaded person. Any action to be taken should not be impromptu but should be the product of highly trained specialists.

Taking A Barricaded Person Into Custody

In instances when a barricaded person has opted to come out and surrender to the authorities, he should be directed to come out with hands held high in the air and fingers spread far apart in open view. The officers involved should not leave their positions of cover to advance toward the subject. Even hostages should be directed to advance toward the officers with their hands held high above their heads so that it can be conclusively determined that they are in fact unarmed hostages and not accomplices of the barricaded person.

EMOTIONALLY DISTURBED PERSONS

When law enforcement officers encounter persons who suffer from mental illness, they must remember that by and large such persons are not criminals. They are simply in need of medical attention. The job of the officers, therefore, is one of assistance and certainly not one of punishment. Actually their role involves protecting such persons who do not voluntarily seek medical attention until they can be safely delivered to medical authorities.

Definition of an Emotionally Disturbed Person (EDP)

"There are lots of difficulties with the term mental illness, which arise from the subjectivity and arbitrariness which are often present in judging who is and who is not mentally ill."[7] Existing individual agency guidelines on what exactly constitutes an EDP along with local legal mandates should be followed. Where none exist, however, the following definition is offered as a guide:

An EDP is a person who through his actions appears to be suffering from mental illness or a temporary derangement and conducts himself in a manner which the responding officer reasonably believes will be likely to cause serious injury to himself or others.

Use of Force

State penal codes and/or state mental hygiene laws usually describe the limits on the use of force when dealing with emotionally disturbed persons. "In addition, civil laws usually provide for temporary custody of individuals who appear to be in need of immediate emergency observation because of some emotional or mental breakdown."[8] However, individual agencies should provide additional guidelines to help officers in such situations so as to protect the officers from injury and civil liability. The following is a sample of such guidelines as used by the New York City Police Department.

"The primary duty of all members of the service is to preserve human life. The safety of ALL persons involved is paramount in cases involving emotionally disturbed persons. If such person is dangerous to himself or others, necessary force may be used to prevent serious physical injury or death. Physical force will be used ONLY to the extent necessary to restrain the subject until delivered to a hospital or detention facility. Deadly physical force will be used ONLY as a last resort to protect the life of the uniformed member of the service assigned or any other person present. IF THE EMOTIONALLY DISTURBED PERSON IS ARMED OR VIOLENT, NO ATTEMPT WILL BE MADE TO TAKE THE EDP INTO CUSTODY WITHOUT THE SPECIFIC DIRECTION OF A SUPERVISOR UNLESS

THERE IS AN IMMEDIATE THREAT OF PHYSICAL HARM TO THE EDP OR OTHERS PRESENT. If the EDP is not immediately dangerous, the person should be contained until assistance arrives. If the EDP is unarmed, not violent and willing to leave voluntarily, the uniformed member of the service may take such person into custody. When there is time to negotiate, all the time necessary to insure the safety of all individuals will be used."[9]

Actions of Responding Officers

The first thing the responding officers should do is make an assessment of the situation. This assessment should answer the question, "What is the level of threat of immediate serious injury to the subject EDP or anyone else present?" If the EDP is unarmed, not violent and willing to leave voluntarily, the officers may take such person into custody. But if the EDP is acting in a way which constitutes an immediate threat of serious injury to anyone present, the officers should take appropriate steps to terminate and further prevent such action. While such actions on the part of the officers could include the use of deadly force, it should be used only as a last resort to protect the lives of those present.

Threatening actions on the part of the EDP which are restricted solely to damaging property should not necessarily be considered as a threat to life.

In situations where the actions of the EDP do not constitute an immediate threat of serious injury to anyone present, and the EDP is either armed, violent or unwilling to leave voluntarily, the officers should attempt to isolate and contain the EDP. While containing the EDP, a safe zone distance (usually a minimum of twenty to twenty-five feet) should be maintained between the officers and the EDP. The officers should request the response of an ambulance, special equipment and additional personnel, if required, and the patrol supervisor. While awaiting such responses, the officers should establish police lines, if necessary.

Actions of Responding Supervisor

The responding supervisor should ensure that firearms discipline is maintained and police lines, if required, have been established. If special equipment is on the scene and is necessary, he should supervise its distribution and use. Sometimes the assistance of family, friends, or clergy can aid in the voluntary removal of the EDP. When the EDP is restrained, he should be removed to a hospital in an ambulance. Restraints may be required based on his being violent or upon the direction of a physician. An officer should accompany the EDP to the hospital along with medical personnel. The supervisor should not allow the EDP to be removed to a law enforcement facility. The EDP is not a criminal. He is in need of medical assistance. At the medical facility, attending medical personnel should be informed if non-lethal devices were used in subduing or restraining the EDP.

DOMESTIC DISPUTES

Law enforcement officials have become increasingly aware of the violence which takes place in the home. Often this violence carries over to the officers who respond to such incidents. Because of this potential for violence and the frequency of such calls for assistance, it is important to be extremely familiar with the issues and tactics involved:

What Is a Family?

Local laws define what exactly constitutes a family. Usually one can find included in such legal definitions:

    a. persons who are or have been related by formal legal marriages.
    b. persons who are related by blood (e.g., brothers and sisters).
    c. persons who may have never been married or never even lived together but have had a child in common.

These categories of persons, often defined as families, find protection and jurisdiction under a state's various laws intended to deal with families. However, progressive agencies realize that

348

different domestic arrangements may also demand the protection of law enforcement. Thus these agencies now include in their procedures to deal with domestic disputes the following domestic arrangements:

a. common law marriages.
b. relatives of common law marriage partners who reside in the same household.
c. same sex domestic partners.
d. relatives of same sex couples who reside in the same household.

It would be wise for agencies to expand their definition, so that "families" include a broader living arrangement for those who need law enforcement protection. The frequency of such dispute calls and the potential for violence demands such an expansion.

Actions of Responding Officers

Because of the frequency of such calls, officers tend to develop a certain laxity when handling domestic disputes. The reality is that such assignments have the potential for being extremely dangerous and volatile. At times the use of alcohol by one or more of those involved compounds the potential for violence. In addition, those involved often turn their anger toward the officers, holding the officers responsible for what they are experiencing, and make the officers a target for their violent acts.

Responding officers should strive to obtain as much advance information as possible, such as a call-back number for the complainant and information about reported injuries and weapons. Full information can go a long way in strengthening the officers' ability to successfully handle the incident.

When a weapon is involved, officers must be careful since often one of the parties involved will falsely indicate that the other party is in possession of a firearm merely to provoke a confrontation between the police and the person who is the subject of the complaint. Sometimes a helpful way of verifying information is by the receipt of numerous calls about the complaint. If, for example, a complainant indicates that her son is beating his sister who is screaming for help, there is obviously a good chance that neighbors will be calling in and making a similar complaint. Another way of verifying that information received about a domestic dispute is valid is to ask nearby neighbors and tenants. Often they will not be willing to verbalize any information but are quite willing to give information through gestures and facial expressions.

Officers should not approach the entrance to the place of the dispute shoulder to shoulder. This initial approach places the officers in a vulnerable position. Their actions should always be geared toward presenting the smallest target possible. Noise emanating from inside the premises should alert the officers to the level of violence and the presence of multiple disputants. When the officers announce their presence, they should not stand directly in front of the entrance door. Just because a door exists between the officers and those inside does not guarantee cover and offer complete safety. The same care must be exercised if there are windows adjacent to the entrance door.

The officers should be confident and professional and avoid being officious and overbearing. After all, they are in the home of someone who is experiencing a difficult situation. Quite often at least one of the parties will see the officers as interfering and meddlesome. The officers should attempt to separate the parties involved and get the facts. However, the officers should remain within sight of each other so that assistance can be rendered should the need arise. Rooms which have the greatest potential for impromptu weapons should be avoided. Typically, the best example of such a room is the kitchen. The officers should avoid the appearance of favoritism. When interviewing the parties, an officer should be constantly aware of his own weapon and position himself in such a way so that the weapon is kept out of reach of the party being interviewed. The officer's weapon should be securely holstered so that it can not be pulled from the officer's holster by one of the parties present. Being constantly alert is key since even though a party being interviewed appears to be responding calmly, it must be remembered that there is great underlying stress in such situations, and this could cause an eruption of violent actions at any time.

350

Arrest or Mediate

Here the policy of each agency must be clear and in keeping with all applicable laws of the region. Some experts describe a "frequently used alternative to advise the parties to come into the office of the police department or the prosecuting attorney (depending on your own department practices) during the next business day and to discuss the matter at that time. Then, if it is determined that an arrest should be made, steps will be taken to secure a warrant and effect the arrest."[10]

However, more and more agencies are developing policies which are NOT geared toward mediating the incident on the scene but which instead are opting to make summary arrests. For example, the mandates given to the officers of the New York City Police Department: "An arrest must be made when officers determine there is probable cause that a felony was committed, an Order of Protection was violated, a misdemeanor was committed and the victim wants an arrest, or a violation has occurred in the officer's presence and the victim wants an arrest."[11]

It is reasoned that by bringing the dispute before a magistrate, the full services of the government can be applied to correct the situation. The old arguments that making such arrests would unnecessarily clog the courts are being pushed aside as more and more incidents of spousal assaults and severe child abuse receive attention. Possibly the best argument against the officer mediating domestic disputes is the question, "Would they be expected to mediate a burglary?" If criminal conduct has taken place, the responding officers should be encouraged by law and agency policy to make the arrest as in any other criminal situation where the level of proof sufficient to make an arrest exists.

BOMB THREATS

Most bomb threats turn out to be unfounded. Nonetheless there have been numerous recorded instances where anonymous bomb threats turned out to be the real thing and have resulted in injuries and death. Agency guidelines should be created for dealing with these situations.

Duties of Responding Officers

Officers responding to a bomb threat should interview the person who received the threat and obtain as much information as possible such as:

1. the exact location or premises which was the object of the bomb threat.
2. the exact location of the alleged bomb, if available.
3. the time the bomb is expected to explode.
4. a description of the bomb.
5. any reason given or suspected for the threatened bombing.

This interview should not be delayed since the facts will be fresher in the mind of the person interviewed, and important points may be forgotten as time passes. Careful interview of the specific person who received the threat may lead to identifying the caller. Questions geared to identifying the following should be asked about:

1. the caller's voice.
2. repeated word or phrases.
3. unusual word patterns.
4. when the call or calls were made (i.e. time of the day and day of the week).
5. any background noises.

The responding officers should request the response of the supervisor. However, this should be done by landline telephone and not portable radio since radio transmissions from the scene could cause detonation.

Conducting the Search

The supervisor should respond to the scene and set up a command post to act as a central location for information and a location for the assembling and assigning of responding personnel. Such supervisor should organize and instruct search teams. Because of the inherent dangers of conducting such a search, personnel assigned to the search should be kept at the minimum number able to efficiently carry out the search. The search team should be constantly aware of what appears to be "out of the ordinary" and not "normal."

Custodial personnel can prove helpful in discovering objects which are out of place or would normally be foreign to the premises. Stairs instead of elevators should be used by the search team. This ensures that stairwells will be examined for any suspected explosive device. If an elevators must be taken, those not used by the public should be used. This allows for the search of an area possibly overlooked and provides a method for evacuation for the building occupants if necessary. The decision whether to evacuate a private premises while a search is conducted should be made by the person in charge of the premises. If there is a threatened time of explosion, and the decision is made to evacuate, then all persons including search teams should leave the area at least twenty minutes before the threatened time of explosion and not return until at least one hour after such time. When persons are evacuated from the scene, they should move to a safe distance of at least one thousand feet. When leaving the premises, lights should not be turned off since this has caused detonations. During such periods thought must be given to preventing thefts from the now evacuated premises.

The search teams should look behind articles such as office furniture in reception areas and be instructed against disturbing anything that resembles a possible explosive device. If such a device is found, they should not touch it and should immediately notify the command post. The notification should not be made by portable radio, because as previously indicated a radio transmission from the scene could cause detonation. Specialized units should be dispatched, and the search team should continue its search, because even though a suspected explosive device may have been found, it may not be the only one. The supervisor should have the bomb squad or other specialized unit respond and remove the device.

Post Explosion Bomb Scenes

Upon responding to the scene where an explosion has occurred, the supervisor should have personnel conduct an immediate search for dead, injured and trapped persons. Steps must be taken to safeguard the property of such persons who are being removed from the scene. After the initial search efforts have been completed, the supervisor should have all persons evacuated to a safe distance once again of at least one thousand feet and await the arrival of the bomb squad or other specialized unit. Care should be taken in the locating of witnesses, including children who may have seen persons loitering in the area. Vehicular and pedestrian traffic should be diverted from the scene as necessary. A post explosion bomb scene is to be treated as a crime scene and therefore should be safeguarded. No one should be allowed through the police lines into the crime scene until the bomb squad or other appropriate unit has declared the scene safe from other devices. The only exception is the fire department engaged in putting out an active fire.

AREA AND BUILDING SEARCHES

Searching is commonly understood as generally seeking or examining. However, in law enforcement, two additional factors must be added to this understanding of searching. They are:

1. whom you are looking for and
2. where should you look.

In addition to the legal guidelines of when and where it is permissible to search areas and buildings, there are general tactical guidelines which can prove useful to law enforcement officers when conducting searches of areas and buildings.

Outside Searches

Searches conducted outdoors, outside of premises, can follow certain tactical guidelines. How well the search will be conducted depends on how well it is organized. It will be well organized if it is coordinated and systematic.

Coordinating an outdoors search is the job of the supervisor. Personnel assisting in the search must be clearly and specifically identified as participating in the search and then given specific tasks. For example, personnel assigned to the search must be told three things:

1. That they are being assigned to a search

Here the supervisor should clearly indicate to the personnel selected that they are being relieved of their normal duties to be part of a search effort. This can be done by having them report to a command post set up by the supervisor or can be accomplished merely through radio communication notifications.

2. Whom they are looking for

Is it a search for a missing person, or a wanted person? Aside from identifying the person sought, a complete, full and detailed description as possible should be given along with the location where last seen and any background information about the subject. For example, when searching for a missing child, information such as his play interests can prove helpful.

3. Where they should be looking

Personnel assigned to the search must be told exactly where they are to search, either by street indications or in other open areas by map grids.

The supervisor further coordinates the search by ensuring that the entire area in question is ultimately searched, that a record is made of each segment of the area searched, and that personnel who have completed a search of one area are promptly reassigned to another area which has not yet been searched. The supervisor also ensures that each area is searched systematically. In systematically searching outside of a premises, such as an outdoor area, many methods or techniques are available. Each of them requires the supervisor to assign the personnel available into search teams with specific duties. Search teams should consist of two to four officers depending on the area to be searched, the purpose of the search (e.g., missing person or wanted felon), and of course number of personnel available. Care must be taken by the supervisor to properly motivate the search teams by stressing the importance of, and also the possible dangers involved in the search. Too many officers when pulled away from their normal duties see a search assignment as merely time away from the usual stresses of the job. Nothing could be further from the truth. In addition to the importance of finding the subject of the search, there is the potential for injury to members of a search team.

The Convergence Method

Though there are many methods or searching techniques for outdoor searches, the convergence method is often used with effective results. In this method, the supervisor determines the outdoors area to be searched by referring to either a street map or a field map. Using the location where the person sought was last seen as the center, the supervisor draws a circle on the map. The radius of the circle is the maximum distance the person could have traveled in the time elapsed between the time he was last seen and the time that the search begins. Then supervisor divides the circle into sectors (similar to pieces of a pie) based on the number of search teams. Each team starts at the perimeter of its sector and works its way to the center recording blocks and areas searched. The supervisor also assigns an appropriate number of personnel to act as perimeter guards to prevent the person sought from leaving the encircled area. Helicopter patrol can be of great assistance in assisting perimeter guards in their duties.

Area residents may be informed of the purpose of the officers in their neighborhood. Although some officers may argue that informing area residents only serves to possibly supply the person sought with information which might aid in his escape, as in the case of a wanted felon, by and large most citizens are law-abiding and may prove to be of some assistance to the search team. A word about interaction with area residents. When communicating with an area householder, it is recommended that the communication be conducted outside and away from the householder's home. The reason is that the person sought may have taken refuge inside the home and may be forcing the householder to give false information to the search team.

Inside Building Searches

Because of the numerous variety of situations that can be found indoors, it is not possible to offer only one way to conduct a search indoors. However, certain general guidelines can be established.

Often criminals are trapped in a building during the commission of their criminal conduct or criminals take refuge in a building while attempting to escape from the scene of their crime. The supervisor should establish and assign search teams as is done when conducting outside searches. Officers should be placed at diagonally opposite corners of the building to seal off any avenue of escape at the perimeter. Uniformed officers should be used exclusively if at all possible. If officers normally performing duty in civilian clothes must be used, they should wear some type of distinguishable outer garment to readily identify them as officers to prevent any misidentification between officers and to remove any claims by the person sought that he did not know members of the search team were officers. The best assignment for non-uniformed officers is maintaining the perimeter.

The supervisor should take into account factors peculiar to the building being searched such as its size and the general characteristics of its interior in determining the number of officers in a search team and the number of search teams. Whatever his determination, the number should be kept at the minimum number to effectively conduct the search. Any assistance from janitorial personnel who are familiar with the layout of the building should be incorporated in the supervisor's briefing of search teams.

The search of a multi-level building should begin at the top and continue downward with each area secured by an officer after being searched. This is done to prevent backtracking by the person being sought. To search from the bottom to the roof might allow the person sought to escape to adjacent roofs or become more violent if trapped at the top. If officers are not available to remain in an area after it has been searched, pieces of electric tape can be put it across the crack of doors to rooms that have been searched. If the tape is broken or moved, the person sought may have backtracked.

Extreme caution must be taken when dealing with abandoned buildings, since they pose special hazards such as exposed electrical wires, holes in floors and broken staircases. Search of roofs mandate attention to debris and other obstructions. Also when an officer enters a darkened roof from a lighted stairwell, his body becomes a full silhouette. Prior to opening the door to the roof, it may be advisable to remove the light bulb from the stairwell landing. Fire escapes are also dangerous areas, because they may have become weakened by age and place the officer in a confined area full of obstructions, such as flower pots and clothes, with little cover available. In multi-level buildings where stairways are to be used, officers should not use hand railings which allow the person sought to look down from higher floors and observe a uniform glove or sleeve. In climbing several flights of stairs, it is not advisable to run up and become over fatigued. An officer in a search team not only is required to find the person sought but also to be able to take him into custody once the person is found.

TEST YOUR UNDERSTANDING

1. Why are guidelines necessary in handling field operations?

2. Explain why officer discretion is a necessary part of law enforcement.

3. How do written guidelines protect an officer?

4. What is probably the most important factor in determining whether or not an incident should be considered an unusual occurrence?

5. What is the goal of a supervisor at the scene of an unusual occurrence?

6. What characteristics should a location chosen for a field command post possess?

7. Describe the duties of the member assigned to maintain the field command log.

8. What are the duties of a field supervisor at the scene of a labor dispute?

9. Who should definitely not be a considered missing person?

10. What is the difference between a missing person and an unidentified person?

11. When should a pursuit by a law enforcement vehicle not be initially undertaken or continued?

12. Describe some general recommended guidelines concerning a high speed pursuit.

13. Why is time important regarding a hostage/barricaded persons incident?

14. What are the general traits that should be exhibited by hostage negotiators?

15. What should generally be considered not negotiable at the scene of a hostage/barricaded person incident?

16. What actions should officers take when responding to the scene of an EDP?

17. What actions should a supervisor take when responding to the scene of an EDP?

18. Why have some law enforcement agencies chosen not to mediate domestic disputes?

19. What kind of information should an officer responding to a bomb threat attempt to obtain from the specific person who received the threat?

20. Describe the actions to be taken when conducting an actual search for an explosive device.

21. What is the convergence method of searching?

22. What are some recommended tactics to follow while searching a building?

FOOTNOTES

1. William G. Bailey, editor, *The Encyclopedia of Police Science.* (New York and London: Garland Publishing Co., 1989), p. 147

2. "Patrol Guide." New York City Police Department, 116-07, p. 2.

3. William G. Bailey, editor, p. 331.

4. "Hostage Negotiations - Organizational and Tactical Guide." New York City Police Department, October 1986, p. 14.

5. Captain Frank Bolz and Edward Hershey, *Hostage Cop.* (New York: Rawson, Wade Publishers, Inc. 1979), pp. 304-305.

6. Bolz and Hershey, Op. Cit., p. 313.

7. Ray Bull, *Police Psychology.* (New York: John Wiley and Sons Ltd, 1983), pp. 78-79.

8. Thomas Francis Adams, *Police Field Operations.* (Englewood Cliffs, NJ: Prentice Hall, Inc., 1985), p. 285.

9. "Patrol Guide." New York City Police Department, 106-11, p. 1.

10. Thomas Francis Adams, *Police Field Operations.* p. 212

11. William J. Bratton, *Police Commissioner.* New York City Police Department, FYI, (New York: April 27, 1994), p. 1.

SUGGESTED READINGS

Adams, Thomas Francis.
Police Patrol - Tactics and Techniques.
Englewood Cliffs, NJ: Prentice-Hall, 1971.

Brown, Michael K.
Working The Street - Police Discretion and the Dilemmas of Reform.
Los Angeles, CA: Russell Sage Foundation, 1981.

Foley, Vern L.
Police Patrol Techniques and Tactics.
Springfield, IL: Charles C. Thomas, Publisher, 1973.

Goldstein, Arnold P., Philip J. Monti, Thomas J. Sardino and Donald J. Green.
Police Crisis Intervention.
Kalamazoo, MI: Behaviordelia, Inc., 1977.

Larson, Richard C.
Synthesizing and Extending the Results of Police Patrol Studies.
Washington, D.C.: U.S. Department of Justice, National Institute of Justice, 1985.

Larson, Richard C.
Urban Police Patrol Analysis.
Cambridge, MA: MIT Press, 1972.

Leonard, V.A.
Police Patrol Organization.
Springfield, IL: 1970.

Levine, Margaret J.
Patrol Deployment.
Washington, D.C.: U.S. Department of Justice, National Institute of Justice, Office of Communication and Research Utilization, 1985.

Miron, H. Jerome.
Managing Patrol Operations - A Trainer's Handbook.
Washington, D.C.: University Research Corp., 1981.

Reuss-Ianni, Elizabeth.
Two Cultures of Policing - Street Cops and Management Officers.
New Brunswick, NJ: Transaction Books, 1983.

Wingate, Anne, Ph.D.
Scene of the Crime - A Writer's Guide to Crime Scene Investigations.
Cincinnati, OH: Writer's Digest Books, 1992.

CHAPTER 15
THE USE OF PHYSICAL FORCE

More than anything else, what separates law enforcement officers from others in the community is their extraordinary legal authority to make arrests and to use force. This two-edged legal authority is the reason for a great deal of public dissatisfaction with law enforcement agencies.

It is the first-line supervisor who is the key figure in the agency's effort to ensure that the use of force by officers is consistent with existing statutory and case law and with agency policy

WRITTEN POLICY GOVERNING THE USE OF FORCE

Unfortunately, some administrators feel it is unnecessary to create specific written guidelines to govern the use of force. They argue that such guidelines are instead the province of state lawmakers and federal and state judges. Statutory law makes conduct otherwise considered criminal justifiable and not criminal when committed by law enforcement officers under certain circumstances. Federal and state courts then create case law which amends such statutory law. But agency policy must supplement the use of force used by officers. Deadly force policies that, in both philosophy and substance, emphasize the sanctity of life over the need to apprehend suspects have reduced killings by law enforcement personnel—and the backlash that often follows—without negative effects on the safety of citizens or the safety and effectiveness of officers.[1]

Many Use of Force Considerations Are Not Covered by Law

The primary reason why agency policy must be created and why it must be more restrictive than the law is that there are many use of force considerations which are simply not covered by the law. For instance, only agency policy can address: Who in the agency should be held responsible and accountable for the proper use of force? and Should officers be allowed to discharge their firearms at or from a moving vehicle? The need for a definitive written agency policy becomes most apparent during personnel complaint investigations and civil liability suits.

All law enforcement agencies should have a detailed written use of force policy, and this policy and any subsequent amendments, including pertinent court decisions, should be made available to every member and should be covered during formal, in-service training programs.

THE CARDINAL USE OF FORCE RULE

The primary duty of all law enforcement officers is to preserve human life. Therefore, the cardinal rule of any use of force policy must be that excessive force by officers will never be tolerated. It should be made clear that even when the use of force is appropriate, only that amount of force that is necessary should be used. It must be stressed that this rule applies at all times, even when preventing a crime. Too many law enforcement officers feel that the prevention of a crime justifies the unbridled use of force. However, many civil court juries across the country are taking the position that if an officer uses excessive force—even while preventing a violent crime—the victim is entitled to damages.

ACCOUNTABILITY

All sworn law enforcement personnel, regardless of rank, should be responsible and accountable for the proper use of force. But how should this rule be enforced at the scene of an incident where force is being used by an officer in the presence of other officers? In such a situation, all officers present are obligated to ensure that the requirements of the law and agency policy are upheld.

Intervention Should be Mandated

Law enforcement officers at the scene of an incident where inappropriate use of force is clearly being applied by another officer CANNOT be relieved of their sworn duty to value human life and respect the dignity of individuals. This means that all officers present are required to intervene if the use of force against a subject clearly becomes excessive. Shortly after the Rodney King incident, Chief Daryl Gates spoke at a press

366

© 1995 by J. & B. Gould
Printed in the U.S.A.   Ms

conference and stated, "What they [LAPD members at the scene of the King incident] should have done, if they really loved their Brother officers [was to] have stepped in and grabbed them and hauled them back and said 'Knock it off!' That's what the sergeant should have done [and] that's what every officer there should have done."[2] Failure to so intervene should result in disciplinary action and may also result in both criminal and civil liability.

Even if an officer was not directly involved in the original incident, upon observance of a fellow officer's excessive force he is required to intervene. This intervention can take many forms. One can intervene without resorting to the use of physical force. However, the intervening officer must always request the immediate response of a supervisor to the scene of the incident. If a supervisor is already present, then the intervening officer must call the supervisor's attention to the situation.

Some officers feel that a rule which requires them to intervene against another officer is a radical departure from traditional law enforcement procedures and is a divisive force in an occupation where teamwork is essential. Those officers have to be reminded that they are sworn to uphold the law and that it is a criminal offense for an officer to use force that is "clearly" excessive. When an officer engages in unjustifiable criminal conduct, he or she must be treated as a criminal. It is as simple as that. Officers are not above the law.

REQUIRED PROCEDURES

Instances of the inappropriate use of force are extremely detrimental to an agency for many reasons. Primary among these reasons are the unwarranted suffering to the victim and the resulting breakdown of trust between the agency and the community. But, surprisingly, even the appropriate use of force can result in damaged community relations. Often this is caused by a lack of definitive procedures which require the investigation of the facts surrounding instances of the use of force. Nothing counters allegations of cover-up better than proof of a professionally conducted investigation made at the time of occurrence, as opposed to the time of allegation. Unfortunately, the opposite is also true. Allegations of cover-up appear credible and warranted in the absence of such a timely investigation.

Supervisor Involvement

A supervisor must be notified by the officer involved whenever force is used to accomplish the agency mission. Management should analyze all department forms to insure that, where appropriate, the forms directly address if and how force was used. The specific form should request the name of the supervisor who was notified. This rule is not meant solely for arrest situations but for all incidents which could appropriately give rise to the use of force. These include: arrests, investigative stops, domestic disputes, and situations involving mentally ill and emotionally disturbed persons.

In turn, the investigating supervisor notified about the use of force must be required to conduct an immediate investigation. The extent of required investigations will vary depending on the circumstances. But in each investigation a written report of the results of investigation must be made. When appropriate, this requirement may be met by entries in department records, as well as in the supervisor's official notebook. In other cases, such as when an officer discharges his firearm or when the subject is physically injured, the investigating supervisor must be required to submit a detailed report to his commanding officer.

Involvement of the Senior Officer Present

The nature of law enforcement work is such that it is impossible to ensure the presence of a supervisor at every incident. The overwhelming majority of incidents, including many which involve the use of force, are handled in the absence of direct supervision. In recognition of this, all law enforcement agencies should have a rule which mandates that, when no supervisor is present at the scene of an incident, the senior member present at the scene will direct and coordinate agency operations pending the arrival of a supervisor.

DEADLY PHYSICAL FORCE

When an officer uses deadly physical force and takes, or attempts to take, the life of another he, in effect, usurps the authority of the courts in that he pronounces guilt and administers punishment in the absence of due process. This is not meant in any way to be a negative statement about the authorized use of deadly physical force by law enforcement officers. It is part of their job. Instead it is meant to emphasize the enormous power society has seen fit to delegate to law enforcement officers, as well as the tremendous responsibility it places on law enforcement agencies to ensure that such power is not abused. To meet this responsibility every law enforcement agency must, at a minimum: (1) have detailed written guidelines in place regulating the use of deadly physical force, and (2) take the necessary steps to ensure that every sworn member of the agency is fully aware of these guidelines.

The Laws of Many States Are Not Restrictive Enough

The most common instance of the use of deadly physical force by law enforcement officers occurs when they discharge their firearms. The issue of when deadly physical force should be used is one that, more than any other, emphasizes the error of relying strictly on the law to control the use of force by officers. This is so since the laws of many states grant wide latitude to law enforcement officers to use deadly physical force. Take New York State as an example. If officers in the New York City Police Department used their firearms in every situation where they were authorized to do so by the laws of New York State, there would be a huge outcry of indignation from the community. Let's by specific example examine why this is so.

According to the Defense of Justification as contained in Article 35 of the New York State Penal Law, a police officer acting in the performance of his duty may use deadly physical force when he reasonably believes it is necessary to prevent or terminate the commission or attempted commission of a burglary. As is the case in many states whose use of force rules had their origins in Common Law, the New York State Law does not require a showing of danger to any person as a result of the burglary before the use of deadly force is legally justified.

In other words, according to the written law in New York State, a burglar could be shot even though that burglar did not present a specific threat of danger to human life. Legally, in New York and many other states, such a shooting is permissible if it can be shown that it was necessary to prevent or terminate the commission of a burglary or some other felony. But such a course of action by an officer is in conflict with the primary duty of all law enforcement officers, which, as mentioned above, is to preserve human life.

To deal with this conflict, the New York City Police Department, like so many other law enforcement agencies, formulated a "use of deadly physical force" policy, similar to the one described below, which had the effect of placing greater use of force restrictions on its officers than those contained in the laws of its state. It is strongly recommended that all law enforcement agencies examine the applicable laws of their state and create similar restrictions, if not already in place.

The Deadly Physical Force Rule

The authority to carry and use firearms is an awesome responsibility. Respect for human life dictates that, in all cases, firearms should be used ONLY as a last resort, and then ONLY to protect life. Law enforcement officers should NEVER be authorized to use their firearms strictly in the defense of property. Therefore, the ONLY justification for the use of deadly physical force by law enforcement officers in the performance of duty, including the discharging of a firearm, is to protect life and, even then, such action should be the last resort available. If, for example, other reasonable alternatives, such as non-lethal weapons, are available to protect human life, then the use of firearms would NOT be appropriate. Also, an element of this deadly physical force rule must be that law enforcement officers should not discharge their weapons, even if otherwise authorized to do so, if doing so will unnecessarily endanger innocent persons.

It is incumbent upon all supervisors to constantly advise their subordinates that the safety of the public and law enforcement officers must be the overriding concern whenever the use of firearms is considered. "Since line supervisors are closest to their personnel and have the greatest day-to-day effects on their work, they must also be accountable for seeing that officers do their jobs in the most humane ways possible."[3]

THE SELF-DEFENSE RULE

Law enforcement officers are sworn to protect others and are most certainly entitled to protect themselves. Therefore, the use of force by an officer upon another person is indeed appropriate when and to the extent such force is necessary to defend himself or a third person from the use or imminent use of unlawful physical force by such other person. And, if the person using the unlawful force is using or about to use deadly physical force, then the law enforcement officer can use deadly physical force in defense of himself or a third person. This is consistent with the rule stated above that the only justification for the use of deadly physical force by law enforcement officers is to protect life.

The Use of Force Must Be Justified by Articulable Facts

Any law enforcement officer using force must be able to articulate the facts which led him to conclude that such force was necessary. The use of force by officers cannot be justified by mere suspicion or "gut" feelings. Articulable facts known to an officer at the time the force was used is the only acceptable manner of establishing the necessary belief that the use of force was required.

The Ramifications of Uncertainty

Supervisors must be absolutely certain that all of their subordinates are extremely well trained in the agency's use of force policy. Of all of the technical skills training a supervisor is responsible for conducting, none is more important because uncertainty about the use of force policies can have tragic ramifications. This is especially true for those policies governing the use of deadly physical force. For example, consider the following results which could occur if an officer is not fully acquainted with the use of force policy of his agency:

1. An officer could act prematurely and unintentionally use deadly physical force in a situation where the use of such force was not appropriate. Such premature use of deadly physical force could then result in unwarranted physical injury or even death, as well as criminal and civil liability sanctions against the officer.

2. An officer could wait too long in a situation where the use of deadly physical force is appropriate, which could result in physical injury or even death to the officer or to an innocent third party.

Supervisors must keep in mind that whenever an officer uses deadly physical force prematurely or waits too long to use such force, the probability exists that the officer involved was uncertain of the department's policy at the time of occurrence. This possibility is addressed by the Indianapolis Police Department in their detailed and well written departmental firearms policy:

"This [departmental firearms] policy is not intended to create doubt in the mind of an officer at a moment when action is critical and there is little time for mediation or reflection. It provides basic guidelines governing the use of firearms so an officer can be confident in exercising judgment as to the use of deadly force."[4]

THE FLEEING FELON RULE

At the beginning of this chapter it was noted that federal and state courts often create case law which helps to define an agency's use of force policy. This is exactly what occurred in 1985 when the United States Supreme Court issued its decision in the landmark case of *Tennessee v. Garner*. In that case, the Supreme Court ruled that "the use of deadly force to prevent the escape of all felony suspects, whatever the circumstances, is constitutionally unreasonable. Without an imminent threat of death or serious bodily injury directed toward an officer or another, the harm resulting from failing to apprehend the suspect does not justify the use of deadly force to do so."[5] It should be noted that the rule established by the Supreme Court in this case is consistent with our general rule that the ONLY justification for the use of deadly physical force is the protection of life.

Probable Cause Is Required

In its ruling in *Garner* the court also fixed the level of information that must be present to establish the required imminent threat of death or serious bodily injury before deadly force can be lawfully used against a fleeing felon. The court ruled that "deadly force may not be used unless it is necessary to prevent a felon's escape and the officer has probable cause to believe that the suspect poses a significant threat of death or serious physical injury."[6]

An officer's authority to use deadly force to subdue a fleeing felon does not stem from the nature of the felony that was committed. The rule is clear. Law enforcement officers may NOT use deadly force to prevent the escape of an unarmed, non-dangerous felon. However, where law enforcement personnel have probable cause to believe a fleeing felon poses an imminent threat of death or serious bodily injury, either to them or to others present, it is not constitutionally unreasonable to prevent the escape by using deadly force. Remember, however, that even in this situation, agency policy should stipulate that such use of reasonable force must be the last resort available.

The Development of Probable Cause

Knowing that probable cause has to be present before an officer may use deadly physical force in fleeing felon cases is extremely important but not sufficient in and of itself. What is also needed is a good understanding of what constitutes probable cause and how probable cause is established. Far too often these issues receive appropriate attention during entry-level training and then little or no attention thereafter.

The question of what constitutes probable cause is complicated immensely by the fact that there is no clear cut definition of probable cause. But there are certain factors which assist officers in determining whether probable cause is present in any given situation. The single most important source of these factors is court decisions rendered in cases where the court determined whether probable cause existed. Such cases often result in the promulgation by the courts of additional guidelines which can then be of assistance in the future under similar situations. But, the promulgation by the courts of these guidelines is of value ONLY if agency supervisors are knowledgeable of them and inform their subordinates about them.

Decisions of the Court Must Be Monitored

In turn, the top-level management people in every law enforcement agency have a responsibility to assist all members of their agency in this very important matter of monitoring the decisions of the court, not only in use of force cases, but in every significant case involving the legal authority of officers to do their job. An essential ingredient necessary in meeting this responsibility is the publication and dissemination within the agency of a detailed analysis of all such court decisions. It is vital that supervisors understand that, from a legal standpoint, officers cannot be excused by claiming ignorance of the law. But who is truly at fault when such a situation occurs? Is it the individual officer involved because he resisted the agency's efforts to keep him properly informed? Or is it the fault of the agency because it failed to disseminate much needed information on a timely basis? Or is it the fault of supervisors because they failed in the performance of their training responsibility?

Whenever the courts rule that law enforcement personnel used force without sufficient authority, an attempt must be made to determine why, and corrective action must be taken. This is not to suggest that there will never be an instance when an officer operates in good faith and in accordance with existing guidelines which are then subsequently revised when examined by the court. Because of the dynamic nature of the regulation of the conduct of law enforcement personnel, this has occurred in the past and will continue to occur in the future. However, when analysis shows that this has occurred, it is more important than ever to inform all members of the agency of the new guidelines via the formal

374

training program which then must be supplemented by one-on-one training between supervisors and subordinates.

Guidelines to Aid in Establishing Probable Cause

As stated above, there is no clear cut definition of what constitutes probable cause. In effect, probable cause must be developed on a case-by-case basis. However, the following guidelines can be of assistance in establishing probable cause in all cases:

a. The courts will not accept "gut" feelings or "hunches" as a basis for establishing probable cause.

b. An officer who wants to establish probable cause must be able to articulate the specific facts he relied upon to conclude that probable cause existed.

c. The articulable facts which led an officer to conclude that probable cause was present should be reduced to writing as soon as possible after the incident.

d. All factors which might indicate probable cause should be included in the officer's notes. Many of these factors by themselves will not be sufficient to establish probable cause, but when considered together, they may become a powerful defense of the officer's actions.

MISCELLANEOUS CONSIDERATIONS

The following considerations are not usually found in statutory law, but they should be contained in every agency's written policy governing the use of force.

Giving Warnings

Respect for human life dictates that, where feasible and when consistent with personal safety and the safety of innocent parties, some warning, such as, "POLICE - DON'T MOVE," should be given before the police use necessary force. This warning should never be given by firing a warning shot. Also remember that force should only be used as a last resort. A person should, whenever possible, be given the opportunity to submit of his own accord to lawful authority.

Warning Shots

It must be stressed that agency policy should absolutely prohibit firing warning shots. Agency policy should define warning shots so that the policy is crystal clear. Part of the problem comes from the multiple meanings of "warn". One such meaning is to caution a person about certain acts. It is this definition that it used in the term "warning shots." They are shots fired to caution a person that their continued engagement in certain illegal acts will result in their being the subject of deadly force.

The disadvantages of warning shots far outweigh the advantages. Any discharge of a firearm can result in unnecessary death or serious injury. This is especially true in densely populated urban areas. Other officers who hear warning shots often conclude that they are being fired upon and react. Such a reaction often results in tragedy.

Discharging Firearms To Summon Assistance

There is some confusion among officers about the difference between firing warning shots and discharging a firearm to summon assistance. Warning shots, as used in the context of this discussion, means discharging a firearm to caution a person to discontinue their present illegal actions. Discharging a firearm to summon assistance is defined as firing a weapon to signal that the officer or a third party is in need of assistance. Law enforcement officers should be prohibited from discharging their firearms to summon assistance EXCEPT in emergency situations when someone's personal safety is endangered, and unless no other reasonable means is available to obtain the needed assistance. So, for example, in an emergency situation where an officer's personal safety is endangered, firing a shot to signal for help would be a violation of agency policy if the officer was equipped with an operable portable radio which he could have used to call for assistance.

The rule against firing warning shots is an absolute rule in that there should be no exceptions. The rule concerning the discharging of firearms to summon assistance is conditional, there are exceptions to it.

Shooting at or from a Moving Vehicle

Shooting at or from a moving vehicle should only be authorized in those situations where there is an immediate threat of death or serious physical injury to an officer or others. Even under the best of circumstances, it is a difficult task to achieve accuracy with a firearm. And every officer who has been to a modern law enforcement firing range knows that accuracy falls off considerably when the distance between the shooter and the target increases and when the target is moving. Supervisors should use this common knowledge to justify the "moving vehicle use of force" rule. Accuracy virtually disappears when shooting at or from a moving vehicle.

Shooting at Animals

Officers should be prohibited by agency policy from shooting at dogs or other animals, except when necessary to protect themselves or another person present from physical injury, and there is no other reasonable means to eliminate the threat.

Cocking a Firearm

To reduce the possibility of accidental discharge, agency policy should make it clear that officers should not, under any circumstances, cock a firearm. Firearms must be fired double action at all times.

Unholstering Weapons

Agency policy should not preclude an officer from unholstering a firearm in a potentially dangerous or life threatening situation. The difference between drawing a gun and firing it is as big as the difference between showing the fleet and using it to launch an invasion. "Police officers in well-run departments are trained to draw guns only when circumstances present a reasonable expectation that they will encounter life-threatening violence."[7]

The Use of Force Guidelines Are Not Mutually Exclusive

First-line supervisors have an ongoing responsibility to keep their subordinates fully informed and up-to-date concerning their agency's use of force guidelines. In so doing, these supervisors must stress to their subordinates that the rules outlining the use of force guidelines are not mutually exclusive. Officers must be taught to consider the totality of the circumstances before discharging their weapons.

As an example of the necessity to consider the totality of the circumstances, consider the following. Suppose an officer is pursuing a fleeing felon who clearly presents a threat of imminent death to other persons present. In such a situation the fleeing felon rule authorizes the discharging of firearms in order to subdue that felon. But, further suppose that at a certain point in the pursuit it is clear that the fleeing felon is going to a location where a number of other officers armed with non-lethal devices are waiting for him. At this point, while one rule, the fleeing felon rule, allows the use of deadly force, another rule, the one that states that firearms should be used ONLY as a last resort, prohibits the use of deadly force.

This example, as well as the overall seriousness and complexity of use-of-force guidelines, emphasizes what has been said over and over in this discussion. The need to train subordinates in the appropriate use of force is a never-ending responsibility of supervisors. Any such training must, of necessity, include simulations in the form of "shoot—don't shoot" situations which should be based on actual occurrences from the jurisdiction where the training is being conducted.

TEST YOUR UNDERSTANDING

1. Should law enforcement agencies have written policies governing the use of force? Why?

2. Who should be held accountable for the proper use of force?

3. Who is responsible for intervening at the scene of an incident when the use of force by an officer against a subject clearly becomes excessive?

4. Which use of force incidents should supervisors become involved in?

5. What is the cardinal use of force rule?

6. What is the deadly physical force rule?

7. What is the self-defense rule?

8. What is the fleeing felon rule?

9. Are warning shots a valuable law enforcement tool?

10. Should shooting at or from moving vehicles be restricted?

FOOTNOTES

1. See James J. Fyfe, "Police Use of Deadly Force: Research and Reform." Justice Quarterly, 5 (1988): 165-205.

2. Los Angeles Times, March 8, 1991. p. 3.

3. Jerome H. Skolnick and James J. Fyfe, *Above The Law - Police and the Excessive Use of Force.* (New York: The Free Press, 1993), p. 192.

4. "Departmental Firearms Policy." Indianapolis Police Department General Order Number 30.00, October 15, 1990.

5. *Tennessee v. Garner*, 475 U.S. 1, 105 S. Ct. 1694, (1985), as quoted in *New Jersey Law Enforcement Handbook.* Larry E. Holtz, (Binghamton, NY: Gould Publications, 1994.), p. 54.

6. Ibid., p. 53.

7. Skolnick and Fyfe, op cit, p. 41.

SUGGESTED READINGS

Armstrong, Terry R., Ph.D. and
Kenneth M. Cinnamon, Ph.D.
Power and Authority in Law Enforcement.
Springfield, IL: Charles C. Thomas, 1976.

Chevigny, Paul.
Police Power: Police Abuses in New York City.
New York: Vintage, 1969.

Fletcher, Connie.
*What Cops Know: Cops Talk About What They Do, How They Do
It, and What It Does To Them.*
New York: Villard, 1991.

Hevesi, Dennis.
"After Prison, Ex-Officer's Advice on Police Violence:
'Don't do it!' "
New York Times, July 12, 1991.

Merola, Mario with Mary Ann Giordano.
Big City D.A.
New York: Random House, 1988.

Skolnick, Jerome H. and James J. Fyfe.
Above the Law - Police and the Excessive Use of Force.
New York: The Free Press, 1993.

CHAPTER 16
UNDERSTANDING THE PROMOTION PROCESS

A DUAL INTEREST

Supervisors in law enforcement agencies should have an interest in, and familiarity with, the promotion process that exists in their agencies. Promotion rarely comes to those who do not seek it. But seeking promotion isn't enough. Without a good understanding of what it takes to get promoted, the road is extremely difficult. Therefore, an essential step for a supervisor who wants to be promoted is to understand the promotion process in his agency.

Not all law enforcement supervisors desire further promotion. Nonetheless, all supervisors should be familiar with the promotion process in their agency so that they can, insofar as possible, assist their subordinates in obtaining their own career objectives. In those agencies which utilize examinations to select those who get promoted, the use of assessment exercises as part of the promotion process has drastically changed the exam format. The supervisor should be up-to-date on these developments so he can effectively further his career goals and/or the career goals of his subordinates.

The Supervisor's Responsibility to His Subordinates

"The supervisor is responsible for the development of subordinates who are capable of reaching their true potential. This should enable the organization to improve its productivity, and it will also prepare the subordinates to assume positions with more complex duties eventually."[1] "Every organization...has the obligation of developing its employees to their maximum potential; and in most cases this responsibility must fall to the supervisor."[2]

This does not mean that a supervisor should assume that each one of his subordinates wants to get promoted. The primary reasons why many workers do not seek promotion are: (1) they believe that the benefits of promotion are not worth the time and effort required, or (2) they are not interested in assuming the additional responsibilities of a higher rank. This does not change the fact that supervisors have a responsibility to their subordinates who seek promotion, especially when promotions are based on examinations.

A supervisor should encourage realistic aspirations for promotion. This encouragement, in addition to building the job satisfaction of workers, without question aids in the achievement of organizational goals via the development of worker morale and loyalty. But supervisors should avoid building false expectations of promotion. Instead, they should emphasize that any individual's chance of achieving promotion increases in direct proportion to the amount of quality time and effort they devote to that end. Note the use of the word "quality." It's not enough to study and prepare. It is essential that the studying and preparation are properly focused. An informed supervisor, therefore, can help prevent wasted study time and effort by advising promotion candidates as to how to properly focus their efforts. But to do this correctly the supervisor must fully understand the promotion process himself.

TWO BASIC TYPES OF PROMOTION SYSTEMS

In agencies which select their supervisors and managers from among the rank and file of their employees, there are two basic types of promotion systems in use throughout the country. Most law enforcement agencies rely on externally controlled civil service systems to select their first-line supervisors and most of their other managers. A significant number of agencies, however, especially smaller ones, use an internally controlled promotion system. While, in theory, either of these two types of promotion systems is capable of identifying those most qualified to advance to the next level of the organization, there is one significant advantage of relying on an externally controlled system. A promotion system based on civil service law is the best way to eliminate patronage from creeping into the promotion process. This consideration is as important today as it was many years ago when the civil service system concept was born.

GENERIC SKILLS AND TECHNICAL SKILLS

Supervisors who are either preparing themselves to take a promotion examination or who are advising subordinates concerning such preparation should understand the distinction between generic skills and technical skills.

Generic skills refers to knowledge and/or abilities that are general in nature, they apply to any law enforcement agency. A primary example of generic skills are the general principles of management and supervision which do not change from one agency to another. For example, the rule which requires a supervisor to, insofar as possible, obtain all of the available facts before making a decision is a generic rule. Other examples of generic skills are those needed to be effective interviewers, counselors, disciplinarians, and problem solvers.

Technical skills refer to knowledge and/or abilities which are peculiar to a particular jurisdiction. Primary examples of technical skills are knowledge of internal agency procedures and criminal law. The exact procedure to follow, for example, when dealing with an emotionally disturbed person in all likelihood differs somewhat from agency to agency. And, of course, what is criminal conduct in one jurisdiction may not be in another jurisdiction.

Sometimes a question on a promotion examination can be answered by using either technical skills or generic skills. When this occurs, technical skills rule. A question on a promotion examination should not be answered by using generic skills if there is a technical skills answer. For example, suppose a law enforcement agency had a rule requiring a supervisor at roll call to read the names of his subordinates who were the subject of disciplinary action. Then if a test question on a promotion test in that agency asked if the reading of names at roll call of those officers who were the subject of disciplinary action was proper, the answer would be yes despite the generic rule which states that it is best for supervisors to criticize their subordinates in private. There is, therefore, a hierarchy of answer sources on promotion examinations in which technical skills answers have priority over generic skills answers. It is only when there is no technical skills answer to a question that a test taker should rely on his generic skills to arrive at the answer.

TESTING IN THE PROMOTION PROCESS

Testing is at the heart of most law enforcement promotion systems. Supervisors who aspire to promotion or who are guiding the promotion efforts of subordinates should have a basic understanding of the legal aspects of test development.

The Legal Definition of a Test

According to federal guidelines, a test is any device which is used as a basis for making personnel decisions, such as those which are made in the selection of personnel, their assignment and/or their promotion. Therefore, to conform to federal laws such as Title VII of the Civil Rights Act of 1964, the scope of a test goes far beyond a paper and pencil examination. It includes such things as interviews, application forms, and performance appraisals if they are used to make personnel decisions.

The cardinal rule in test development is that a test must measure only the knowledge and/or abilities that are essential for successful performance in the position to be filled by the results of that test.

Disparate Impact Is Prohibited by Federal Guidelines

Tests which are used to make personnel decisions must not have a disparate impact. "Applicants who do not generally 'test well' may do poorly on an examination even though they have the required skills or aptitudes. Tests that fail a higher than normal number of individuals in protected classes have an adverse impact and are considered to be discriminatory."[3] This means that tests will not stand up to judicial review if they yield significantly different results for women and/or minorities as compared to non-protected groups.

Tests Must Be Valid

A test must be valid or it will not stand up to judicial review. In very simple terms, a valid test is one that accomplishes what it is supposed to accomplish. A promotion test, for example, is supposed to identify those candidates who have the required knowledge and abilities to most effectively perform the duties

386

of the rank for which they are being tested. According to law, any testing device used to select or promote employees is required to be a valid predictor of performance in the future. "Guidelines issued by the Equal Employment Opportunity Commission require that anything used to aid in the selection of candidates for promotion must be validated. That is, there must be statistical evidence to demonstrate that there's a direct relationship between performance on the selection device and performance in the target position. You should never use a device that hasn't been validated."[4]

The problem that this legal requirement has created is the same today as it was in 1978 when the provisions of Title VII of the Civil Rights Act were made applicable to the public sector as well as the private sector. That problem is how to establish to the satisfaction of the courts that a test has validity. The problems involved in establishing validity are demonstrated in these contrasting examples:

Example 1. *Creating a Valid Test for a Typist*

Examiners who are preparing a test for a typist position have an objective, measurable goal. The test they devise will require candidates to type the same material under the same conditions. The material and conditions under which it is to be typed should approximate the demands of the actual job. For them to develop any other type of test would be foolhardy.

In this example, the development of the test was relatively simple because the job description of the position being tested is also quite simple. No one would disagree with the fact that a good typist has to know how to type well.

Example 2. *Creating a Valid Test for a Law Enforcement Supervisor*

Preparing a test for a supervisor's position in a law enforcement agency is a much more difficult task. The scope of duties required for a supervisor takes in both objective and subjective qualities. It is harder to quantify and empirically measure all the personal and intangible qualities that go into the profile of a good supervisor. A good typist has to know how to type. But what does a good law enforcement supervisor have to be good at to function effectively? Among other things, good law enforcement supervisors have to possess technical skills, interpersonal skills and analytical skills; they have to play an ambivalent role; they have to have certain managerial skills; they have to be good leaders, trainers, communicators, interviewers, problem solvers and counselors; they have to be able to evaluate the performance of others, accept and investigate personnel complaints and resolve grievances; and they have to be able to maintain an acceptable level of discipline. Therefore, it should be obvious that it is quite difficult to develop a test that accurately predicts which candidates taking the test will be the most effective supervisors in the future.

Two Basic Methods of Establishing Validity

While there are many ways to establish the validity of a test, the two methods of establishing validity that have emerged as being most predominant are criterion-related validity and content validity.

Criterion-related validity involves an empirical demonstration that those who do well on a promotion test are the same individuals who eventually perform well on the job upon being promoted. If there is a direct correlation between test score and eventual job performance, then the test is valid. While, in theory, this is the preferred method of establishing test validity, for a number of reasons it is not the kind on validity that examiners most commonly rely on. One reason why it is difficult to use criterion-related validity is the difficulty involved in finding an acceptable technique to rank job performance so that the required correlation study can be made comparing the rank order of the candidates resulting from an examination against a rank order of the same candidates resulting from job performance.

The most common method used to measure the validity of promotion examinations is content validity. Content validity is established by proving that a test is a fair reflection of the content of the job. Content validity is built into a test by having trained experts perform a job analysis to identify the tasks performed by incumbents in the job for which the test is being developed. The knowledge and abilities needed to perform these tasks are isolated and then tests are constructed which accurately measure the needed knowledge and abilities.

The Ramifications of Inappropriate Testing

Personnel examiners have always had a moral responsibility to develop valid promotion tests which are fair and which identify those candidates with the most potential to succeed. But since 1978 they have also had a legal responsibility to do the same thing. Prior to 1978, there was no recourse for candidates who thought a test was invalid. Since then there have been numerous lawsuits which have forced personnel examiners to develop a promotion system which is in accordance with the law. As a result, the typical promotion process in progressive law enforcement agencies has undergone significant change. Gone are the days in these agencies when a simple multiple choice examination testing technical skills was the primary vehicle used to select candidates for promotion. What has evolved is a more complex promotion process.

A RECOMMENDED PROMOTION PROCESS

There are a number of critical steps involved in the development of a promotion test which has content validity. These basic steps are as follows:

a. Conducting a job analysis to determine task statements.
b. Analyzing the task statements.
c. Deciding the format of the test.
d. Publishing a pre-test study guide.
e. Writing the test questions.
f. Administering the test.
g. Considering appeals and issuing a final answer key.

Please note that there is no one specific way to develop a valid promotion examination. What follows is one way of developing such a test. While the approaches may vary, the concepts are the same. The following information, therefore, is offered as a way of presenting and explaining these concepts so that those supervisors seeking promotion can understand the process and thus be better able to prepare. In addition, it will enable them to assist subordinates who may be seeking promotion via a similar process.

a. Conducting a Job Analysis

A test for a particular job cannot have content validity if the test does not reflect activities that are performed in that job. These activities are determined by a careful analysis of the job as it is actually performed. The result of the job analysis is the development of a series of task statements. "A job analysis begins with a description of what employees holding the job do. Next, the job analysis tells what is required in order to successfully carry out the necessary duties. These are the actual job requirements. At this stage focus attention on qualities that spell the difference between success and failure and list them in terms of knowledge, skills, and behavior."[5]

Suppose, for example, the field auditor conducting the job analysis observed a supervisor reviewing written reports and forms prepared by subordinates. The following task statements might be developed regarding the supervisor's actions:

1. Reviews written forms and reports completed by subordinates for accuracy, completeness, grammar, and clarity of ideas and thoughts.

2. Makes corrections, or directs subordinates to make corrections, to forms or reports that have been completed improperly.

These two task statements provide a basis for test questions on the accuracy and completeness of department forms and reports. Note that task number one points out the need for questions on grammar. Learning to read and interpret task statements in this manner, helps to concentrate study efforts in areas as needed.

Each Task Statement Must Be Classified

Once a complete series of task statements is developed, the next step is to classify each statement according to its frequency and importance. From this a test is designed to assess these tasks. Importance is measured by considering the impact of

390

inappropriately handling a task. For example, consider the following two task statements:

1. Answers questions of subordinates related to the performance of their duties.

2. Investigates incidents involving line-of-duty deaths to law enforcement personnel and, if appropriate, makes recommendations to prevent recurrences.

Further consideration of task number one reveals that it is performed often enough to be a task that should be the subject of one or more questions on an upcoming test. And, while task number two is not performed as frequently, inappropriate handling of this task is serious. As a result, this task could most certainly be the subject of a test question.

b. Analyzing the Task Statements

After the task statements have been formulated and classified, each one has to be analyzed to determine what knowledge or ability is needed to perform it. For example, consider the following individual task statements:

1. Determines that legal and department guidelines are followed when officers conduct searches and make arrests.

2. Interviews members of the department as part of official investigations.

In order to perform task one a supervisor must have the necessary knowledge of the legal and departmental guidelines which apply to conducting searches and making arrests. This knowledge would then be included in an overall list of technical knowledge that will serve as the basis for questions on an upcoming test. Analysis of task number two, however, reveals that in order to perform it a supervisor must have a special ability as opposed to a special knowledge. The ability involved is generally known as "oral fact finding/interviewing." It is defined as the "ability to gather and interpret facts and information from individuals, through questioning, interviewing, and interrogation." Therefore, analysis of task number two would result in the ability of "fact finding/interviewing" being included on the listing of abilities for any upcoming test for that supervisor's position.

c. Deciding on the Format of the Test

Without question, the biggest change in the promotion process involves the format of the test. Progressive law enforcement agencies no longer rely on one comprehensive, multiple choice, technical skills test to rank order candidates for promotion. "For some positions, it is equally important to test ability to make adjustments to new situations or to profit from training."[6]

The reason why new testing formats have evolved is the necessity to test for abilities as well as knowledge. Although not a new concept, it had not been pursued by examiners. Instead, it took judicial review coupled with new legal responsibility for valid tests to literally force some personnel examiners to develop new ways of testing. As a result, promotion examinations now contain, or should contain, a number of components to measure the varied knowledge and abilities needed by a law enforcement supervisor.

Assessment Center Exercises

It is not unusual for some promotion tests to contain up to four components. One or more of these components could be what are known as "assessment center exercises." "An assessment center is a series of exercises in which management candidates perform realistic management tasks under the watchful eyes of expert appraisers. Each candidate's potential for management is thereby assessed or appraised. An assessment center is based on the idea that the best way to evaluate how a person will do on a job is to observe that person's behavior on the same or similar jobs."[7] While there are many variations of assessment exercises in use, they all have one thing in common. They all involve some sort of job simulation. "Simulation exercises attempt to place the candidate in a real-life opportunity to display qualities considered important in the job."[8]

There is one feature of an assessment exercise that many candidates for promotion have great difficulty understanding.

While assessment exercises are often designed to test a candidate's technical skills and generic skills sometimes the answer to a question does not come directly from either of these two skill areas. Rather, the answer could be contained in the material that creates the job simulation.

A recent promotion exam in a large law enforcement agency, for example, conducted what can best be described as an Incident Management Test. The directions for that test explained that the candidate would be asked questions relating to an airplane accident. Included in the package of information each candidate received was detailed instructions concerning the handling of such an accident. What puzzled many candidates was that, although their agency had detailed procedures for airplane accident, the procedures given out on test day were, in many ways, different from the agency's official procedures. Uninformed candidates were, therefore, not sure of which way to answer the questions.

These candidates were not familiar with the hierarchy of answer sources. According to this hierarchy, information in the test packet takes priority over all other sources. This special feature of assessment exercises emphasizes the need for promotion candidates to seek out professional coaching schools to obtain special training prior to taking a promotion examination.

COMMON COMPONENTS OF PROMOTION EXAMINATIONS

The most common components currently in use in the typical promotion examination are described below. Some components are assessment type exercises, while others are not.

1. Closed-Book Technical Knowledge Test

This test utilizes the traditional multiple-choice format that has been used for many years, and which once served in many law enforcement agencies as the one and only test component. The candidate is asked a series of multiple-choice questions based on information which has been identified by the job analysis as necessary in situations which do not allow the supervisor to look up the information. Some information must be committed to memory. We call this knowledge "street knowledge." Examples of such knowledge are firearms policies, procedures governing the handling of vehicle accidents, and legal guidelines concerning search and seizure.

2. Open-Book Technical Knowledge Test

In law enforcement work there is certain knowledge that does not need to be committed to memory. In recognition of this fact, candidates for promotion are often asked multiple-choice questions that can be answered by referring to reference materials which are made available to the candidates on the day of the test. The knowledge needed in these situations, where time is not of the essence, is what we call "inside knowledge," because it is needed by supervisors when present at a police facility in non-emergency situations. Examples of this knowledge are internal procedures governing the booking of arrested persons, information concerning the exact degree of criminal charge to use when booking prisoners, internal procedures governing the seizing and recording of property, and attendance, leave, and payroll reporting systems.

3. Video Work-Sample Tests

The work-sample test, commonly referred to as a video test, is a form of assessment exercise which is constructed to test abilities that are difficult to test using the traditional multiple choice question format. In these tests, video scenarios depicting job simulations are shown to the candidates. Then, depending on the jurisdiction, each scenario is followed either by a series of multiple-choice questioner by one or more open-ended questions which the candidate responds to either in writing or orally.

4. In-Basket Tests

In-basket tests, also known as administrative tests, are designed to test the candidate's administrative skills. "In an in-basket exercise the candidate receives a packet of materials containing instructions, background material (such as an organization chart and a calendar), and a series of items to handle. It's as though the candidate arrived at work and began

394

handling the items in an in-basket."[9] In most in-basket tests a candidate must review all of the items before answering any questions because the answers to some questions depend on information from more than one item. As is true with all assessment exercises, the simulation involved can reflect actual official material, or it can reflect artificial material created specifically for the test. The test questions can be presented in either a multiple choice format, or they can be open-ended questions which require the candidate to give his answer either in writing or orally to one or more examiners.

5. Scheduling Exercises

A scheduling exercise is an assessment exercise usually given to those supervisors whose job analysis indicated a need to account for and assign personnel at the start of a tour of duty, and to re-assign personnel during the tour as the need arises. The format of a scheduling exercise closely follows that of an in-basket exercise. The candidate must adjust a roll call in response to various pieces of information that are supplied in a packet of material which the candidate reviews before answering any questions. For example, the packet may contain approved requests for last minute excusals by employees who are listed on the roll call as working, information about officers who have recently reported sick, and information about officers who have been newly assigned to, or recently transferred from, the command.

6. Incident-Management Tests

This exercise requires the candidate to answer multiple-choice or open-ended questions based on a large-scale incident or on a number of somewhat routine incidents, or both. In addition to receiving specifics about the incident or incidents, the test material often includes a detailed procedure outlining how certain incidents should be handled. This detailed procedure could be an agency procedure, or it could be artificial and created specifically for examination purposes. Some of the answers appear in the test material, in other cases, the candidate must rely on either his technical skills or generic skills to determine an answer.

7. Oral-Interactive Interview

In this exercise, candidates review materials distributed beforehand to prepare for and to participate in oral interactions with one or more role players. The candidate interviews a role player who is prepared to give carefully worded responses when certain questions are asked of him. In all other cases, the role player gives neutral responses to the candidate. The role player may play the role of one of the candidate's subordinates, a civilian complainant or a representative of the media. The interview is either video or audio taped. Subject matter experts then review the tapes and score it in accordance with a standard scoring system.

8. Fact-Finding Exercise

A fact-finding exercise requires the candidate to, through a series of questions, obtain the essential facts of an incident from a role player who is trained to respond only to properly framed questions. The exercise is either video or audio taped, and the candidate's score is based on the number of pertinent facts about the incident that he uncovered during the timed exercise.

9. Report-Writing Exercise

In this very simply structured assessment exercise, the candidate is required to prepare a written report or reports based on material presented to them on the day of the test. The candidate's writing efforts are then scored based on style, format, and content.

d. Publishing a Pre-Test Study Guide

In this step, all of the pertinent information compiled to this point is condensed into a pre-test study guide and made available to all candidates who have filed to take the test. Only recently has the value of this step been recognized by personnel examiners. Candidates for promotion are entitled to know well in advance of the test both the content matter of the test and the format of the various components of the test. There is simply no justification to withhold this information.

A recent pre-test study guide one from a progressive personnel department of a large city contained the following information for its candidates. (This particular study guide was twenty-three pages long.)

1. The weights of each of four components of the test;
2. Knowledge to be tested in a closed book technical knowledge component;
3. Knowledge to be tested in an open book technical knowledge component;
4. A listing of the abilities to be tested in the in-basket component of the test;
5. A listing of the abilities to be tested in the report writing component of the test;
6. A detailed description of each of the four components of the test;
7. A listing of each of the task statements from the job analysis that would be used as the basis for evaluating the knowledge and abilities to be tested;
8. Sample technical knowledge questions;
9. Sample in-basket items.

Our research reveals that candidates who receive detailed pre-test study guides are more apt to believe in the fairness of the test as opposed to candidates in agencies where there was little or no prior information about the test. Supervisors in agencies which do not supply study guides to promotion candidates should request, through channels, that such guides be made available for future tests.

e. Writing the Test Questions

Test questions should measure critical job knowledge and ability. These questions have to be effectively written so that tasks that were identified by the job analysis are specifically targeted and assessed.

It is unrealistic to expect personnel examiners with no actual law enforcement experience to write valid test items without input from those who have experience and who are subject-matter experts. Progressive personnel examiners who are responsible for developing promotion tests should, therefore, enlist the aid of either incumbents in the rank being tested or retired personnel with equal or greater rank. In the past, fears about the security of the test prevented personnel examiners from seeking this up-front assistance. Whereas test security is always an important consideration, the price for overemphasizing security can be excessive litigation due to poorly written questions and exams.

f. Administering the Test

Test administration is the step in the promotion process that, with one exception, has undergone the least amount of change as a result of legal mandates to develop valid promotion examinations. The exception is assessment exercises, such as the fact-finding interview and the oral interactive interview, which require the use of role players. When role players are used it is essential that they be adequately trained. "If assessors act as role players or provide feedback to candidates, they must have demonstrated competence in these areas during training."[10] Where possible using incumbents or retired ranking officers as role players is recommended.

g. Considering Appeals and Issuing a Final Answer Key

A progressive promotion process should contain an appeals procedure which allows candidates to have input into the final answer key. For multiple-choice parts of the exam, an answer key should be published, and candidates should then be given a period of time to protest the proposed answers. Candidates who lodge protests should be required to submit documentation in support of their protest. After considering all protests, the examiners should amend the key, if necessary, and then promulgate the final answer key.

Some components of an examination—those which do not utilize a multiple-choice format—require an unstructured answer key. For example, the answer key for an oral interactive interview contains a number of statements that earn or lose points for the candidate. For these components, the appeals process should be two-phased. First, candidates should be allowed to review the statements on the proposed answer key and lodge protests directed at amending them. In the second phase, which occurs after the final answer key is established, candidates should be allowed to challenge the scoring of their exercise. The candidate does not try to change the final key but, instead, maintains that his answer is reflective of the final key answer. In effect, the candidate maintains that what he said or wrote should be interpreted as meaning the same as a statement that is included on the final answer key. After considering all the appeals from the second phase of the process, a final promotion list should be established.

FREQUENCY OF PROMOTION TESTS

Top-level administrators should make it a priority to ensure frequent promotion testing. It is recommended that promotion tests be given at least every two years. It is unfair to require employees to wait for extended periods of time for an opportunity to get promoted. Unfortunately, even in larger law enforcement agencies, it is not uncommon for as much as five years to pass between promotion examinations. This is obviously an undesirable situation.

One way of planning for promotion tests more frequently, such as every two years, is to predict how many openings for promotion can be expected for a certain rank in a two-year period, and then set the pass mark for a promotion test for that rank accordingly. For example, if statistics show that there is going to be approximately one hundred openings at the rank of sergeant over the next two years, then the pass mark on a test for that sergeant's position should be set at the top hundred scores plus ties.

Also, by having promotion tests frequently, the agency is afforded a continuous and effective training vehicle at little or no cost. In preparation for promotion tests, a significant percentage of employees who are extremely motivated use their off-duty time to study such things as the law, supervisory principles, the policies of the agency, and any other material which appears on the examination announcement and/or in the pre-test study guide.

A RECOMMENDED STRATEGY FOR CANDIDATES

Law enforcement supervisors who are seeking promotion or who are advising subordinates as to how best prepare for promotion should be familiar with the following strategy.

a. Utilize a Structured Approach

Be organized. Start by allowing sufficient time to prepare. As a general rule, those who begin studying sooner are more successful that those who wait until the last minute to prepare. But don't overdo your efforts at the beginning, or you will "burn out." A few hours of study each week one year in advance of a test then progressing up to as many as twenty hours a week just prior to the test is the best way to proceed. Don't build your study time around your other responsibilities, it becomes too easy for study time to be neglected. And, don't forget to seek the support of your spouse and/or close family members and friends. Impress upon them that sacrifices from all concerned will probably be needed, but also explain that your long-range success will benefit all members of the family.

b. Focus Your Studying Efforts

The most common studying error is lack of focus. Study only what you need to know! For example, a promotion candidate must know the duties and responsibilities of the rank being sought and of the subordinates of those in that rank, but is not responsible for knowing everybody's duties and responsibilities. For example, if a candidate is studying for the rank of lieutenant, he is not responsible for knowing the captain's job.

Prior to the publication of a pre-test study guide, the best barometer of what to study is the content matter of the last test for the same rank. If the test was released, get a copy of it and let it guide your study efforts. If the test was not released, speak to someone who was successful on it and be guided by what they tell you about it. Once a pre-test study guide is available, let it be your guide for content matter you should be studying. If your agency does not publish a comprehensive pre-test study guide, then you should request through channels that one be made available.

c. Develop Appropriate Test-Taking Strategies

It is not enough to concentrate your study efforts exclusively on content matter. If your test contains a number of components, you must become familiar with them, and you must develop a specific test taking strategy for each such component. This is especially true if one or more of the components are assessment type exercises. Unfortunately, we know of many candidates who were extremely well-versed in content, but who did not do well on their promotion examination, because they were not properly prepared to participate in assessment type exercises.

Professional Coaching Schools

It is our opinion that professional coaching schools can be of great assistance to the promotion candidate. This is especially true for those candidates who are preparing to take assessment exercises. But there are two caveats that must be mentioned. First, the school must be conducted by true professionals who know what they are doing and who tailor their lesson plans to the specifics of each situation. Given the many variations of assessment exercises available for use by examiners, coaching schools which keep teaching the same general course over and over often prove to be of little value to their clients. Second, it is a mistake for promotion candidates to believe that regular attendance at such a school is sufficient preparation.

401

The truth is that there is no substitute for individual effort. The school's function should be to guide the candidate's efforts, to teach test taking strategies, and to act as a sounding board for the candidate to evaluate his private efforts. The time honored formula for promotion has not changed: work hard, concentrate on the appropriate material, learn test-taking strategies, and attend the appropriate school on a regular basis. Those who follow that regimen will almost always be successful.

GOOD LUCK!

TEST YOUR UNDERSTANDING

1. Why should supervisors have an interest in the promotion process that exists in their agencies?

2. What is the difference between generic skills and technical skills?

3. What is the legal definition of a test?

4. Identify and discuss the steps in the promotion process.

5. Identify and discuss the most common components of promotion tests.

6. Discuss a strategy to follow for those seeking promotion.

FOOTNOTES

1. Hy Hammer, *Supervision,* 9th ed. (NewYork: Arco, 1983), p. 108.

2. Frank P. Sherwood and Wallace H. Best, *Supervisory Methods in Municipal Government.* (Chicago, IL: The International City Manager's Association, 1958), p. 9.

3. Robert W. Wendover, *Smart Hiring For Your Business.* (Naperville, IL: Small Business Sourcebooks, 1993), p. 115.

4. Marion E. Haynes, *Managing Performance - A Performance Guide to Effective Supervision.* (Los Altos, CA: Crisp Publications, Inc., 1990), p. 211.

5. Ibid., p. 204

6. The Passbook Series, *Passbooks For Career Opportunities - Captain, Police Department.* (Syosset, NY: National Learning Corporation, 1991), p. 3.

7. John A. Reinecke, Gary Dessler, and William F. Schoell, *Introduction to Business - A Contemporary View,* 6th ed. (Boston, MA: Allyn and Bacon, 1989), p. 239.

8. Haynes, p. 209.

9. Ibid., p. 210.

10. Kim J. Kohlhepp, "The Police Chief." June 1992, p. 54.

SUGGESTED READINGS

Byham, William C.
"Assessment Centers for Spotting Future Managers."
Harvard Business Review, July-August, 1970.

Coleman, John L.
Police Assessment Testing: An Assessment Testing Center Handbook for Law Enforcement Personnel, 2nd ed.
Springfield, IL: Charles C. Thomas, Publisher, 1992.

Koplack, B.D.
"The Assessment Center Approach to Police Officer Selection."
Police Chief, September, 1991.

Moulton, Harper W. and Arthur A. Fickel.
Executive Development - Preparing for the 21st Century.
New York: Oxford Press, 1993.

Parsloe, Eric.
Coaching, Mentoring and Assessing: A Practical Guide to Developing Competence.
East Brunswick, NJ: Nichols Publishing, 1993.

Scherer, G.
How Candidates Perceive Assessment Centers.
Police Chief, February, 1990.

Snyder, E. Kenneth.
Employee Matters.
Chicago, IL: Probus Publishing Co., 1991.

Spencer, Lyle and Signe Spencer.
Competence at Work: Models for Superior Performance.
New York: John Wiley and Sons, Inc., 1993.

Trevor, Malcolm.
The Japanese Management Development Systems.
New York: St. Martin's Press Inc., 1983.

INDEX

© 1995 by J. & B. Gould
Printed in the U.S.A.   Ms

Rules and Procedures

Index

© 1995 by J. & B. Gould
Printed in the U.S.A. Ms

NEW from GOULD!

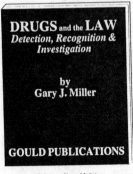